If everybody had an **ocean** . . .

All I need are some **tasty waves and a cool buzz** and I'm fine.

— *Sean Penn as Jeff Spicoli,* Fast Times at Ridgemont High, *1982*

It's about art.

— *Laird Hamilton, 2004*

I honestly can't remember the first time I rode a wave. I suppose it was while playing in the shore break and I must have come to it so gradually that the memory has faded. It was probably inevitable that I'd learn to surf, for the ocean was my backyard. It was where I played every day from one season to the next and riding waves was a part of it. I'm sure it's the same for anyone who grows up in close proximity to the sea—**it becomes your home, your mother, the very essence of life.**

— *Nat Young,* Nat's Nat and That's That, *1998*

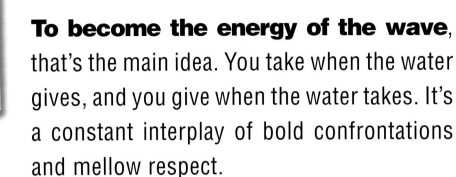

To become the energy of the wave, that's the main idea. You take when the water gives, and you give when the water takes. It's a constant interplay of bold confrontations and mellow respect.

— *Billy Hamilton*

I stood, high like on a mountain peak and dove down, but I stood it. The only sound in the vast moving green was the hissing of the board over the water. A couple of times it almost dropped away under my feet, but I found it again and stood my ground. **"Shoot it, Gidget. Shoot the curl!"**

— *Gidget in Frederick Kohner's* Gidget, *1957*

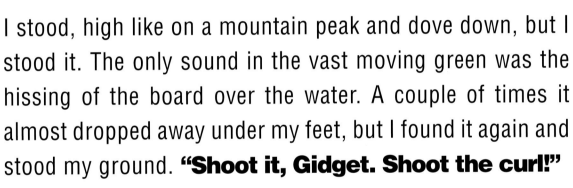

It's an insatiable desire.

— *Kelly Slater,* Pipe Dreams: A Surfer's Journey, *2003*

CONTINENTAL RECORDS PRESENTS

the del-vamps play with fire

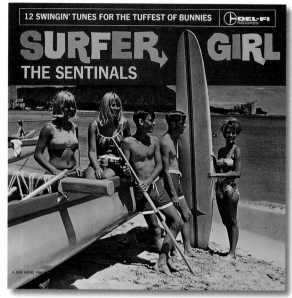

12 SWINGIN' TUNES FOR THE TUFFEST OF BUNNIES · DEL-FI RECORDS

SURFER GIRL
THE SENTINALS

A BOB KEENE PROD.

SURF STOMPIN'
DON DAILEY

CROWN RECORDS

HANG 10
CLOSE OUT
MORNIN' AT MAKAHA
SURF STOMPIN'
MAILE
MALIBU
I'M STOKED
WAY OUT
ALA-MOANA
WAIMEA WIPE OUT

surf rider

Recorded on the beach at Waikiki, Hawaii by Waikiki Records Co.

SURFER'S STOMP!
LIBERTY
The Original Hit

THE MAR-KETS

SURFER'S STOMP · SURVIVAL STOMP · THE BRISTOL STOMP · HERE
COMES THE HO-DADS · LET'S GO TRIPPIN' · STOMP, LOOK AND LISTEN
STOMPIN' AT THE SAVOY · STOMPIN' ROOM ONLY · BALBOA BLUE
SURFIN' · IF YOU GOTTA MAKE A FOOL OF SOMEBODY · STOMPEDE

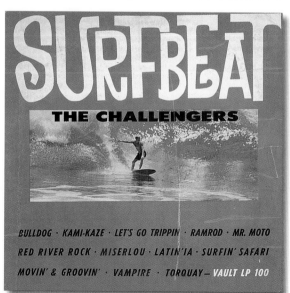

SURFBEAT
THE CHALLENGERS

BULLDOG · KAMI-KAZE · LET'S GO TRIPPIN' · RAMROD · MR. MOTO
RED RIVER ROCK · MISERLOU · LATIN'IA · SURFIN' SAFARI
MOVIN' & GROOVIN' · VAMPIRE · TORQUAY — VAULT LP 100

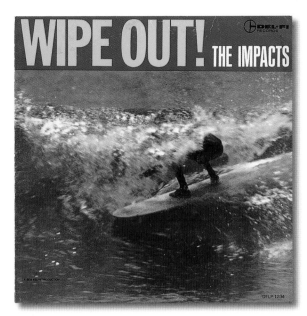

WIPE OUT! THE IMPACTS

DFLP 1234

Surfin' with the Astronauts

BOB DEMMON · JIM GALLAGHER · STORMY PATTERSON · DENNIS LINDSEY · RICH FIFIELD

RCA VICTOR
DYNAGROOVE
RECORDING

LPM-2760

STEREO
LES JAGUARS
VOL-2

TOURNESOL STL-402

CST 313   STEREO
CROWN RECORDS

SURF ROCKIN'
JOE HOUSTON

WIPE OUT
GREMMIE
NIGHT LAMP
DIG
HO DADS
HALEIWA
SURF ROCKIN'
MAME
HOOKED
POPOREA

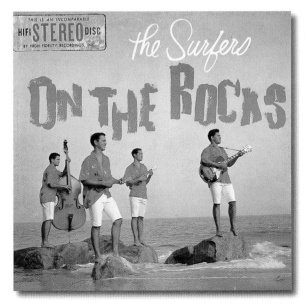

THIS IS AN INCOMPARABLE
HIFI STEREO DISC
BY HIGH FIDELITY RECORDINGS, INC.

the Surfers
ON THE ROCKS

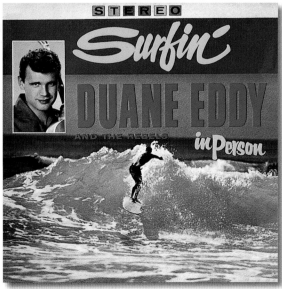

STEREO

Surfin'
DUANE EDDY
AND THE REBELS
in Person

SurFING

AN ILLUSTRATED HISTORY OF THE
COOLEST
SPORT
OF ALL TIME
BY BEN MARCUS

Foreword by
Steve Pezman of *The Surfer's Journal*

Photographs and Artwork by
Jeff Divine, John Severson, LeRoy Grannis,
Ron Dahlquist, Rick Griffin, Greg Noll,
Doc Ball, and more

MVP
BOOKS

First published as *Surfing USA!* in 2005 by Voyageur Press, an imprint of
MBI Publishing Company, 400 First Avenue North, Suite 300, Minneapolis, MN 55401 USA.

This edition published 2013.

ISBN-13: 978-0-7603-4451-4

Library of Congress Cataloging-in-Publication Data

Marcus, Ben, 1960-
  Surfing USA! : an illustrated history of the coolest sport of all time / by Ben Marcus ;
photographs and artwork by Jeff Divine ... [et al.].
     p. cm.
  Includes bibliographical references and index.
  ISBN 0-89658-690-1 (hardcover)
  1. Surfing--United States--History. 2. Surfing--United States--History--Pictorial works. I. Divine,
Jeff. II. Title.
  GV839.6.M37 2005
  797.3'2--dc22
                        2005011655

Editor: Michael Dregni
Designer: Julie Vermeer

Printed in China

Cover photo: Evan Valiere rides a wave at the Billabong Pipe Masters on December 9, 2011, at Pipeline, Hawaii. (Photo © Mana Photo/Shutterstock.com)

Page 1: Surfers charge the waves. (Photo © Ron Dahlquist)

Pages 2–3: Darrick Doerner rides Peahi. (Photo © Jeff Divine)

Pages 4–5: Classic surfing decals and stickers. (Keith Eshelman Collection/Voyageur Press Archives)

Page 6: The image of the woman surfer, circa 1930s: Tap-dancing starlet Eleanor Powell poses with a surfboard prop. (Surfing Heritage Foundation Archives)

Page 7: The image of the woman surfer, circa 1990s: Lisa Andersen cuts a curve. (Photo © Jeff Divine)

Pages 8 and 9: Classic surf music album covers. (Voyageur Press Archives)

Page 10: Surfer Lauren Spalding in Tavarua, Fiji. (Photo © Ron Dahlquist)

Page 11: Woody Brown, still surfing at 89 years young. (Photo © Ron Dahlquist)

Title page: The end of another perfect day at Kuau Cove on Maui. (Photo © Ron Dahlquist)

Title page inset: Hawai'ian travel decal, circa 1920s. (Voyageur Press Archives)

Above: The glory days of Hawai'ian surfing at Waikiki Beach, circa 1927: from left, Harry Rebello, Blue Makua, Turkey Love, David Kahanamoku, Ox, Curley Conley, and Louie Kahanamoku.

Contents pages: Waikiki surfing postcard, circa 1950s. (Voyageur Press Archives)

Contents

Surfing and the Meaning of Life

Surfing is the antithesis of organized social behavior. Ethereal. Amorphous. Non-tangible. As we hang it with trappings, the outline becomes more discernable. The ride is everything, and then it is gone. Essentially the riding of a wave is all about the individual, "alone with the surf and his thoughts," experiencing a profound sense of connection with nature, truth, life, and death, while having a ton of fun.

Ironically, that essence made it into a movement, then an industry. Surfers early on were a strange bunch of outcasts and renegades who rejected normal behavior to chase waves on cumbersome hundred-pound craft. Being human, they banded together with their brethren, becoming tribal in the process, and the non-conformist trappings came to represent their renegade style to the mainstream. What they did was non-productive, but also non-depletive. It is done of the sake of sensation, entirely for self-satisfaction—hedonism to the max.

Contrary to common perception, early surfers were not a dumbed-down bunch of irresponsible louts, but more often brainy types who exercised a curiosity to escape the herd and try different things. Operating to the demands of living comfy but staying free for when the surf was good required ranging outside the box. Being generally clever and resourceful types this was no problem. Surfers realized that outside the box were navigable waters and began to see society's conventions as false gods. So, they made new rules.

"Lifestyle" was coined to explain their colorful and uniquely functional garb, specialized lingo, inventive forms of affordable transport, and an overall approach that said, "ride life like it's a wave." When surfing exploded from a few thousand eccentrics into "legions of the stoked" in the mid-twentieth century, surfer mannerisms became the topic of media attention. We were cool stuff.

The trappings of surf culture began to appeal to a broadening base of youth far from shore. By the end of the century, it had been exploited into a multi-billion-dollar industry. This imbued some surfers with a profit motive, but most still rode waves for the pure joy of it. True, it was harder to be alone with your thoughts when out in the home surf, but as conditions grew more and more crowded a travel mode revealed the globe to be covered with perfect curling waves and the search was on, in earnest.

As a tribe we have now probed the furthest corners of the oceans. Surfboards have become small, light, spontaneous, free-flying little spears. We have conquered ten-story waves and lived to tell about it. Our lifestyle is now a universal option in the kitbag of humanity. We are featured in movies. Our dance has been diagramed, choreographed and fed back to us. Surfing soap operas are on television and we cut-back huge on freeway billboards. Ironically, the riding of waves has become absorbed by the mainstream we once shunned.

Our saving grace is that the lone surfer is still free to paddle out to catch and ride a wave no matter how surrounded he or she is by other lone surfers. That is as it has always been and always will be. The ride is at the core of our culture, and the sensation of the ride is still the most bitchin' thing you'll ever feel. Better than sex.

This book is an attempt to explain, share, illustrate, and define that elusive mode of being, a surfer. Just don't call me that to my face.

Steve Pezman | Publisher | *The Surfer's Journal*

"Jaws Dimension": John Severson's fantastical watercolor of tow-surfing at Jaws, on Severson's home island of Maui. (Artwork © John Severson/surferart.com)

Catching the First Waves

From Polynesia with Love • The Dawn of Time to 1940

Left, **"Surf-Board Riding,"**
1870s: This drawing appeared
in Reverend J. G. Wood's
exposé *The Uncivilized Races*
of Man in All Countries of the
World. They may have been
lacking a Westerner's concept
of "civilization," but those
wave-riders sure looked happy.
(Bishop Museum)

Above, **Hawai'ian Surfer**
Girl, 1920s: A label from
Hawaiian Girl canned pine-
apples depicting a surfing girl
of days past. (Voyageur Press
Archives)

All this surfing sensation— the culture and fashion, the movies and music, from *Gidget* to the Beach Boys and those bushy, bushy blond hairdos—goes back as far as the 1770s. And beyond.

Captain James Cook was sailing the HMS *Discovery* on his third voyage into the Pacific when, on January 18, 1778, he discovered an uncharted Polynesian archipelago. The natives called their home Owhyhee— later transliterated as "Hawai'i"—but Cook christened them the Sandwich Islands in honor of his friend and supporter, John Montague, first Lord of the Admiralty and fourth Earl of Sandwich. The Islanders greeted Cook with reverence, believing the Englishman was a white-skinned, red-bearded god. Cook traded iron nails and other geegaws for supplies and was in turn offered the chieftain's daughter, whom the good captain politely accepted. Yet these Hawai'ian Islanders would soon prove Cook's undoing. Returning to the Big Island of Hawai'i in January 1779, Cook found the natives restless. In the midst of ritual warfare for their god Lono, the Islanders stole one of Cook's precious "cutters," a small sailboat essential for exploring in advance of the main ships. Cook retaliated by kidnapping a chief. The result was a mêlée, leaving Cook and two of his marines dead.

Cook's discovery of Hawai'i may not have been fortuitous for the good captain, but it did lead to the world-at-large's discovery of the sport of surfing.

Lieutenant James King took over the *Discovery* and the task of completing the ship's journal. Before fleeing Hawai'i, King devoted two full pages to describing his bizarre findings as practiced by the Islanders at Kealakekua Bay on the Kona coast:

Whenever from stormy weather or any extraordinary swell at sea the impetuosity of the surf is increased to its utmost heights, they choose that time for their amusement, which is performed in the following manner: Twenty or thirty of the natives, taking each a long narrow board, rounded at the ends, set out together from the shore. The first wave they meet they plunge under, suffering it to role over them, rise again beyond it, and make the best of their way, by swimming out into the sea. The second wave is encountered in the same manner with the first;... as soon as they have gained by these repeated efforts, the smooth water beyond the surf, they lay themselves at length on their board, and prepare for their return. As the surf consists of a number of waves, of which every third is remarked to be always much larger than the others, and to flow higher on the shore, the rest breaking in the intermediate space, their first object is to place themselves on the summit of the largest surge.

By the time of King's observations in 1778, riding waves lying down or standing on long, hardwood

> I could not help concluding that this man felt the most supreme pleasure while he was driven on so smoothly by the sea . . .
>
> — *Captain James Cook on seeing a Tahitian native riding waves in a canoe,* Journals, *December 1777*

surfboards was an integral part of Hawai'ian culture. Surfboard riding was as layered into the society, religion, and myth of the Polynesian islands as baseball is in the modern United States. Chiefs and kings proved their royalty and earned their leadership by their surfing skills, and commoners made themselves famous—and infamous—by the way they handled themselves on the waves.

Anthropologists can only make educated guesses at the origin and evolution of wave-riding and surfboard construction in Polynesian culture, as there's no certainty about the timeline and movements of the Polynesians. The migration of humans out of Asia and into the eastern Pacific began around 2000 BC, and Polynesians established themselves within a large triangle from Aotearoa (New Zealand) at the south, Tonga and Samoa along the west, and Tahiti and the Marquesas Islands to the east. Migrating due to the push of population and the pull of the horizon, the first Polynesians arrived in the Hawai'ian Islands in the fourth century AD.

Polynesians who made the arduous journey from Tahiti and the Marquesas Islands across more than 2,500 miles of ocean to Hawai'i were necessarily

"Surf Swimming by Sandwich Islanders," 1870s: The Reverend J. G. Wood included many illustrations of naked Islanders enjoying their wave-riding in his 1871 tome, *The Uncivilized Races of Man in All Countries of the World.* In fact, there were so many such images, one began to wonder at the good minister's own desires to ride the surf. (Voyageur Press Archives)

Ancient Hawai'ian *Olo*: The long *olo* boards were reserved for royalty—surfing kings and queens. *Olo* were usually crafted from solid koa or wiliwili. (© Malcolm Wilson) SPECIFICATIONS: 16' LONG; 18" WIDE; 6" THICK; 170 POUNDS

Ancient Hawai'ian *Alaia*: A typical *alaia* used by Hawai'ian Islanders, the style dates back hundreds if not thousands of years. These thin planks were shaped from solid ulu (breadfruit tree) or koa, and measured 6 to 12 feet in length. (© Malcolm Wilson) SPECIFICATIONS: 12' LONG; 22" WIDE; 1½" THICK; 50 POUNDS

Ancient Hawai'ian Surfboard-Building Rituals

From Ben Finney and James D. Houston, *Surfing: A History of the Ancient Hawaiian Sport*, 1996

Although surfing was not specifically a religious observance, it was, like other aspects of Hawaiian life, integrally involved with the gods and spirits of the day. The observance of ritual began when a potential surfboard was still an image in the craftsman's mind; it began with the tree. When he had selected a suitable koa or wiliwili tree, a board-builder placed a red fish at its trunk. He then cut down the tree with a stone axe, dug a hole among the roots, and placed the fish therein with a prayer as an offering to the gods in return for the tree he was about to shape into a board. The construction and shaping of the surfboard that followed this ritual was an exacting task that required the experienced craftsmanship of professional native board-builders. The trunk was first chipped away with an axe and roughly shaped to the desired dimensions. It was then pulled down to the beach and placed in a hālau (canoe house) for finishing work. To remove the uneven surface of axe marks the board was smoothed with rough coral. Stone rubbers called 'ōahi were used to polish the boards, much as canoe hulls were polished. As a finishing stain, the root of the ti plant or the juice of pounded kukui bark was used to give the completed board a dark, glistening luster. Stains were also obtained from the soot of burned kukui nuts, charcoal from burnt pandanus leaves, or the juices from young banana buds. To complete the process, a dressing of kukui nut oil was applied when the stain was dry, and the black, glossy board was ready for surfing. Before it was set in the water there were still other rites and ceremonies to be performed in dedicating the board to insure its wave-riding success. And although the common people often disregarded those observances, professional board-builders followed them faithfully.

Carnation Lei Hawaiian Islands. 134.

95. Famous Surf Riders. Hawaiian Islands.

Hawai'ian Lore Post-cards, 1910s–1920s

(Voyageur Press Archives)

But a diversion the most common is upon the Water, where there is a very great Sea, and surf breaking on the Shore. The Men sometimes 20 or 30 go without the Swell of the Surf, & lay themselves flat upon an oval piece of plank about their Size and breadth, they keep their legs close on top of it, & their Arms are us'd to guide the plank, they wait the time of the greatest Swell that sets on Shore, & altogether push forward with their Arms to keep on its top, it sends them in with a most astonishing Velocity, & the great art is to guide the plank so as always to keep it in a proper direction on the top of the Swell . . .

— *Lieutenant James King, logbook of the HMS* Discovery, *1778*

exceptional watermen and -women, and they brought with them a deep love and knowledge of the waves. They also carried along their customs, including playing in the surf on *paipo* (belly) boards. Although Tahitians were reported to have occasionally stood on their boards, the art of surfing upright on longboards was certainly perfected, if not invented, in Hawai'i.

Cook and King arrived in Hawai'i thirteen centuries after the first Polynesians, and found surfing deeply rooted in centuries of Hawai'ian legend and culture. Around the islands, places were named for famous surfing incidents. The *kahuna* (surfing experts) intoned special chants to christen new surf-

boards, bring the surf up, and give courage to riders who challenged the big waves. Hawai'ians had no written language until the *haole* (white-skinned people) arrived, so their genealogy and history were remembered in songs and chants: There were legendary stories of love matches made and broken in the surf, lives risked on the waves, and heroic ocean deeds performed by chiefs and commoners alike.

Wave-riding played a role in the annual three-month celebration the Hawai'ians named Makahiki, ruled over by the great god Lono. As James D. Houston and Ben Finney describe in

Hawaiian Outrigger Canoe Club, circa 1910: Surfers and canoeists stand by their craft in front of the Hawaiian Outrigger Canoe Club headquarters on Honolulu's Waikiki Beach. Founded on May 1, 1908, the club was the first modern group dedicated to the perpetuation of the ancient sport of wave-riding. (Bishop Museum)

Surfing: A History of the Ancient Hawaiian Sport, during Makahiki from October through January, the Islanders halted all work to spend their days dancing, feasting, and surfing. Thousands gathered to watch tournaments where a special god of sport—*akua pa'ani*—presided. At Kahaluu Bay on the Kona coast, a *heiau* (ancient shrine) was erected of black lava rock and known as a "surfing temple" where one might pray for good waves. Anthropologist Kenneth Emory explains, "No important contest was engaged in without approaching the gods with prayers and offerings to win their favor. Some god presided over every sport. When a man felt he was in harmonious relations with the mysterious forces about

Down through the ages surf-riding probably varied in it's degree of popularity. It is most certainly a sport of peace and prosperity and we definitely know that after the invasion of Oahu by Kamehameha I in 1795 the practice of surf-riding declined, so that around 1900 the long board was a lost art.

— *Tom Blake,* Hawaiian Surfboard, *1935*

Duke Kahanamoku, circa 1930: Hawai'i's greatest surfer and swimmer, Duke Kahanmoku stands with his long longboard in front of the Ala Moana Hotel on Waikiki Beach. One of the founders of the Hui Nalu club, Duke became the first ambassador—and star—of surfing, inspiring interest in the sport from Australia to California, and beyond. (Tai Sing Loo/Bishop Museum)

him he was quite likely to accomplish superhuman feats of strength and skill."

Before contact with Cook's crew, Hawai'i was ruled by a code of *kapu* (taboos) regulating most everything, from where to eat and how to grow food to building surfboards and predicting when the waves would be good—or convincing the gods to make them good. Hawai'ian society was stratified into royal and common classes, and these taboos extended into the surf zone. There were reefs and beaches where the *ali'i* (chiefs) surfed and reefs and beaches for the commoners. Commoners rode waves on *paipo* and *alaia* standing boards as long as twelve feet, while the *ali'i* rode waves on *olo*, standing boards stretching an incredible twenty-four feet in length.

Several of Hawai'i's most famous chiefs—including Kaumuali'i, the ruling chief of Kaua'i, and Kamehameha I—were renowned for their surfing ability. *Ali'i* could prove their royalty by showing courage and skill in big waves, and woe betide the commoner who crossed into surf zones reserved for them. On the south shore of Oahu at Waikiki, the surf spot now known as Outside Castles was called

Kalehuawehe (the Removed Lehua) to commemorate an incident in which a commoner dropped into the same wave as a female chief—a taboo punishable by death. To save his skin, he offered her his *lehua* wreath. The gift worked, and he lived to surf another day.

By the time Captain Cook and his ships reached Hawai'i in 1778, the art, sport, and religion of surfing had reached a sophisticated peak. But what Lieutenant King described was the crest of wave-riding in Old Polynesia; in the wake of the *Resolution* and *Discovery*'s voyages, Hawai'i—and Hawai'ian surfing—fell into decline for more than 125 years.

European contact was not good for the Islands. After the publication of Cook and King's journals, the Sandwich Islands became a destination of choice for adventurers, brigands, missionaries, and other opportunists. *Haole* and Hawai'ian cultures collided at the end of the eighteenth century, and within the first two decades of the nineteenth century, Hawai'i was changed forever. The *haole* brought new technologies, languages, and gods—along with vices and diseases that ravaged a society that had evolved in paradisiacal isolation over more than a millennium. In 1819, less than fifty years following Cook's contact with the Islanders, the old system of taboos was dying away due to the *haole*'s influence.

As the *kapu* system crumbled, so did surfing's ritual significance within Hawai'ian culture. This brought the demise of the ages-old Makahiki festival, and now a commoner could drop in on a chief's wave without fear for his life, or even of giving up his *lehua*. Now that the Hawai'ians had been set adrift from the old ways, their culture fell into chaos; as Houston and Finney wrote, "For surfing, the abolition of the traditional religion signaled the end of surfing's sacred aspects. With surf chants, board construction rites, sports gods and other sacred elements removed, the once ornate sport of surfing was stripped of much of its cultural plumage."

Christian missionaries were largely to blame for surfing's demise in Hawai'ian culture, but in truth they only sped up decay that began earlier with the Islanders' contact with other *haole*. The first Calvinist missionaries arrived from England in the

A Thoroughly Modern *Olo*

Greg Noll Builds Ancient Surfboards the Old Hawai'ian Way

Greg Noll's Thoroughly Modern *Olo:*
The Noll *ohana* in their woodshed along California's Smith River. From left, son Jed, wife Laura, and Greg. The ancient Hawai'ians had koa and wili wili, stone adzes and coral; the Nolls use a variety of hardwoods from tropical to temperate and tools from draw knifes to power sanders.
(Photos © Jorge Salas)

In old Hawai'i, before the *haole* washed ashore and whitened the social order, the Hawai'ian *kapu* system controlled everything—including surfing and surfboards. The surfing *kapu* were a combination of localism and apartheid, delegating the mass of commoners to ride the shorter *alaia* boards while the royal *ali'i* rode *olo* boards as long as twenty-four feet. Commoners could only surf at certain beaches while the *ali'i* hogged the best reefs. If a commoner was caught riding an *olo* board, the punishment was decapitation.

Severing a head for riding a surfboard might seem a little severe today, but Greg Noll has a personal angle on the whole business and understands why a Hawai'ian king might get edgy if a commoner ripped his personal stick.

Noll is a renowned surfer who made his name in the 1950s. He was the Pied Piper who led a group of surfers in 1956 to break an old *kapu* on surfing Waimea Bay, and later became famous for bulling his way into big waves at Pipeline and Makaha. Now in his sixties and living on the Smith River in Cres-

cent City, Noll is the John Wayne of surfing, a retired tough guy who has a lucrative hobby carving recreations of ancient Hawai'ian surfboards from exotic hardwoods.

Noll travels to great lengths to collect rare hardwoods in Hawai'i, ship them home, cure and dry them, and then carve classic *olo* and *alaia* using plan shapes that go back to the Adam and Eve of all surfboards. He puts a tremendous amount of care and work into his boards, yet has all the advantages of the modern world on his side. He can only imagine what the ancients went through: "If I were a Hawai'ian prince and put all that work into a board and someone came along and snagged it off the beach and rode it, I might get a little cross myself," he says.

Noll has worn a lot of hats in his day—Olympic-class paddler, surf star, surfboard-manufacturing mogul, movie maker, brawler, troublemaker, commercial fisherman—but underneath it all he is really a woodshop geek with a great love for the Hawai'ian culture and people. He began making surfboards in the days of redwood and balsa, honing his woodworking by reshaping planks down to something a skinny kid could drag to the beach and ride. While still in high school, he moved to Hawai'i from his Los Angeles home and attended some of the roughest schools on Oahu. "I learned the Four R's in Hawai'i: Reading, writing, right crosses, and running," Noll says. His troubles all evened out when he helped a mammoth Hawai'ian named Bongo Alapai get an A on a woodshop project. "After that I had an island full of cousins," Noll grins.

Through the 1960s, Noll supported his surfing habit by making movies and selling boards. Greg Noll Surfboards operated out of a twenty-thousand-square-foot building in Hermosa Beach, and in its 1960s heydays was producing 150 boards weekly, from blowing foam at one end to finished product at the other.

Noll is one of the men who put the "industry" in surfing, but he also played hard. In winter, he went surfing, mostly in Hawai'i. In 1969, he rode one of his own creations—an eleven-foot four-inch, thirty-five-pound monster—on one of the biggest days ever attempted at Oahu's Makaha. He wiped out, survived, and became legend.

There are three manipulations of nature that are fundamentally pleasing to humans—carving rock, channeling water, and smoothing wood—and you will find all three within the Noll compound. He works in a Geppetto-class woodshop overflowing with drying hardwoods, tools, plan shapes, sawhorses, and a great deal of surfing history. Hanging from the rafters is the big-wave gun Noll rode at Makaha, and a similar yellow moose that Noll famously piloted at Outside Pipeline. Scattered among the different boards are some of his recreations carved from exotic hardwoods and polished to a glistening finish. Since 1991, he has spent hundreds of hours in the woodshed, gluing, tractioning, smoothing, and sanding works of art from raw blocks of wood.

Noll's recreations span time from surfing prehistory to the 1960s. There are Hawai'ian big-wave boards, balsa "beach boards" from the 1950s, and a redwood recreation of Duke Kahanamoku's favorite board from the 1920s. There are hardwood recreations of boards by Bob Simmons, Mickey Dora, and Jose Angel, but his favorites are the ancient *olo* boards made from Hawai'ian koa: "I get chills working with that wood because it is so beautiful and rich in Hawai'ian culture, but it is a bugger to get," Noll says. "It is *kapu* in Hawai'i to harvest live koa, so I have to wait for a tree to fall down or die. Then I fly to the Big Island, pick out some wood, and get it roughed into planks. Then I ship it from the Big Island to Oahu and then from Oahu to Oakland and then truck it up to Smith River."

Noll roughs out the planks using templates drawn from boards found in ancient burial mounds in Hawai'ian lava tubes. Those priceless boards are hidden away in locked vaults in Hawai'i's Bishop Museum: "They let me BS my way into a room where they usually allow only graduate students," he explains. "I had to wear gloves and used special pencils to draw the plan shapes, but the hair was standing up on the back of my neck the whole time, thinking about who had made these boards and how they had made them and where they had ridden them."

Once the board is roughed out, the koa has to dry, sometimes for two years; there are koa slabs stored away in the rafters and racks all around his woodshed. Once he gets down to shaping and finishing, he has modern advantages at his fingertips. "I use my favorite Skill 100 planer and boxes of sandpaper to shape and smooth the boards," Noll says. "And again, these boards are a bugger to make. The Hawai'ians made their boards with stone adzes and coral. To finish the boards, the Hawai'ians dipped them in pig slop or coconut oil to seal them. I oil my boards or occasionally fiberglass them."

Noll has averaged eight boards a year since 1991, and has orders lined up into the next decade. He has made *olos* as long as fourteen feet and sold them for fifteen thousand dollars. He regularly gets five to ten thousand dollars for a board, but sometimes can't bear to part with a special beauty and keeps it for his family. He knows his boards are mostly collector pieces, although some of his hardwood recreations have actually been baptized in the briny and slid along waves. "A few guys have paddled them out, ridden a couple of waves, and then hung them on the wall."

Noll feels that building these boards isn't as much about making money as it is about payback to the Hawai'ians for their incredible gift to the world for the sport of surfing. "Making these boards as a tribute to the ancient Hawai'ians keeps me busy and puts a little food on the table," he says, "but mainly it just makes me feel good."

1820s and quickly set about converting Hawai'ians from polytheism to their own one true God. Priests sought to straighten out the heathens, establishing new *kapus* that forbid drinking, gambling, ship visits by native women, and horseback riding on the Sabbath. The Calvinists taught the Hawai'ians to read and write a twelve-letter alphabet, putting the Hawai'ian language on paper. They also banished that lascivious form of native dancing called "hula" and insisted the Hawai'ians wear more clothes. The Hawai'ian chiefs resisted this new God and His messengers for a time, but within a decade the Christians' strict moral code was replacing the Hawai'ians' sensual way of life. Above all, the Calvinists insisted the Hawai'ians work more and play less; restrictions on play included a ban on that wicked sport of surfing.

Those who knew Hawai'i before and after the missionaries' arrival denounced the churchgoers for ruining what was unique and good about the

We came upon a large company of naked natives, of both sexes and all ages, amusing themselves with the national pastime of surf-bathing. Each heathen would paddle three or four hundred yards out to sea, (taking a short board with him), then face the shore and wait for a particularly prodigious billow to come along; at the right moment he would fling his board upon its foamy crest and himself upon the board, and he would come whizzing by like a bombshell. It did not seem that a lightning express train could shoot along at a more hair-lifting speed.

— *Mark Twain,* Roughing It, *1872*

Duke Kahanamoku, Surfing Hero: Duke appeared on everything from this 1920s travel brochure to a 1933 gum card and magazine ads promoting varnish. (Voyageur Press Archives)

Valspar—the Varnish of countless uses—

DUKE KAHANAMOKU of Hawaii, famous athlete, expert on the surf-board and world champion 100-metre swimmer has discovered still another use for Valspar. Duke Kahanamoku writes:

Honolulu, T. H., May 5, 1921
"Have used Valspar on my surf-boards for several years, and find that it preserves the wood, because it is waterproof and prevents the water from soaking in. No matter how long the board is used in the water, the Valspar is not affected and does not change color." DUKE KAHANAMOKU.

Valspar is durable, easy to apply, weatherproof and *waterproof*— "the Varnish that won't turn white."

Valspar's well-known uses—on floors, furniture, woodwork, linoleum, airplanes, boats and railroad trains—are supplemented by countless others such as

Baby Carriages	Golf Clubs
Window-Screens	Tents
Trunks	Fishing Rods
Hand Luggage	Tennis Rackets
Wicker Furniture	Oilskins
Refrigerators	Gun Stocks
Fireless Cookers	Snow Shoes
Draining Boards	and Skis
Boots and Shoes	Etc., etc.

In fact, anything that's worth varnishing is worth Valsparring.

Don't overlook the coupon below.

VALENTINE & COMPANY
Largest Manufacturers of High Grade Varnishes in the World—Established 1832

New York   Chicago   Boston   Toronto   London   Paris   Amsterdam
W. P. FULLER & Co., Pacific Coast

This coupon is worth 20 to 60 cents
VALENTINE & COMPANY, 456 Fourth Ave., New York

VALENTINE'S **VALSPAR**
The Varnish That Won't Turn White

Islands. One of the first *haole* to point a finger was W. S. W. Ruschenberger, who wrote in his 1838 *Narrative of a Voyage Around the World,* "A change has taken place in certain customs. . . . I allude to the variety of athletic exercises, such as swimming, with or without the surfboard, dancing, wrestling, throwing the javelin, etc., all of which games, being in opposition to the strict tenets of Calvinism, have been suppressed. Can the missionaries be fairly charged with suppressing these games? I believe they deny having done so. But they write and publicly express their opinions, and state these sports to be expressly against the laws of God, and by a succession of reasoning, which may be readily traced, impress upon the minds of the chiefs and others the idea that all who practice them secure themselves the displeasure of offended heaven. Then the chiefs, from a spontaneous benevolence, at once interrupt the customs so hazardous to their vassals."

Harsh words, which drew a response from Hiram Bingham, one of the staunchest defenders of the missionary position. In his *A Residence of Twenty-One Years in the Sandwich Islands* from 1847, Bingham righteously proclaimed: "The decline

Duke Kahanamoku
Hawaiian Swimmer

**Duke Kahanamoku
1930s Waikiki
Surfboard:** Typical of
the boards popular at
Waikiki in the 1930s,
this California redwood
plank belonged to Duke
Kahanamoku. (© Malcolm
Wilson)
SPECIFICATIONS: 10' LONG;
24" WIDE; 3½" THICK; 70
POUNDS

Left, **Duke Kahanamoku
Postcard, 1910s:**
Duke became an image
of Hawai'i, promoted on
postcards such as this
to be sent home to lure
others to the Islands. As
the flipside promised, "He
is generally in the surf at
Waikiki Beach Honolulu
every afternoon." (Voya-
geur Press Archives)

Waikiki Surfing Post-cards, 1910s–1930s
(Voyageur Press Archives)

and discontinuation of the use of the surfboard, as civilization advances, may be accounted for by the increase in modesty, industry and religion, with-

out supposing, as some have affected to believe, that missionaries caused oppressive enactments against it."

Yet the "oppressive enactments" of the missionaries were those very things—modesty, industry, and religion. Calvinists forbade wearing the native loincloths and frowned upon the intermingling of the sexes on land and sea. Surfing, naturally, was one of the arch evils, and the missionaries' enforced modesty and morality was quickly applied to wave-riding. Sadly, many Hawai'ians set their surfboards aside.

Surfing wasn't the only thing dying out in Hawai'i; the Hawai'ians themselves were being killed off. After 125 years of European contact, conquest, and contamination, the *haole* controlled just about everything Hawai'ian—the Islanders' gods, culture, magic, land, and their lives. The estimated population of Hawai'i at the time of Captain Cook's arrival was four hundred thousand to eight hundred

> I shall never forget the first big wave I caught out there in the deep water . . . I heard the crest of the wave hissing and churning, and then my board was lifted and flung forward. I scarely knew what happened the first half-minute. Though I kept my eyes open, I could not see anything, for I was buried in the rushing white of the crest. But I did not mind, I was chiefly conscious of ecstatic bliss at having caught the wave.
>
> — *Jack London, "A Royal Sport: Surfing at Waikiki," 1907*

thousand. Within a hundred years, the population was down to a mere forty thousand.

Control over the people was not enough, however; the outsiders wanted it all. In 1893, sugar was Hawai'i's number one export and it had made a number of families rich. But because Hawai'i was still a sovereign foreign nation, the United States imposed a hefty import tariff on its sugar. Now, a cabal of businessmen, plantation owners, and missionaries assisted by U.S. Marines plotted to overthrow the Hawai'ian monarchy led by Queen Lili'uokalani. When the queen fought back against *haole* domination of her Islands, the foreigners imprisoned her. U.S. President Grover Cleveland declared the coup "not merely wrong, but a disgrace," yet his words came too late. In 1898, the United States annexed Hawai'i as a territory.

If all this was inspired by the outraged spirit of Captain Cook, then he had certainly gotten his revenge.

Once surfing gets into your soul, it keeps its hold: Wave-riding hadn't disappeared from the Hawai'ian Islands by the dawn of the twentieth century, but the traditions were being lost. Honolulu had become Hawai'i's largest city, home to one out of every four Hawai'ians, but surfing on the bay's reefs was now a rarity. Most of the enduring wave-riding took place at isolated spots like Kalehuawehe on Oahu's south shore, with a few surfers on Maui, Kaua'i, and the other islands. Several famous photographs from the early 1900s survive of native surfers wearing loincloths with Diamond Head—and little else—in the background. These were solitary men, most likely posing for the camera, surfing alone where once hundreds had cavorted.

At times, even an adventurous visitor caught a wave to sit on top of the world—and then told the world all about it. Reverend Henry T. Cheever celebrated the surfing he witnessed at Lahaina, Maui, in his 1851 journal, *Life in the Hawaiian Islands, or, The Heart of the Pacific, As It Was and Is*: "It is highly amusing to a stranger to go out to the south part of this town, some day when the sea is rolling in heavily over the reef, and to observe there the evolutions and rapid career of a company of surf-players. [The sport of surfing] is so attractive and full of wild excitement to the Hawai'ians, and withal so healthy, that I cannot but hope it will be many years before civilization shall look it out of countenance,

Summer this Winter in HAWAII

You can come to the Islands **NOW!**

Do not delay the trip to **Paradise** any longer— Read how easy and inexpensive the voyage really is.

or make it disreputable to indulge in this manly, though it be dangerous, pastime."

Fifteen years later, Mark Twain sailed to Hawai'i and attempted wave-riding. He described his misadventures in his 1866 book *Roughing It*: "I tried surf-bathing once, subsequently, but made a failure of it. I got the board placed right and at the right moment, too; but missed the connection myself. The board struck the shore in three-quarters of a second, without any cargo, and I struck the bottom about the same time, with a couple of barrels of water in me."

Ironically, it was three *haole* who led the rebirth of surfing in the Hawai'ian Islands, and a fourth man— a native Hawai'ian—who was instrumental in pollinating surfing around the world.

In 1907, Jack London came to Hawai'i a literary lion, having already published three best-selling adventure novels: *The Call of the Wild*, *The Sea-Wolf*, and *White Fang*. London and his wife Charmian were celebrities when they stayed on Waikiki Beach where the Ala Moana Hotel now stands. There were still a few surfers at Waikiki at that time, a loose clique of Hawai'ians and part-Hawai'ians who formed a group called the Waikiki Swimming Club. London met the crew and was introduced to the joy of surfing by Alexander Hume Ford, an eccentric journalist and wanderer. Here, London met the most celebrated Waikiki beach boy of the time, twenty-three-year-old Irish Hawai'ian George Freeth. London was a renowned writer, Ford a habitual organizer, and Freeth a great waterman. What they had in common was a love of surfing, and their combined talents breathed life into the dying-yet-beautiful Sport of Kings.

London penned a tribute to wave-riding, "A Royal Sport: Surfing in Waikiki," published in the October

The First Surfers in California

The young Hawaiian princes were in the water, enjoying it hugely and giving interesting exhibitions of surfboard swimming as practiced in their native islands.

– *The Santa Cruz Surf* newspaper, July 20, 1885

The first surfers to practice the ancient sport of Hawai'ian kings in California were true Hawai'ian princes. There were three of them, and they were seen "surfboard swimming" at the mouth of the San Lorenzo River in Santa Cruz in July 1885.

The Kalaniana'ole brothers—Jonah, David, and Edward—were certified Hawai'ian royalty, the sons of Kaua'i's high chief D. Kahalepouli and Princess Kekaulike.

Jonah Kuhio Kalaniana'ole was fourteen in 1885, the oldest of the three and the one destined for greatness. After leaving Saint Matthews Hall in San Mateo, Jonah attended England's Royal Agricultural College. Childless Hawai'ian Queen Lili'uokalani adopted Jonah and proclaimed him prince, and that

got him into trouble during the *haole* overthrow in January 1895. At age twenty-four, Prince Kuhio aided the Royalist uprising against Hawai'i's new republic. Captured and convicted of treason, he was sentenced to a year in jail.

Released, Jonah Kuhio Kalaniana'ole became the U.S. Congressional delegate from the Territory of Hawai'i, a seat he was reelected to ten times. He did much for Hawai'i, and today there are highways, buildings, and beaches named in his honor. And when Hawai'i celebrates Prince Kuhio Day on March 26, the state pays tribute to the eldest of the three Hawai'ian princes who were "surfboard swimming" at the San Lorenzo Rivermouth in 1885.

1907 *Lady's Home Companion* and again in 1911 as part of *The Cruise of the Snark*. His evocation was pure poetry: "Where but the moment before was only the wide desolation and invincible roar, is now a man, erect, full statured, not-struggling frantically in that wild movement, not buried and crushed and buffeted by those mighty monsters, but standing above them all, calm and superb, poised on the giddy summit, his feet buried in the churning foam, the salt smoke rising to his knees, and all the rest of him in the free air and flashing sunlight, and he is flying through the air, flying forward, flying fast as the surge on which he stands. He is a Mercury—a brown Mercury. His heels are winged, and in them is the swiftness of the sea."

London continued, describing George Freeth riding upon the crests: "I saw him tearing in on the back of [a wave] standing upright with his board, carelessly poised, a young god bronzed with sunburn." Such was London's power of prose that Freeth was invited in 1907 to California by railroad and real estate magnate Henry Huntington to demonstrate wave-riding to promote the Redondo-Los Angeles Railway. Freeth caught a wave in front of an astonished crowd and earned the title of "The First Man to Surf in California."

Meanwhile, Alexander Hume Ford was campaigning on behalf of surfing in Hawai'ian waters. In 1908, he petitioned the Queen Emma Estate trustees to set aside a plot of land next to Waiki-ki's Ala Moana Hotel for a club to preserve the ancient Hawai'ian pursuits of surfing and outrigger canoeing. Ford's fundraising manifesto promised the fraternity would "give an added and permanent attraction to Hawai'i and make Waikiki always the Home of the Surfer, with perhaps an annual Surfboard and Outrigger Canoe Carnival which will do much to spread abroad the attractions of Hawai'i, the only islands in the world where men and boys ride upright upon the crests of waves." The trustees accepted Ford's plan and on May 1, 1908, the Hawaiian Outrigger Canoe Club was founded, the first modern group dedicated to the perpetuation of wave-riding. The clubhouse offered facilities for dressing and a grass hut for board storage right on the beach.

Native Hawai'ians launched in 1905 the informal Hui Nalu—literally "Club of the Waves"—revitalizing Islander interest in the sport. Hui Nalu and the Outrigger Canoe Club began friendly competi-

tions, and by 1911 when the Hui Nalu was formalized, there were as many as a hundred surfboards on Waikiki Beach. In 1915, Jack London returned to Hawai'i and was shocked to find the Outrigger Canoe Club had 1,200 members, "with hundreds more on the waiting list, and with what seems like half a mile of surfboard lockers," as he happily noted.

One of the Hui Nalu founders was a teenager named Duke Kahanamoku. He and his friends began to gather under a *hau* (lowland tree) at Waikiki Beach, spending their days surfing and swimming. According to legend, Duke was sitting on his board with others offshore of Waikiki one afternoon waiting for a rideable swell; Duke pointed seaward and said, "The name of our club is out there. The swells coming in spill into a *hui* (a gathering) and *nalu* (surf) is what we ride. Add them up and you get *hui nalu*—the surf club!"

Duke soon won fame as a swimmer; credited with developing the flutter kick to replace the scissor kick in freestyle swimming, he became the three-time world record holder in 100-meter freestyle competition. As a surfer, Duke was one of Hawai'i's best ocean watermen, a beach boy and a fine figure of Polynesia—slim, muscular, built for speed, and blessed with extraordinarily long hands and feet. He was a natural.

In 1912, Duke passed through Southern California en route to the Olympic Games in Stockholm. He took time out from his travels to demonstrate his surfing style at Corona del Mar and Santa Monica, causing a sensation greater than Freeth. Despite oversleeping and almost missing his heat, Duke won Olympic gold in the 100-meter freestyle in Stockholm and again in Antwerp in 1920. Touted as the fastest swimmer alive, he toured constantly, giving swimming exhibitions around the world. Along the way, he also became a favorite of Hollywood directors, who cast him as an Aztec chief, Hindu thief, Arab prince—any exotic, dark-skinned role. On off days from the shady turf of the studio, Duke led his fellow Hollywood stars into the sunny surf.

My boys and I, we showed them how to go surfing.
— *Duke Kahanamoku*

Hawai'i Travel Brochures and Posters, 1910s–1920s (Voyageur Press Archives)

Hawaii DIRECT FROM **LOS ANGELES**

Hollywood, and proselytizing for surfing around the globe. But it was back home in Hawai'i in summer 1917 that Duke made himself legendary—and with a single ride. He caught a wave of near-mythological size at Kalehuawehe, which was now called Outside Castles. The wave took him well over a thousand yards, from Outside Castles, through Elk's Club, Cunha's, Queen's, and all the way to the beach. It was a wave and a feat that have never been matched.

Following in the wake of George Freeth and Duke Kahanamoku, the population of surfers in California grew slowly but steadily. Surfboards were mostly made of heavy and unwieldy redwoods and hardwoods with designs adapted from Hawai'ian shapes to fit California conditions. By 1928, a Wisconsin-born surfing convert named Tom Blake organized the Pacific Coast Surfriding Championships at Corona del Mar, the United States' first wave-riding competition. The best surfers from all over California competed for the Tom Blake Trophy from 1928 to 1941, when World War II put an end to the event. Blake also became the first photographer to shoot surfing from the water.

Surfing was on its way to becoming more than just a sport in California; the lure of the waves was creating a lifestyle. One of the first Southern California men to become enamored with surfing in the 1920s and 1930s was John H. "Doc" Ball, a dentist who grew up near Hermosa Beach. Doc Ball got hooked by surfing as seriously as any man ever has, finding it "a great stress reliever" away from the confines of an office and the professional sadism of the dentist's chair. He struggled with the early redwood surfboards until he developed the strength and agility to handle them. Like Blake, Doc Ball was also fascinated by photography and he became the second serious surf photographer, shooting wave-riding from the water via a waterproof camera housing. But he also was capturing something more. Doc Ball turned his camera to document the emerging surfing lifestyle as it existed before, during, and after World War II. He was truly catching a new wave.

Surfing had traveled over a millennium from Polynesia to Hawai'i and on to California and Australia. But the love affair was just beginning.

Out of the water, I am nothing.
— *Duke Kahanamoku*

Everywhere he went, Duke rode atop his fame to introduce the world to the sport of surfing. Invited in 1915 by the New South Wales Swimming Association to give a swimming exhibition at the Domain Baths in Sydney, Duke spread the good word on wave-riding to Australia. At the time, Australians were only vaguely aware of surfing, yet the ocean-crazed people thrilled when Duke fashioned an eight-foot six-inch *alaia* board out of native Australian sugar pine and rode it at Freshwater Beach in Manly in February 1915. Duke's ride single-handedly put Australia on a path to superpower status in the surfing world.

Duke was a busy man into the 1920s, competing in the 1920 and 1924 Olympics, hobnobbing in

Tourist at Diamond Head, 1930s: Tourists began making the trek to Waikiki by the scores, and if they didn't learn to wave-ride Hawai'ian-style, they at least posed with a surfboard for the folks back home. (Voyageur Press Archives)

Slow Boat to Paradise

The Long Happy Life of the SS *Lurline*

My first time to Hawaii was 1948. I took the *Lurline* out of San Pedro, and ate for four days straight. I got off the boat, bought trunks and shirts from Nat Norfleet Sr. and surfed Waikiki all summer. I was 17.

– Surf industry pioneer Walter Hoffman

Ask surfers of a certain age what they remember best about Hawai'i in the 1930s, 1940s, and 1950s, and their eyes will get misty as they speak the name of a girl—"Lurline."

The SS *Lurline* was an elegant passenger liner, pride of the Matson Shipping Line. This was the slow boat to Hawai'i, but no one seemed to mind. From the early 1930s, the *Lurline* sailed the San Francisco–Palos Verdes–Hawai'i route, transporting tens of thousands of people to paradise. Some of the passengers were surfers bound for the promised land. Others became surfers after their first trip and the experience of riding waves with the beach boys at Waikiki.

The Matson firm was founded by Swedish immigrant William Matson in 1882. Coming to San Francisco, he sailed the bay and rivers, becoming acquainted with the wealthy Spreckels fam-

ily, who asked him to skipper their family yacht, *Lurline*. The Spreckels helped Matson finance his first ship, the *Emma Claudina*, which made its premiere passage to Hawai'i in 1881. The Islands were producing one hundred thousand tons of sugar annually, and reliable shipping was essential. Matson hauled sugar to California, returning with cargo, machinery, and building materials to help fuel the growth of Hawai'i.

The innovation of safe, comfortable passage to Hawai'i sparked the first boom in travel to the South Pacific in 1910, and William Matson died with fourteen ships in his fleet and a near-monopoly on Pacific trade and passenger travel.

The firm was taken over by William Phillip Roth, the husband of Matson's daughter Lurline. With business booming, the company ordered three glamorous new sister ships between 1930 and 1932—the *Mariposa*, *Monterey*, and *Lurline*.

The *Lurline* was a beauty, gleaming white and sleek of hull. She was 632 feet long, built for style and speed, accommodating 475 first-class passengers and 240 surfer-class passengers with a crew of 359. She began regular service to Honolulu in 1934.

Amelia Earhart became the first to fly from California to Hawai'i, in 1935. The following year, a Martin M-130 flying boat called the *Hawaii Clipper* made its premiere commercial flight from San Francisco to

Honolulu. The plane boasted private compartments, sleeping berths, and gourmet dining, and the seven customers paid $360 each way for what must have been a sketchy twenty-one-hour thirty-three-minute flight. But why bother, when you could take the *Lurline* instead?

In 1935, Earhart was one of many celebrities who cooled their heels in the Islands. During the 1930s, a Hawai'ian voyage aboard the *Lurline* was chic, and the likes of William Powell, Carole Lombard, Jimmy Durante, Claudette Colbert, Myrna Loy, Joel McCrea, Frances Dee, and Shirley Temple all made the trip, hanging out on the beach—often to be photographed with Duke Kahanamoku, Hawai'i's official greeter for several decades.

By 1941, Pan Am's *California Clipper* and five other Boeing B-314s were taking seventy-four passengers each on daily flights to Honolulu. But *Lurline* was still the queen of the Hawai'i run.

During World War II, the *Lurline* and other Matson ships served the country, carrying some 750,000 troops around the Pacific.

After the war, Matson sold the *Mariposa* and *Monterey* but kept the *Lurline,* which returned to service in 1948 after a twenty-million-dollar makeover. Matson continued to expand its operations and in 1951, built the Surfrider Hotel on Waikiki beach. Now *Lurline* passengers had a destination of the same luxurious class.

Postwar, the Douglas DC-4 became the plane of choice for crossing the big water, yet despite increasing competition, the *Lurline* was still operating at 97 percent capacity in 1955. In 1958, the Boeing 707 opened Hawai'i to international travel and in 1959, statehood brought a construction boom that saw the swamps of Waikiki disappear under a concrete jungle.

Statehood and jet service to the Islands spelled doom for Matson and the *Lurline.* In 1963, the ship suffered massive damage to its turbine engines, and

repair costs forced Matson to lay up the original *Lurline* and pass her name on to the *Matsonia.*

Passenger cruises to Hawaii struggled along until 1970, when Matson announced it was selling its flagship *Lurline* to Greek shipping operators. On June 25, 1970, *Lurline* arrived in San Francisco for the last time under the Matson flag. There was a bon voyage party, but it was not a happy farewell.

S. S. LURLINE · S. S. MARIPOSA · S. S. MONTEREY · S. S. MATSONIA

Hawaii

Reproduction from a painting of the S. S. Lurline

⚓ SHIPS . . . a vital part of the Nation's armor . . . SHIPS, and the men who sail them. Matson has proudly forged her fleet into this vital part of National armor. These SHIPS . . . and their officers and men . . . are serving our country's cause, without limit or reservation. MATSON SHIPS will also continue serving Hawaii and their normal routes to the limit permitted by the National Emergency.

Matson Line
TO *Hawaii* · NEW ZEALAND · AUSTRALIA
VIA SAMOA · FIJI

S. S. *Lurline,* 1940s: The Matson Line's S.S. *Lurline* became the mainland's connection to Hawai'i— and surfing at Waikiki. (Voyageur Press Archives)

From Here to Honolulu

Discovering the Secrets of the Sea • The World War II Years

Left, **Woody Brown Goes Hawai'ian, 1940s:** Lean and tan, Woody Brown rides a wave on Oahu. (Mary Sue Gannon and David L. Brown Productions)

Above, **Hawai'ian Wave-Riders, 1940:** Surfing in a Honolulu *Star Bulletin* Christmas gift print by Hawai'ian artist Lionel Warden. (Voyageur Press Archives)

Up until the 1940s, Hawai'i was a distant dream to most mainland Americans—the stuff of Bob Hope and Bing Crosby *Road* movies; exotic isles too far off in time and money for anyone but the wealthy.

World War II changed all that.

Japan's surprise attack on America's naval fleet at a then-little-known base called Pearl Harbor in Hawai'i drew the United States into a war that would

home did so with new ideas on how to live life—and many had firsthand experience on how to get your kicks on top of a wave.

Before 1940 with Hawai'i as remote as Timbuktu, swimsuits made of itchy wool, and surfboards hewn from heavy hardwoods, wave riding was a secret thrill enjoyed by just a coterie of surfers scattered in the Islands, California, and certain select spots

My soul is full of longing for the secrets of the sea, And the heart of the great ocean sends a thrilling pulse through me.

— Henry Wadsworth Longfellow, The Secret of the Sea*, 1850*

expose millions of Americans to the secrets of the sea. The war gave millions of young American men and women a free ride through Hawai'i and out into the Pacific. The armed services trained and transformed city slickers into sailors, laze-abouts into Marines, farmboys into frogmen. Those that came

around the rest of world. Following the war, the thrill was a secret no more.

For every million people who experienced the war there's a story, but of all those millions of stories there is one boy whose personal, perilous course through these years

-171 Surf Riding – Waikiki

linked together the experiences of many. Woody Brown was a rich kid who became a wanderer, adventurer, vegetarian, pilot, sailor, conscientious objector, and surfer. From New York City to La Jolla to Honolulu and now Maui, he usually found himself on the edge of history—sometimes witnessing it, sometimes aiding it, and often times changing it. While most of what he did he did just for fun, along the way he had a profound effect on sailing and sailboats, surfing and surfboards.

Woodbridge Parker Brown was born in 1912 into a wealthy New York City family, the kind of Social Register clan that produces doctors, lawyers, and presidents. His father had one of the original seats on the New York Stock Exchange, so Woody's life was founded on privilege. And yet he rejected the life of a "rich man's son" early on.

Quitting school at sixteen, he ran away from home to pursue his love of flying. He hung around Long Island's Curtiss Field, sweeping hangars and cleaning up oil leaks. It was here he met Charles

Lindbergh in 1927 when the soon-to-be-legendary aviator was training for his historic transatlantic flight in the *Spirit of St. Louis*. "I helped Lindy with his airplane before he took off for Paris," Woody remembers. "He was my hero."

Woody soon became more interested in gliders than powered flight. As he was learning how to glide, he met Englishwoman Elizabeth Sellon. Together, they ran off to California, driving a Chrysler Airflow and towing a glider behind. "We left New York in '35," Woody says. "We drove to La Jolla and lived there five years—the happiest time of my life!" And at La Jolla Beach, Woody launched his gliders right off the sand, Elizabeth faithfully piloting the tow car.

While riding the thermal waves above the beaches, Woody couldn't help but notice all the cool, green

Above, **Wave-Riding in Hawai'i, 1940s:** Woody Brown sliding left, in the Hawai'ian Islands at Waikiki or Yokohama Bay. (Mary Sue Gannon and David L. Brown Productions)

waves breaking down below him. He wondered about riding the ocean the way he rode the air, and that lead him to use his glider-building skills to make surfboards: "I first made these solid redwood planks, you know, like a Boogie board," Woody says. "But I wanted to ride waves standing up, so I made a hollow little plywood box. About 9 feet long and about 4 inches thick, but it was hollow so it didn't weigh much. It was great. I could paddle out there and catch the waves and ride." Woody made an educated guess about surfboards in 1936; nearly seventy years later, his design still stands as a sophisticated guess.

Woody's second board was thicker and wider than the first—and it had a small skeg for stabilization. That skeg started a revolution. Some historians credit Woody Brown with the invention of the surfboard fin, but Woody humbly points to Tom Blake. "I didn't know anything about Blake and his experiments with adding fins to surfboards," Woody says. "See, we were all separated out. I was in San Diego and he was in L.A., way up there."

Woody also started a small surfing craze in La Jolla. He and friends Towny Cromwell and Don Okey pioneered places like Windansea, Pacific Beach, Bird Rock, and Sunset Cliffs. Through the second half of the 1930s, it was virgin territory.

By 1939, Elizabeth was pregnant. Woody was slated to travel to Texas for a glider competition. "I told my wife I'd stay with her, but she told me to go," Woody says sadly. "She said, 'It's important because everybody's expecting you to be there. You're the top man! They all want to compete with you!'" So Woody went.

At Wichita Falls in 1939, Woody flew his Thunderbird glider 263 miles to national and world gliding records for altitude, distance, maximum time aloft, and goal flight. A telegram of congratulations awaited him from President Herbert Hoover when he finally came down to earth.

Then fate interceded. Driving back to California as fast as he could, Woody arrived in time for Elizabeth to begin labor. She gave birth to a boy, but she herself died in childbirth. "And, boy, I just cracked up," Woody remembers. "I just couldn't take it 'cause we were so happily married. Our boy lived but I couldn't take care of him. I couldn't take care of myself. I couldn't sleep; quit flying; quit everything. I told the Lord: 'I can't take it anymore.' So, He goes: 'Why don't you go to Tahiti? You've always wanted to.' You know, we always hear about the magic of the South Seas. Next day, I was on the boat. I got my passport and everything. I left my car, the garage, my home, glider, everything. I don't know what happened to them. I just walked out and left everything. When you're off your rocker that way, you know, you don't know what you're doing."

In September 1940, Woody Brown caught a ship for Tahiti, but the tensions that would soon pop at Pearl Harbor were bubbling all over the South Pacific. "They wouldn't give you a passport to get out

You catch the wave as it curls. We take it earlier, perhaps half a dozen yards away from the point of turning, and accumulate speed by scooping the water with the right hand and using the left in the ordinary way, putting in the while at least the speed you saw me finish my world record in last Saturday afternoon. Then the velocity of the shoot is materially increased and its duration rendered greater. We begin on our sides and find we get more control over the effort, then we turn on our backs or breasts as fancy suggests.

— *Duke Kahanamoku, 1915*

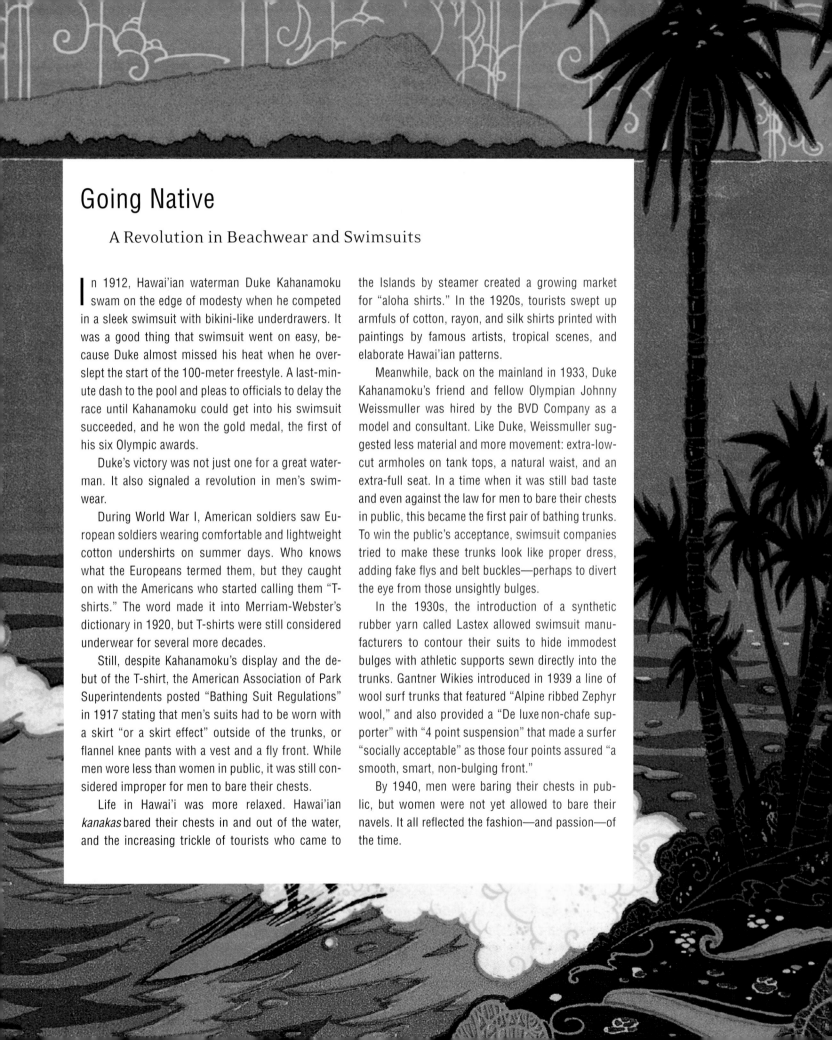

Going Native

A Revolution in Beachwear and Swimsuits

In 1912, Hawai'ian waterman Duke Kahanamoku swam on the edge of modesty when he competed in a sleek swimsuit with bikini-like underdrawers. It was a good thing that swimsuit went on easy, because Duke almost missed his heat when he overslept the start of the 100-meter freestyle. A last-minute dash to the pool and pleas to officials to delay the race until Kahanamoku could get into his swimsuit succeeded, and he won the gold medal, the first of his six Olympic awards.

Duke's victory was not just one for a great waterman. It also signaled a revolution in men's swimwear.

During World War I, American soldiers saw European soldiers wearing comfortable and lightweight cotton undershirts on summer days. Who knows what the Europeans termed them, but they caught on with the Americans who started calling them "T-shirts." The word made it into Merriam-Webster's dictionary in 1920, but T-shirts were still considered underwear for several more decades.

Still, despite Kahanamoku's display and the debut of the T-shirt, the American Association of Park Superintendents posted "Bathing Suit Regulations" in 1917 stating that men's suits had to be worn with a skirt "or a skirt effect" outside of the trunks, or flannel knee pants with a vest and a fly front. While men wore less than women in public, it was still considered improper for men to bare their chests.

Life in Hawai'i was more relaxed. Hawai'ian *kanakas* bared their chests in and out of the water, and the increasing trickle of tourists who came to the Islands by steamer created a growing market for "aloha shirts." In the 1920s, tourists swept up armfuls of cotton, rayon, and silk shirts printed with paintings by famous artists, tropical scenes, and elaborate Hawai'ian patterns.

Meanwhile, back on the mainland in 1933, Duke Kahanamoku's friend and fellow Olympian Johnny Weissmuller was hired by the BVD Company as a model and consultant. Like Duke, Weissmuller suggested less material and more movement: extra-low-cut armholes on tank tops, a natural waist, and an extra-full seat. In a time when it was still bad taste and even against the law for men to bare their chests in public, this became the first pair of bathing trunks. To win the public's acceptance, swimsuit companies tried to make these trunks look like proper dress, adding fake flys and belt buckles—perhaps to divert the eye from those unsightly bulges.

In the 1930s, the introduction of a synthetic rubber yarn called Lastex allowed swimsuit manufacturers to contour their suits to hide immodest bulges with athletic supports sewn directly into the trunks. Gantner Wikies introduced in 1939 a line of wool surf trunks that featured "Alpine ribbed Zephyr wool," and also provided a "De luxe non-chafe supporter" with "4 point suspension" that made a surfer "socially acceptable" as those four points assured "a smooth, smart, non-bulging front."

By 1940, men were baring their chests in public, but women were not yet allowed to bare their navels. It all reflected the fashion—and passion—of the time.

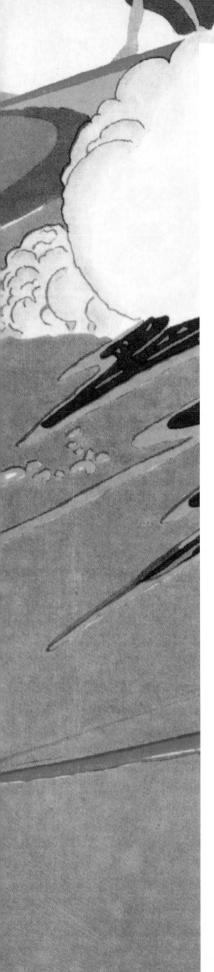

The Aloha Shirt

Wearing Hawai'i Proud

The aloha shirt is a true product of modern Hawai'i—a combination of Polynesian images, Asian fabrics, and *haole* technology and marketing.

In the late 1920s, Chinese merchant Ellery Chun ran King–Smith Clothiers & Dry Goods in Waikiki. Among his inventory were rolls of kimono fabric for his Japanese customers. At some point, a Chinese lantern flashed over Chun's head and he began cutting and sewing shirts from the leftover pieces. The first notice for Chun's newly named "Aloha Shirts" appeared in the *Honolulu Advertiser* newspaper on June 28, 1935.

Aloha shirts were an instant hit with locals, tourists, military personnel, and surfers. Within a couple of years, small tailor shops throughout the Islands began manufacturing and selling aloha shirts en masse.

"Aloha Shirt" became a registered trademark in 1936. Hawai'ian resident Herbert Briner saw the alarming production of these shirts, bought an existing uniform manufacturer, and transformed it into Hawai'i's first ready-to-wear garment manufacturer. He named his firm for the great Island king, and Kamehameha aloha shirts became famous.

In 1937, Nat Norfleet and George Brangier got in on the act at 1704 North King Street, next to one of the pioneers of Hawai'ian garment manufacturing, Wong's Products. "We began like nearly everybody else in the business—not with a pair of shoestrings but with one shoestring between the two of us," says Norfleet. "Red McQueen had brought back from the 1932 Olympics in Japan some shirts made out of silk kimono cloth. We copied them to produce our first aloha shirts. They were absolutely horrible, but Elmer Lee had a stand in front of the old Outrigger Canoe Club where he sold coconut milk and pineapple juice, and he sold our horrible shirts." Norfleet and Brangier called their company Kahala. In 1939, they moved into a factory on Kapiolani Boulevard, perfectly situated to supply the endless line of servicemen soon flocking to the Islands to fight the Japanese.

World War II was ended by a man who liked aloha shirts. President Harry S. Truman was just one of many celebrities and public figures who proudly wore aloha shirts and inspired their worldwide popularity. John Wayne and Duke Kahanamoku endorsed major designer labels while Bing Crosby, Arthur Godfrey, and Johnny Weissmuller entertained in their loose, flowing sportshirts printed with everything from palm trees to ukuleles to wave-riders.

In 1948, seventeen-year-old California surfer Walter Hoffman took his first trip to Hawai'i. "The first thing I did was go to Kahala and buy my trunks and shirts. Then I spent the summer surfing," he remembers. That trip changed Hoffman's life. He returned to California with a steamer trunk full of aloha prints to steer the family business—Hoffman Fabrics—away from woolens and into the brave new world of rayon and polyester. Hoffman Fabrics went on to supply material to almost every major clothing company, including start-up money for Ocean Pacific, which would become the mother of all surfwear firms.

Out of the 1940s, the aloha shirt's popularity grew as travel to Hawai'i became easier with faster ocean liners and then air travel. *From Here to Eternity* also gave the aloha shirt a kick in the pants. The movie was nominated for thirteen Academy Awards including Best Costume Design—a good call as costume designer Jean Louis made Montgomery Clift look good lying dead in a ditch in an aloha shirt. In black and white.

By 1959, the world was bubbling for the Islands and aloha shirts. The first passenger jet arrived in Honolulu that year as Hawai'i became a state. Hawai'i's tourist industry was about to explode: Kahala did one million dollars in sales in 1959 while in 1960, Kamehameha shipped thirty-five tons of garments to the mainland.

Gidget hit the big screen in 1960, but strangely, few of the movie's California surfers were wearing aloha shirts; madras was the rage at the time. That fashion changed a year later when Kahala introduced a Duke Kahanamoku line of aloha and t-shirts advertised in *Surfer* magazine featuring surfers like Greg Noll, Fred Hemmings, and Paul Strauch.

And then in 1961, Elvis Presley starred in *Blue Hawaii* as Chad Gates, a young Hawai'ian who gets out of the Army and returns to the Islands to surf, chase chicks, and hang out at his shack at Haunama Bay, playing the ukulele and slack key guitar with his buddies. Elvis was in his prime in 1961, and he made the aloha shirt look even better.

In vivid Technicolor.

Left, **Woody Brown at Makaha, 1950s:** Accidents would happen to Woody Brown. He crashed a few gliders in his day and nearly drowned on Oahu's North Shore. Here's Woody stepping into oblivion at Makaha. (Mary Sue Gannon and David L. Brown Productions)

Below, **Fran Heath and Tom Kelly 1934 "Cut-down" Surfboard:** Fran Heath and Tom Kelly were frustrated by the performance of their slab board, so they cut down the tail one day in 1934. The result was immediate; as Kelly remembers, "I caught a wave and the tail just dug in and I went right across, and we figured something had just happened." (© Malcolm Wilson)
SPECIFICATIONS: 10' 10" LONG; 19½" WIDE; 3¼" THICK; 60 POUNDS

of the country," Woody says. He made it only as far as Hawai'i, arriving in the U.S. territory at the start of interesting times.

Flying was not available in Hawai'i at that time, so Woody tried to surf the sadness out of his system: "Surfing saved my life because I'd go out all day—Waikiki. I'd just go out on my board in the morning and sit out there all day long and surf. Lunch time, I'd dive down and get seaweed off the bottom to eat and just stay there 'til late evening, sunset. Then, I'd go in and I'd be able to sleep a little 'cause I was so damn tired from being in the sun and surfing all day. And, I survived!"

Akin to T. E. Lawrence in his prewar years as a student archaeologist in Arabia, Woody wandered the Islands on foot and bicycle, seeing places at ground level, meeting people, and enjoying an *aloha* that doesn't really exist anymore. "The old Hawaiians were such wonderful people," Woody said. "I'd stop in front of a house and ask if I could stay for the night and they'd say, 'Oh sure! Sure! Come in!' They'd treat me like a king and didn't want me to go."

Then Pearl Harbor was attacked. Every able-bodied man and woman fell in to avenge the Day that Would Live in Infamy. Woody, however, was a paci-

fist. He had family contacts he could have used, a name and reputation as a flyer, and even his age could have leveraged him into any position he wanted in the military. But Woody stood firm as a conscientious objector when that was a dangerous thing to be in Hawai'i, as some objectors were beaten and even killed by Hawai'ian natives and military personnel enraged by the Japanese.

During the war years, Woody lived on Waikiki Beach, surfing with a small band of friends including John Kelly, Fran Heath, and Wally Froiseth. They surfed everything Oahu's South Shore had to offer, including some big days when ships couldn't even get out of Honolulu Harbor.

The boards they rode were clunky, ten- to twelve-foot-long creations with wide tails and no skegs. They worked okay in the small surf but in the big stuff they'd slide ass, which meant a long swim back to the beach. Just before Woody arrived in Hawai'i, Kelly, Froiseth, and company came in from a day of sliding ass in big waves and decided to take action:

"Kelly got mad, picked up his axe and said, 'I'm gonna start chopping the board right *here*!'"

Woody says. "He hit it and he whittled

> We believe there is not another place in the world equal of Waikiki—that little cove lying in the shelter of Diamond Head—for surf shooting purposes, and thousands of travellers who call at our picturesque island every year endorse that opinion.
>
> — *Duke Kahanamoku, 1915*

Tom Blake 1940s "Cigar-Box" Surfboard: Built by surfer and shaper Tom Blake for Gene "Tarzan" Smith, this mahogany pointed-tail surfboard was known as a "cigar-box" for its hollow construction. (© Malcolm Wilson) SPECIFICATIONS: 13' LONG; 23" WIDE; 45 POUNDS

Facing page, **"Getaway":** Artist John Severson's watercolor of a surfer's getaway summed up the lure of the Islands. (Artwork © John Severson/surferart.com)

the tail down to about this big and said, 'Now I got it.'" What John Kelly created with his axe was an innovation called the Hot Curl. He reshaped the wide tail to a pintail; now the boards would hold in: "That changed the whole of surfing, see," Woody says. "Now, you could go out in big waves and control it."

Although Woody and Tom Blake started putting fins on surfboards in the mid-1930s, the innovation was not accepted for another decade, and Hot Curl boards filled the meantime. "Blake first put those skegs on his hollow boards, which were no good in anything but small surf," Woody remembers. "Those hollow boards were terrible and no one wanted anything to do with them or the skegs on the bottom. I think that is why it took us so long in Hawai'i to start using fins on our surfboards."

Hawai'ians were riding Hot Curls when Woody arrived and he used his natural-born knowledge of aero- and hydrodynamics to improve the design: "I learned to whittle mine down like theirs, because mine would slide ass. Wally helped me, he showed me. Then, I perfected it more and more, because I was interested in the speed. From my aerodynamics, I knew that too steep a curl will suck air, will drag, eh? The more you flatten out the curve, the faster you can go. So, with my boards, I'd flatten out the belly and get it flatter and flatter. Well, that made it stiff and hard to turn, but it made it fast."

Woody devised a board that was twelve feet long and weighed eighty pounds—Mack-truck heavy by today's standards but featherlight for the times. Fashioned from chambered redwood, it had a three-inch vee tail, thin rails made of spruce, and a nose and tail of oak. It was greased lightning in the big stuff. "Boy, when that bugger would drop into the wave, man, you'd just have to hold on to stay with it," he says. "You'd take off so fast, which is great when you've got a half mile of curl to get across!"

Woody rode out the war riding the waves of Waikiki. "I'll tell ya: in the old days, only the kings were allowed to surf at Castle Surf. You know, when I used to ride my board out there, I'm telling ya the truth: I felt somebody on the board with me. Boy, I didn't see anything, but, boy, it was there! With me, riding that wave. . . . It was spooky, I tell ya. Just like the king was there on my board, riding again. . . ."

By 1943, Woody was married to a Hawai'ian woman named Rachel and they were raising their two kids above the Waikiki Tavern, dead center in the surf scene. Oahu's South Shore is best for surfing in the summer months. During the rest of the year, Woody and his band of Merry Men—including Froiseth, Kelly, Fran Heath, Rus Takaki, and younger surfers like George Downing and Rabbit Kekai—explored other Island beaches looking for new breaks. The point at Makaha on Oahu's West Side became a favorite for these pioneering big-wave surfers, and they all struggled to evolve surfboards that would handle the super-fast steep walls of the Point. There were a lot of waves breaking on Oahu's North Shore as well, between the town of Haleiwa and Kahuku Point, and Woody was one of a small number of guys who bothered to drive all the way to Sunset Beach, which soon became the most popular break.

During the war, Woody was working as a surveyor for the Navy on Christmas Island, 1,160 miles south of Honolulu and just 105 miles north of the equator. He was probably there to check for surf on the Navy's dime, but what he saw ended up being his main contribution to the twentieth century.

In the lagoon, Woody watched in amazement as two South Pacific natives sailed a double-hulled canoe. Over the years Woody has described those sailors as both Melanesians and Tongans, which is a little confusing, but whoever they were, they

Modern "Outrigger," 1947: Inspired by ancient Polynesian outrigger canoes, Woody Brown engineered his modern "outrigger"—a glorious catamaran sailboat christened the *Manu Kai*. Brown's rediscovery of the ocean worthiness and speed of multihulls led to everything from the Hobie Cat to the Catalina Express. Woody waves from the rear while Ma Brown, in the big hat, grins at the launching of the *Manu Kai* in Hawai'i. (Mary Sue Gannon and David L. Brown Productions)

The art of the surfboard is coming back and the future will see contests and surf-riding that will rival any that took place for the old Hawaiian kings.

— *Tom Blake,* Hawaiian Surfboard, *1935*

were flying in their little boat, and Woody loved to fly. He described how the outrigger canoe could outrun Navy motor launches it was so sleek and fast in the surf. As he swore, "I sailed sailboats, and there was nothing like this anywhere." He made plans to build one of his own when he got home.

And he did. When Woody returned to Hawai'i he teamed up with Hawai'ian boatbuilder Alfred Kumalae, Hawai'ian boat designer Rudy Choy, and Californian Warren Seaman to establish C/S/K Catamarans. In 1947, they went to Hawai'i's Bishop Museum to measure ancient double-hulled canoes, then used modern engineering and materials to build the world's first asymmetric double-hulled sailing catamaran, the thirty-eight-foot *Manu Kai*.

Their catamaran was as fast as the sea bird for which it was named. "We went out and sailed circles around all the stuck-up guys from the Yacht Club," Woody laughs. "They couldn't go near that fast. They hated us!" Working with C/S/K Catamarans, Woody built multihulls from ten to one hundred feet in length, including one for the now famous Duke Kahanamoku. "Duke was a member of the yacht club and he used to race that catamaran I built for him," Woody says. "So, I got to know him pretty well, but I never got to surf with him too much because by the time I came along, he was getting kind of old, already. He didn't care to go out to Castle, anymore. He'd stay in there at First Break."

From the 1940s into the 1950s, Woody was in heaven. His noodling around in the South Pacific brought a rediscovery of the speed and oceanworthiness of ancient multihull outriggers, leading to

The Infamous Waimea Bay *Kapu*

In December 1943, Woody Brown drove to Oahu's North Shore with young Hawai'ian-born surfer Dickie Cross. These were pioneering years for surfers on the North Shore, yet the two were about to get involved in an incident that would resonate for a decade.

The most popular break on the North Shore was—and still is—the point at Sunset Beach. On December 23, 1943, Woody and Dickie Cross paddled out at Sunset during a rising swell. At that time, there were no satellite photos of weather reports to warn a surfer that a rapidly building swell was approaching, and Woody and Cross soon found themselves stuck outside at Sunset. "All of a sudden the waves were twenty feet," Woody remembers. "So, we got caught out there! It kept getting bigger and bigger and finally, we were sitting in this deep hole where the surf was breaking on two sides and coming into the channel.

"Then, all of a sudden, way outside in the blue water, a half mile out from where we were—and we were out a half mile from shore—way out in the blue water this tremendous wave came all the way down the coast, from one end to the other. It feathered and broke out there! We thought, 'Oh boy, so long, pal. This is the end.' But, we were sitting in this deep hole and the huge swell came through, but didn't break. Oh, boy! Scared the hell out of us!

"Well, there was a set of about five or six waves like that. So, after the set went by, we said, 'Hey, let's get the hell inside. What are we doing out here? This is no place to be! Let's get in!'"

They couldn't get in at Sunset Beach and their only option was to paddle west about five miles to Waimea Bay, a deep crescent that might give them a chance to get to the beach. Woody was thirty-one years old and wiser than Dickie Cross, who was only seventeen: "Dickie was just a gutsy young guy. . . . We dodged some big sets on the way to Waimea and when we got down there I wanted to sit in the channel and watch the sets. Well, Dickie just started paddling in and I tried to stop him but he wouldn't pay any attention. It seemed like it was his time; just like something was calling him, you know? It was just like it was his time to go. I don't know."

Cross paddled in and lost his board, and as Woody was paddling in to rescue him, another giant set came, forcing him to turn around and paddle outside. "I told him, 'Come out, come out!' It sounded like he said, 'I can't, Woody, I'm too tired.'"

The last Woody Brown saw of Dickie Cross, the young Hawai'ian was swimming in through giant surf at Waimea Bay. Woody got caught inside again and lost his board. As the sun was setting, he took off his trunks for less drag and swam for the beach: "For a moment I thought about sharks and then I thought, 'Well, that's stupid. I'll probably drown first.'"

Woody Brown somehow made it to the beach, but Dickie Cross was never seen again. Woody remembers having to go to the Cross family home two days before Christmas to tell them their boy had drowned.

The death of Dickie Cross in giant surf at Waimea Bay put a *kapu* on the spot that stood for more than a decade.

If the Swell drives him close to the rocks before he is overtaken by its break, he is much prais'd. On first seeing this very dangerous diversion I did not conceive it possible but that some of them must be dashed to mummy against the sharp rocks, but just before they reach the shore, if they are very near, they quit their plank, & dive under till the Surf is broke, when the piece of plank is sent many yards by the force of the Surf from the beach. The greatest number are generally overtaken by the break of the swell, the force of which they avoid, diving and swimming under the water out of its impulse. By such like exercises, these men may be said to be almost amphibious.

— *Lieutenant James King, logbook of the HMS* Discovery*, 1778*

everything from the Hobie Cat to the Catalina Express. Woody had his family, business, and enough time to chase wind and waves. Woody and his buddies Froiseth, Kelly, Heath, Downing, Henry Lum, and a handful of others were surfing those big Waikiki and Makaha waves on progressively advanced equipment. Skegs had caught on—finally. "For big waves you need a vee in the tail for the board to hold in, but the smaller the vee the faster the board goes," Woody explains. "Well, we wanted to go as fast as possible for Makaha and we also wanted to hold in, and eventually I dropped my rebellion against the skeg. George Downing and I made a super board for big waves at Makaha. It had a pretty flat back end, with little curves on the sides. Georgie said, 'I'll make a slot, so we can put a skeg in or take it out. We can try it and see the difference.' So, we went to Makaha. They were about 15-foot peaks that day. He went out there without the skeg first, and he rode it. It rode beautiful; fine, oh, just no trouble at all. Georgie came in and said, 'Well, let's put the skeg in and just try it, anyway. See the difference. See what it's about.' So, he puts the skeg in and went back out. It looked like he was riding the same, but he came back in and said, 'Hey, Woody, it's much better with a skeg.' I asked, 'How is it better?' He said, 'Well, it's not any faster, but it's more solid and you can turn it real easy with a skeg,' which we couldn't do before. Our boards were real stiff turning.

"Most surfers avoided the North Shore and looked to the point at Makaha to get their kicks," he remembers. "Makaha was a better surf than the North Shore. We had nice, long lines! There's a peak, see, and then you could slide all the way across the bay. I've seen 25 feet there, and you could make every damn one! In fact, we were making every one. We kept moving more over to the point, more in the boneyard. We kept moving over and still we were making 'em! Move further; still make 'em! And move wa-a-ay over 'til we were way out in front of that point and still make 'em across!"

In 1953, Honolulu photographer Skip Tsuzuki took a famous photo of Buzzy Trent, Wally Froiseth, and George Downing riding a fifteen-foot wave at Makaha. True to the rest of his life, Woody was probably on the beach or somewhere on the fringes when that photo was taken. Distributed by the Associated Press all over the United States, the image woke up a growing population of young California surfers to the possibilities awaiting them back in Hawai'i. Some had been in the Islands during the war and now longed to return; others were younger and the lure of Hawai'i was fresh.

Woody remembers those days: "California surfers started coming over, after that picture. That went to the mainland and, boy, that drove everybody crazy. They couldn't believe that. So, they all wanted to come out here and see for themselves.

"But I didn't know any of those guys. I didn't go with 'em then. I just went with Wally and them. I just never got to know 'em. We were kind of separated into two bunches, then. Wally, Kelly, and me, and those guys. We would go to Makaha. California guys went more for the North Shore. I don't know why—probably because the waves were more peaks and you could play around on the peak, where Makaha had this wall and, man, you had to have a good, fast board and had to really trim it to get going, to get across. That, maybe, didn't appeal to them."

Woody was happily on the fringes when the first wave of surfers flocked into Hawai'i from the mainland. As Ricky Grigg, Peter Cole, Greg Noll, and Buzzy Trent made names for themselves, Woody was happy to let it all flow past and enjoy what he had enjoyed all along—a free ride on the wind and waves.

Woody Brown, 2000:
Still surfing after all these years: Woody Brown in California, ready to charge some waves. (Mary Sue Gannon and David L. Brown Productions)

Hawai'i Travel Posters and Decal, 1940s–1960s (Voyageur Press Archives)

The Golden Years

From the Fall of Hitler to the Rise of Gidget • 1946 to 1959

Left, **San Onofre, 1963:** After a long gestation in Hawai'ian waters, surfing's heart moved to California and beaches such as Malibu and San Onofre. The early days in California were idyllic and uncrowded, but soon everyone was catching a wave. (Photo © LeRoy Grannis)

Above, **California Travel Decal, 1960s** (Voyageur Press Archives)

Blame it on Gidget.

In real life, she was just a perky and pertinacious California teen obsessed with surfing. But when her story was told by her father in the 1957 novel *Gidget* and then made into a 1959 movie starring Sandra Dee, the whole country went crazy for surfing.

Gidget was Kathy Kohner, a sixteen-year-old girl who learned to surf at California's Malibu Beach under the tutelage of a gang of board bums. These surfers christened her "Gidget"–a surf slang contraction of "girl" and "midget." Kathy came home from the beach with tales of "bitchen" wave-riding alongside sunburned gods with monikers like the great Kahoona and Moondoggie.

Gidget's real-life dad, Hollywood screenwriter Frederick Kohner, knew a good story when he heard one. A Jewish native of what is now the Czech Republic, Kohner escaped Hitler's rise to come to America in the 1930s. He soon was writing Broadway plays and then Hollywood scripts, earning himself a long list of writing credits including a 1938 Academy Award nomination for *Mad About Music*. But his teenager's world was something completely foreign and new to him. Kohner deciphered his daughter's slang and even listened in on her phone conversations–with her consent, or so he said–to learn more about this surfing thing. Then he sat down to write a romantic coming-of-age novel, told from Gidget's perspective and in her charming voice. It was like *The Catcher in the Rye* catching a wave, California's sunny answer to Françoise Sagan. At the time, *Gidget* was shocking–as was this whole, strange surf culture that was blossoming on the beaches.

Gidget was a best-selling book, and in 1959 Columbia Pictures invested some of its better talent into a movie version starring heartthrob Cliff Robertson as the great Kahoona, tall-dark-and-handsome crooner James Darren as the surf-happy Moondoggie, and blond queen Sandra Dee as "that troublesome teen" Franzie Lawrence, a.k.a. Gidget.

Gidget was an ambitious production–part romantic comedy, part action movie, part musical–that all added up to good, clean fun. The first movie was followed by two sequels: 1961's *Gidget Goes Hawaiian* and 1963's *Gidget Goes to Rome,* as well as a television series.

Yet Gidget did much more than just make money for Hollywood. As one critic smartly stated, if all American literature comes from *Huckleberry Finn*,

WATCH OUT BRIGITTE... HERE COMES GIDGET!

COLUMBIA PICTURES presents **GIDGET**

SANDRA DEE · CLIFF ROBERTSON · JAMES DARREN
ARTHUR O'CONNELL with MARY LaROCHE JO MORROW and THE FOUR PREPS

The joyous movie based on that book!

Screenplay by GABRIELLE UPTON · Based on the novel by FREDERICK KOHNER
CINEMASCOPE Produced by LEWIS J. RACHMIL · Directed by PAUL WENDKOS EASTMAN COLOR

Facing page, **"Malibu 1950":** The way it was: John Severson painted this water-colored remembrance of things past at Malibu. (Artwork © John Severson/surferart.com)

Left, ***Gidget* Movie Poster, 1959:** Blame it on *Gidget:* If all American literature derives from *Huckleberry Finn*, all American surf culture comes from *Gidget.* (Columbia Pictures)

> Surf-riding is not playing Monopoly and the more I got the knack of it, the more I was crazy about it and the more I was crazy about it, the harder I worked at it.
> — *Gidget in Frederick Kohner's* Gidget, *1957*

all American surf culture comes from *Gidget.* Kathy Kohner's story introduced the surfing lifestyle to the world.

Gidget also marked the end of an era and the start of a new one. By gazing back at the idyllic life of California surfers in the 1950s, *Gidget* launched a surfing craze that would ironically change that lifestyle forever.

After a long gestation in the warm waters of the Hawai'ian Islands, surfing's heart moved to California, as the men and women who had survived the war in the Pacific came home. Materials for surfboards and wetsuits improved thanks to wartime technology, and as surfboards got lighter and wetsuits got better, more and more people were riding

Le Bikini

The Bomb on the Beach

World War II ended with a bang, so to speak, and then more bangs that sent shock waves to all ends of the Earth and changed the way the world did just about everything—including what we wore to the beach.

On July 1, 1946—almost a year after the United States dropped two atomic bombs on Japan—American atomic-weapon testing continued with a pair of twenty-three-kiloton explosions on Bikini Atoll, a small archipelago in the Marshall Islands. The two bombs—dubbed Able and Baker—were detonated near a collection of ninety-five surplus warships, the blast of Baker sending a water column a mile high and tossing the aircraft carrier USS *Saratoga* more than eight hundred yards. "As soon as the war ended," Bob Hope joked, "we located the one spot on Earth that hadn't been touched by the war and blew it to hell."

The shockwaves from the Bikini Atoll tests reverberated all the way to the garment district of Paris. Five days later, French couture designers Jacques Heim and Louis Réard were nervously preparing to unveil their shocking new women's swimsuits to the world. Both ideas were a play on the material shortages that plagued the globe during World War II, their suits using minimal material and thus offering maximum exposure.

Heim dubbed his suit "l'Atome," and described it as "the world's smallest bathing suit." Réard fired back: His design was "smaller than the world's smallest bathing suit" and he claimed it could be pulled through a wedding ring. Réard was clever—and very French. Looking for a name for his creation, he took a clue from the explosion in the tropical South Pa-

cific and christened it "le Bikini." Réard promised his bikini would "reveal everything about a girl except her mother's maiden name."

Réard hired a nude dancer from the Casino de Paris to model the suit at the public Piscine Molitor swimming pool in Paris. Her name was Michelle Bernardini and she was game. In 1946, the bikini made its debut. Réard and Bernardini started a sensation, while the half-life of the Atome was short.

The bikini was a *succès de scandale*; the world was just recovering from the brutality of war and wasn't ready for any more shocks. In 1951, bikinis were banned from beauty pageants after the Miss World Contest. Spain, Italy, and Portugal outlawed the bikini in 1953, while decency leagues pressured Hollywood not to expose the suit on the silver screen. Amphibious starlet Esther Williams righteously huffed, "A bikini is a thoughtless act," whereas *Modern Girl* magazine sniffed, "It is hardly necessary to waste words over the so-called bikini since it is inconceivable that any girl with tact and decency would ever wear such a thing."

Little did they know.

In 1956, a bikini-bound Brigitte Bardot bounced across the world in a film suitably titled *And God Created Woman*. Perhaps she lacked decency and tact, but she had everything else. The bikini was off to the races.

The bikini was a war baby. It was something old and something new, something borrowed and, as the French would say, something *bleu*—as in, more than somewhat naughty. And in the history of beach fashion, the bikini was as big as a nuclear bomb.

Le Bikini, 1956: Scandalous or not, Brigitte Bardot showed off what the good Lord made in *And God Created Woman*. (Voyageur Press Archives)

Dale Velzy 1943 Redwood-Balsa Surfboard:
Dale Velzy shaped early boards such as this on sawhorses set up in the sand at California's Malibu, Hermosa, and Manhattan beaches. (© Malcolm Wilson)
SPECIFICATIONS: 11' LONG; 24" WIDE; 4" THICK; 80 POUNDS

waves. Because humans gravitate toward places that are beautiful and have good weather, a lot of them came to Los Angeles. And as the population of Southern California boomed, little pockets of surf scene began to take root along the coast from Santa Barbara to San Diego. The surfers of the 1950s were tribal, loyal to their local beaches with language, customs, and styles unique to their turf. You'd see them surfing at Trestles, Palos Verdes, Windansea, and Rincon. There were large pockets of surfers as far north as Santa Cruz and San Francisco, but out of the 1940s and through the 1950s, the most influential surf scene in California—and indeed, the world—was Malibu Beach.

A perfect little sand-and-cobblestone point facing south within easy reach of the huddled millions of the Los Angeles basin, Malibu has its face in the sun and its feet in the tingly cool waters of the Pacific Ocean. The cobblestone point was created by a clear creek where steelhead flourished while there were abalone and lobster on the rocks, fish in the surfline, and it seemed like the sun was always out, the sky always blue. The name of the spot was derived from a Native American tribe, the Chumash, who called the point *Humaliwu*, meaning literally, "Where the surf sounds loudly." When the surf is sounding loudly at Malibu, it is one of the prettiest waves anywhere.

Because of its proximity to the City of Angels, Malibu was the original perfect wave, first surfed by Tom Blake and Sam Reid in 1926. They had to sneak onto the point then, because Malibu was still a part of Rancho Malibu, a giant land grant passed from the Tapia family to Boston Brahmin Charles Rindge. The Rindge clan owned a vast tract of prime Southern California land that was at one time the most valuable piece of private real estate in the United States. Beginning in the early twentieth century, the federal government and then the state of California attempted to manifest their destiny through Rancho Malibu in various forms—a lighthouse on Point Dume, a railroad along the coast, and a highway from Oxnard to Santa Monica. The Rindges loved their property and privacy, and they fought all these intrusions. They kept out the lighthouse and built their own railroad to halt any other line. But by the 1920s, the pressures of population in California overwhelmed the Rindges, and they were forced to sell parcels of the Rancho to pay off the enormous legal bills they ran up fighting the state and federal governments.

The first surfers had to sneak in by sea in 1926, paddling down the coast to get past gunslinging cowboys who rode the fences and kept everyone out. Blake and Reid were the vanguard of many surfers, as the Malibu Colony was one of the first public habitations within Rancho Malibu, and the surf that broke there just to the east would start attracting more devotees out of the 1920s and into the 1930s. The Roosevelt Highway was officially dedicated in 1929, and as surfing became more popular in the 1940s, the waves at Malibu were perfectly located to provide the alchemy of surfing, from secret thrill to something much bigger.

In the late 1940s, Malibu was the beach of the gods. Marilyn Monroe tandem-surfed the breaks with Tommy Zahn. Peter Lawford was riding the waves there, too. Gary Cooper's wife, Rocky, persuaded her husband to take up surfing, and she took lessons from one of the top beach boys of the time. Child actor Jackie Coogan lived at the Colony and surfed every day. In those years, many actors shuttled back and forth from Malibu to Hollywood between shoots. Surfing kept them young, kept their skin clear, kept them trim.

These surfers needed a new type of board for Malibu. In 1947, Malibu wave-riders were going very straight and very fast on eleven-foot-long Pacific System Homes redwood-balsa planks that weighed a whopping eighty pounds. Those guys were having a ball, but those mean, green, humping walls inspired the likes of Bob Simmons, Joe Quigg, and Matt Kivlin to shave down the eleven-foot hardwood planks of their forefathers into something smaller, lighter, better. Within five years, "Malibu Chips" were as short as eight feet, twenty pounds lighter, made mostly of balsa, and some even boasted channels and twin fins. That fast transition in length, weight, materials, and design was inspired by Malibu and the surfers'

**Still Life with Mickey
Dora and Friend 1960s:**
Mickey Dora and friend get
the tandem thing wired on
land before taking it to the
waves, sometime during
the Roaring Sixties. (Surfing Heritage Foundation
Archives)

The Great Kahoona Speaks

Malibu in the Mid-1950s As Seen through the Eyes of Terry "Tubesteak" Tracy

Architect of the Malibu Shack, model for the great Kahoona in *Gidget*, trusted friend and confidante to Mickey Dora, co-originator of the Royal Hawai'ian, surfing's first masterpiece of performance art—Terry "Tubesteak" Tracy's is a tale worth telling.

Through the 1950s, Tubesteak was as much a fixture at Malibu as the lagoon, pier, sand, and that close out section between Third and Second Points. For two summers, he lived the life of a modern-day Robinson Crusoe on the point at Malibu in a driftwood shack. To this day, Tubesteak is regarded with humor and fondness by those who were in the Pit—and those who have only read about the Golden Years at Malibu.

If you look at the Malibu crew of the 1950s as a Dionysian cult, then Mickey Dora was clearly Dionysus and Tubesteak was Silenus—a satyr regarded as Dionysus' foster-father, companion, and teacher. Silenus had the powers of prophecy—he was said to know the past and the future—but this power had to be forced from him, and taken with a grain of salt. Silenus was a little too fond of wine, and it was sometimes hard to get any sense out of him or trust his wine-soaked prophecies.

And so it is with Tubesteak, who can reveal great truths and spread great stories, all in the same breath.

The Kahoona in Gidget: *Was that based on you?*

The hideous Kahoona character was Gidget's father's fantasy of the Malibu Guru, a.k.a. Tubesteak.

It is true you lived in a shack on Malibu for a couple summers.

I did.

Not a myth.

Nope.

Where was the Malibu Shack?

About halfway between the Adamson House and that area that was not yet known as the Pit. We built it for the summer of 1956, and it was beautiful. Not far up Malibu Creek there was an orchard of Phoenix palm trees. The palms were over 10 feet in length when harvested. They were stacked on longboards, then barged to the final resting place 200 feet north of the yet-to-be-named Pit. When they were discharged, there were 2x4s stacked eight feet high. The Shack was around 12x12 feet. It was the size of a small bedroom. . . . The interior was a discarded mattress, davenport, coffee percolators, sleeping bags, straight back chair with a cane back, all donated. . . . As the days slid by that summer, other items were added:

Flags, surfboards-for-hire signs, a hangman's noose swung from a lanyard, and the pièce de résistance was a four-foot-high roll of barbed wire surrounding the structure to keep out the riffraff, if you know what I mean. There was a poster of Manolete the bullfighter inside and outside there was a sign that said, "Uptown Surf Club. Members Only."

What happened to that one?

Somebody burned it down. Maybe some cowboys, maybe the lifeguards, I don't know. We rebuilt it the next summer on stilts and telephone poles. It had a picket fence and lift-off doors and it was an architect's dream.

Malibu is nice now; it must have been great then.

It was great.

Could you rinse off in the lagoon?

I guess if you wanted to. No one did. The nearest freshwater spigot was across the street at Tube's Steak & Lobster House, where the Malibu Inn is now. Well, I spent a lot of time over there.

Is that where you got the handle "Tubesteak"?

Maybe.

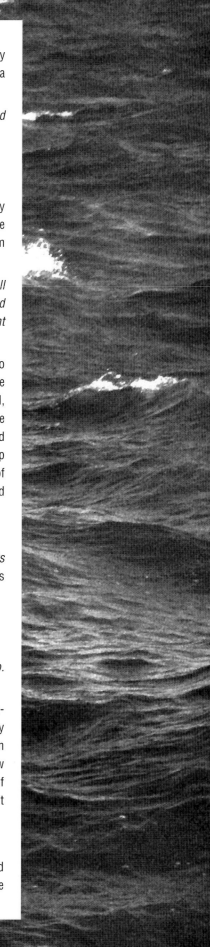

Describe an idyllic day at Malibu, during summer 1956.

Well, Tubesteak wakes up in the shack in the early morning, and when he looks out he sees the sun coming up over the mountains there. The first thing he hears is one of those big, green horseflies. And the surf, well, the surf is perfect, of course.

Cranking from Third Point to the Pier.

Third Point? No one surfed Third Point back then. No one had to. We surfed Malibu, man: From the flagpoles in front of the Adamson House.

Is there anyone else sleeping in the Shack?

Sometimes. Maybe. Depends on what went on the night before. So I wake up in the Shack and I grab my surfboard and I'm the first to paddle out. So I am in the water all by myself and maybe I am getting lonely and then Mickey Muñoz comes down from Santa Monica Canyon or Dora comes down from Hollywood and then we've got a couple of friends in the water.

Was the wave different then?

I think so. The wave has changed over the years because of sand and storms and how they have rearranged the creek. But Malibu is Malibu.

So you surf and then as you come in you casually pick up a lobster off the reef and cook it for breakfast.

Yeah, there were lobster and abalone on the reef and there were steelhead in the rivers but we weren't divers or fishermen, we were surfers! Breakfast, lunch, and dinner always showed up eventually. It came to us on two legs.

Groupies? Hangers on? Wannabes?

No, nothing like that, just people. Good people would come to the beach and they would bring food with them and cold beer and that was that. We were always taken care of.

Surf in the morning. Breakfast. Did you ever leave the beach?

No. Most of the day was taken up with the demon bottle.

Drinking.

Beer. Cold beer. It came down in an endless supply line from friends and strangers. Beer was 12 cents a can then and we liked it cold.

You've got Dora and Muñoz, you've got beer and food. What is missing?

Women.

There were women on the beach?

There were women. One girl's name would be Beverly Beercan. Another girl's name would be Sally from the Valley. Another girl's name would be Ramona from Pomona.

Sounds like Guys & Dolls. *So you're at the beach all day. All the perfect surf you could want. Free food and beer. What did you get up to when the sun went down?*

In the evening what would happen you would go probably up the hill to where Pepperdine is. You've heard of Wilson's House of Suede & Leather? Well, the people who started that company had a house up on the hill. The guy's name was Harold Fred and he would let us have parties, barbeques. We'd be up there as the sun was going down and the lights of Santa Monica and Palos Verdes were twinkling and we'd be listening to Harry Belafonte.

Calypso.

(Singing) *Dayo! Down the way where the nights are gay.* . . . That type of stuff. That's Malibu. That's Malibu music.

Were there pranks at Malibu?

There were pranks.

The Statute of Limitations ran out a long time ago. Speak freely.

You know those big doors, I mean gates at the entrance to the Malibu Pier? One night it was really sultry up there, like '56. All these people were on the pier, so a few of us went up to the pier and saw all those people and we each grabbed a big side of those gates and locked the people in. They couldn't get off the pier. What a bunch of pranksters.

Not bad.

Mickey Dora had this girlfriend named Ditzi and Ditzi had a credit card and she invited us to go to the

Malibu Sports Café. We ran up a $150 tab in 1956 drinking Stingers. You know what a Stinger is?

A shoulder-fired missile?

It *is* a strong drink, but back then cost like 75¢ or 80¢. And we bought about a $150 worth on Ditzi's credit card.

Top Five at Malibu?

Mickey Dora, of course. Kemp Aaberg. He was easily that good. Tom Morey was hot. Really good. Now Matt Kivlin was awfully good but too tall. And there were just a lot of other guys that no one has heard of: Hugh Foster, the Jaw guys. Larry Goin: He had a lot of atmosphere and was a good surfer. Moondoggie. Kenny Price. Freddy Fowler when he came up to Malibu. Freddie Hopkins was a really good surfer but no one ever heard of him or a lot of these guys unless they were there. Who am I leaving out? Oh man, Lance Carson.

Where is Tubesteak in all this?

Well, I look at it this way. If Tubesteak were 5' 6" and 145 pounds, he would have been in the Top Five. When I was there, Kivlin was already 27 years old and on the down stroke. Dora was the same age as me but he was getting everyone pissed off at him. Compared to Dora, I was medium and compared to Kemp, I was medium and compared to Morey, I was medium but you have to remember that there are two parts to surfing: There is the water and there is the sand. In the water it was Dora and on the beach it was Tubesteak.

Was Gidget *the downfall of Malibu?*

No, it was before that. It was the lifeguards. When there was atmosphere the people were neat and the place was neat, but then the lifeguards showed up with their stinking badges and screwed it all up, "Tubesteak you're making a spectacle of yourself! And what is this shack doing here and hey put out that fire!" Well, Kemp Aaberg was the only cool lifeguard because he let us store our drinks under his tower and hang out. But when the badges showed up, that was it for the atmosphere.

Is there a heaven?

Yes.

What's it like?

Malibu.

What is the music you hear on the stairway to heaven?

"Louie, Louie."

You answered that fast. Are you sure?

For sure. Because in my experience, when you walk into a party and they're playing "Louie, Louie," that's going to be a good party.

Facing page, **Hotdogging, California Style, 1959:** Los Angeles County lifeguard and ace waterman Kemp Aaberg pulling a stylish turn at Rincon. (Photo © John Severson/surferart.com)

desire to do justice to those sparkling walls, to do more than just go straight. What Simmons, Quigg, and Kivlin began in the 1940s was taken to the next level by the likes of Greg Noll, Dale Velzy, Hap Jacobs, Hobie Alter, and Dewey Weber. It was these surfers/shapers who combined with test pilots like Mickey Dora, Lance Carson, and Tom Morey to take the Hawai'ian concept of hotdogging and make it something California-grown.

Malibu was the right wave at the right time in the 1950s. Those great green waves became the melting pot where a new generation of athletes and designers came together, continuing to make surfboards lighter, faster, and better—and ride them lighter, faster, and better. The Malibu Crew of the 1950s was a loose affiliation of geniuses and rogues, rich kids and poor, Lancelots and Merlins—men and women who shared their love of surfing and had a profound effect on the sport and the culture as they shaped it into the sensation that would sweep the nation in the 1960s.

Mickey Dora ruled Malibu. A truly beautiful surfer, Dora was the Sovereign of Style and he laid down aesthetic rules during the 1950s that are still being followed today—grace, speed, and lack of body movement. Surfing had its Duke; now it had a King.

Dora loved to ride waves and he broadcast that love with his body English. Fast and fluid, he complimented every wave he rode by riding it well. He

Above, **Quasimodo:** Mickey Muñoz at Secos break, pulling a move known as the "Quasimodo." (Photo © John Severson/ surferart.com)

called attention to himself by not calling attention to himself, keeping his arms below his waist and steady. There was no excess movement in his turns and cutbacks, and every cell of his body was concentrated on speed and grace and riding beautiful waves as beautifully as possible. His nickname was Da Cat because that was how he moved. He was truly a great surfer.

He was also a sociopath.

A native of Budapest, Hungary, by birth, Dora was a native son of the Golden West by nurture. He grew up in Los Angeles in the 1940s when the city had all the advantages of location and weather but few of the frustrations of overcrowding and traffic. "The '50s were the best times to be a surfer in California," claims Terry "Tubesteak" Tracy. "You could buy a bitchin' car for $200. Gas was like two cents a gallon, or something. A bottle of beer was like four cents, or something. We had the roads to ourselves, the beaches to ourselves. The squares all thought surfboards were airplane wings, or something. Malibu was our oyster." The ascent of surfing

I flew down the face, past the lip of the wave, and when I got to the bottom, which is where I wanted to be, I looked ahead and saw that sonofabitch starting to break in a section that stretched a block and a half in front of me. I started to lay back, thinking I could dig a hole and escape through the backside of the wave. The wave threw out a sheet of water over my head and engulfed me. Then for a split second the whole scene froze forever in my mind. There I was, in that liquid green room...

— *Greg Noll on surfing Makaha in 1969,* Da Bull: Life Over the Edge, *with Andrea Gabbard, 1989*

paralleled the ascent of rock'n'roll, and it's fun to imagine someone like Dale Velzy, flush with cash from his surfboard business, driving his rodded '56 Ford F-100 pickup down the Pacific Coast Highway to Malibu, listening to Elvis howling "Hound Dog" on the radio, checking out the surf at Topanga, and angling for The Malibu, where he might find a handful of guys in the water—all friends, all some of the Happy Few who were tuned in to surfing. If that sounds good, it's because it was good, and Dora lived that time as well as anyone.

Mickey Dora was the Wild One of surfing. He was Marlon Brando's leather-jacketed antihero Johnny Strabler, but instead of a Triumph motorcycle, he rode a board. He was an outsider and a nonconformist and a rebel without a cause when that little part of mainstream society that paid any attention at all to surfers wrote them off as beach bums. Dora lived the life immortalized in *Gidget.*

In later years, Dora was appalled by the commercialization of surfing and what it did to those Golden Years of the 1950s—and yet he was also in part responsible for it. Dora, Mickey Muñoz, and others of Malibu's finest were all involved in the production of the film version of *Gidget.* That's Dora surfing as a stand-in for James Darren's Moondoggie as he brings a half-drowned Gidget into the beach on the nose of his board. Dora can be seen surfing throughout the movie, recognizable for his "nose tweaks" and other nervous tics as well as for his sheer speed and class on the board. He is easy to spot because he stands out from every other surfer.

Gidget caused the explosion that blew the cover on the surfing lifestyle, and Dora lit the fuse. It's tragically ironic that Dora was a part of the movie

that immortalized his 1950s lifestyle and then effectively ended it. Where Malibu and all of those Southern California breaks had been the Private Idaho of Mickey Dora and those Happy Few throughout the 1950s, suddenly the beaches were crowded with Moondoggie wannabes modeling their moves on those of Dora. If he had only known he was opening a Pandora's box by riding a board through *Gidget,* he might have stayed home that day.

Within just a few years after *Gidget,* a long string of waxploitation flicks clogged the silver screen—Elvis's *Blue Hawaii, Ride the Wild Surf* featuring Fabian, Bobby Vinton in *Surf Party,* and the whole *Beach Party* series starring Frankie and Annette. Mickey Dora and others from the Malibu crew worked on these movies as stunt doubles and actors and made easy money that allowed them to finance their low-cost beach life for months, if not years. But the repercussions from those first movies are still reverberating, and Dora and Muñoz must have felt like the first mountain men in the Wild West watching the last lonely swarms of buffalo killed off by all who followed. In the 1960s, Malibu became a free-for-all as Valley cowboys, gremmies, kuks, Barneys, and hodads bumped rails with the pioneers.

Perhaps this is what drove Mickey Dora around the bend and into a life of crime.

Shakespeare would have had a field day with Dora. He was equal parts Richard III, Hamlet, and Macbeth, and if Dora became a misanthrope, no wonder. Perchance it was the fall of Malibu that made him a man not too keen on his fellow man. Dora witnessed,

Dale Velzy 1950 "Balsa Chip": Seeking better performance, Dale Velzy re-shaped his redwood-balsa longboards: "I tried to get as much curve into the planshape as possible, but it was still too parallel. I've always tried for as much curve as I could get. They just work better." (© Malcolm Wilson)
SPECIFICATIONS: 10' 6" LONG; 23½" WIDE; 3½" THICK; 65 POUNDS

played a hand in, and suffered from Malibu's transition from undiscovered country to a troubled sea without any more secrets. Anyone with imagination who has surfed and suffered the sometimes outrageous frustrations of battling the masses for a few yards of empty, green wall, can only wonder what it was like for Dora and the crew who once had Malibu to themselves. To sit in the lineup at Malibu now and imagine it all in the 1950s—few houses in the hills, no traffic roar or Code Three sirens on PCH, no lifeguards on the beach, almost no human flotsam or jetsam clogging the lanes from the pier to the colony—is to suffer ancestor worship. Those who have struggled with the calamities and thousand shocks

of modern Malibu can only wonder how it would have been to be bobbing around out there with just a few friends, letting the less-than-perfect six-footers go through, and paddling into the pick of the litter. Malibu before the deluge meant not constantly looking over your shoulder to see if anyone was behind you, or dropping in afraid of the wolf pack waiting to pounce on the inside. Back then, it was one man, one wave, and Dora was the Man.

Malibu was paradise lost for Dora, and to lose something like that is more than enough to make a chap snap. And, like Hamlet, it might make him wonder if there wasn't better surf in the "undiscover'd country, from whose bourn / No traveller returns…."

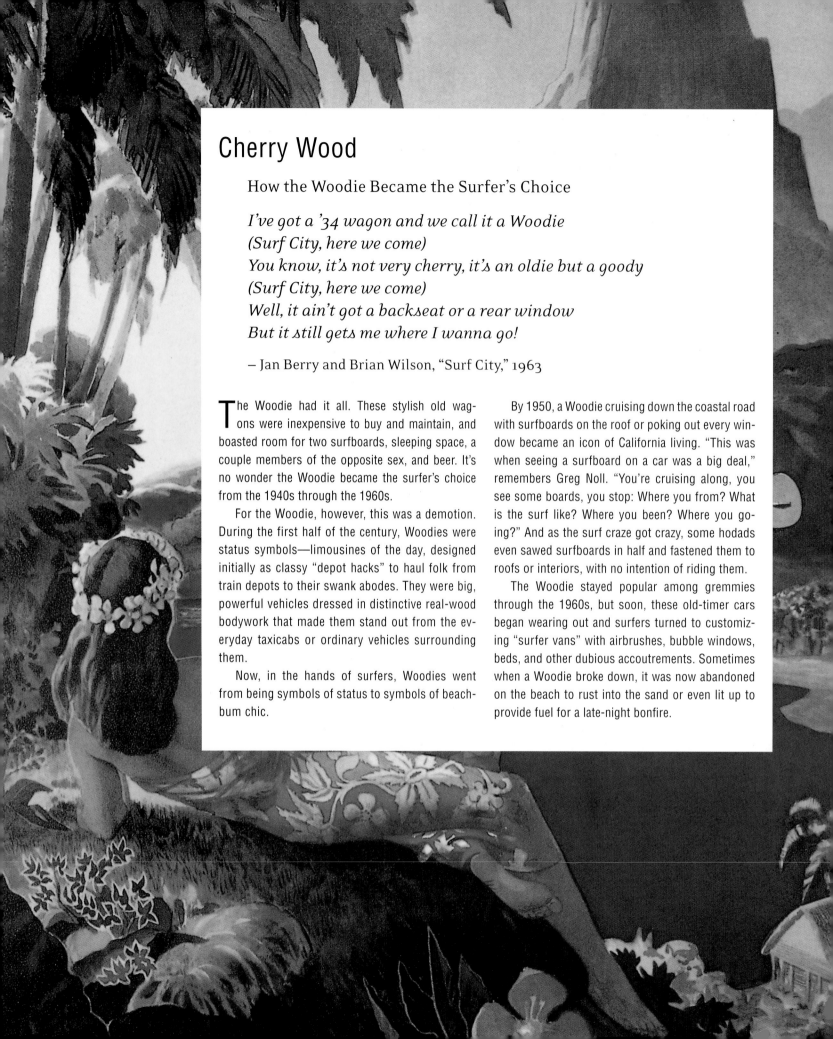

Cherry Wood

How the Woodie Became the Surfer's Choice

I've got a '34 wagon and we call it a Woodie
(Surf City, here we come)
You know, it's not very cherry, it's an oldie but a goody
(Surf City, here we come)
Well, it ain't got a backseat or a rear window
But it still gets me where I wanna go!

– Jan Berry and Brian Wilson, "Surf City," 1963

The Woodie had it all. These stylish old wagons were inexpensive to buy and maintain, and boasted room for two surfboards, sleeping space, a couple members of the opposite sex, and beer. It's no wonder the Woodie became the surfer's choice from the 1940s through the 1960s.

For the Woodie, however, this was a demotion. During the first half of the century, Woodies were status symbols—limousines of the day, designed initially as classy "depot hacks" to haul folk from train depots to their swank abodes. They were big, powerful vehicles dressed in distinctive real-wood bodywork that made them stand out from the everyday taxicabs or ordinary vehicles surrounding them.

Now, in the hands of surfers, Woodies went from being symbols of status to symbols of beach-bum chic.

By 1950, a Woodie cruising down the coastal road with surfboards on the roof or poking out every window became an icon of California living. "This was when seeing a surfboard on a car was a big deal," remembers Greg Noll. "You're cruising along, you see some boards, you stop: Where you from? What is the surf like? Where you been? Where you going?" And as the surf craze got crazy, some hodads even sawed surfboards in half and fastened them to roofs or interiors, with no intention of riding them.

The Woodie stayed popular among gremmies through the 1960s, but soon, these old-timer cars began wearing out and surfers turned to customizing "surfer vans" with airbrushes, bubble windows, beds, and other dubious accoutrements. Sometimes when a Woodie broke down, it was now abandoned on the beach to rust into the sand or even lit up to provide fuel for a late-night bonfire.

Dora spent most of his later life on the run, always on the lookout for an experience as pure and as great as Malibu in his golden youth. From the mid-1960s, he was an incessant wanderer, a criminal, a scammer who lived by the motto, "A dollar scammed is better than ten dollars earned." Suddenly, he was a rebel in this new being called the "surf industry," and while he was flipping off the surfing industrial complex with one hand, he was accepting money with the other. It is sad to read Dora revile the Hollywoodizing and commercialization of surfing, then see him in the background of the Frankie and Annette movies, pulling faces and dancing the Frug.

During the 1960s, Dora used the newborn surf media mostly to his advantage. Accused of being ruthless in the waves of Malibu, Dora turned up the heat in an interview with *Surfer* magazine: "It's a lie. I'm vicious. We're all pushing and shoving, jockeying for position, and if I get the wave first—if I'm in the best position—then I feel I deserve it."

In 1967, Mickey Dora made his parting statement while competing at the Malibu Invitational Surf Classic. For a couple of years he had been calling contest judges "senile surf freaks" and at that contest, he made his ultimate statement. He took off on a wave, trimmed along a beautiful wall, and then dropped trou and bare-assed the judges.

And that was that. Like the Cheshire cat, that image of Dora's grinning butt hung in the air, while Dora himself disappeared. He traveled the world during the 1970s, a vagabond and desperado, scamming his way from one surf spot to the next, living the life of a surfisticate. Australia, New Zealand, Hawai'i, South Africa, France. Occasionally he would write angry, eloquent articles for the surf magazines, cynically writing off the media while using their money to finance his adventures.

In the 1980s, Dora's lifestyle caught up with him when he was arrested for making illegal international telephone calls in France. He was deported to the United States, where he faced the music for traveling the world on a Diner's Club card that did not belong to him. The judge was not sympathetic, and Dora did more than a year of federal time—some of it at Lompoc Prison, within smelling distance of the ocean.

Mickey Dora's existential dilemma came to an end on July 1, 2004, after a six-month battle with pancreatic cancer. This wasn't a scam, and Dora is now exploring that "undiscover'd country" that Hamlet pondered. Hopefully, he's scoring some surf, with his faithful dog Scooter Boy alongside him on the beach.

The Malibu Dora left behind is as complicated as the man, but less tragic. Malibu is gorgeous and frustrating, entertaining and maddening. Nature is beautiful, while sometimes human nature is not so. The sky is blue about 360 days a year and the water at Malibu is cool and clear, if not always clean.

All in all, Malibu is doing a surprisingly good job of fighting off the slings and arrows of the twenty-first century. A trip to Malibu is a trip back to the source, back to one of the crucibles of surfing. Paddle out and maybe you will get lucky. Maybe you will slide into one of those uncrowded slots, when the surf is good and for one reason or another, everyone is somewhere else. On these days, it is just possible to imagine Malibu as it was and appreciate it as it is: There are almost always dolphins and seals frolicking in the surf line, whales passing offshore. There is that million-dollar view across the Santa Monica Bay to Palos Verdes and Redondo Beach. The Malibu Pier is there, looking as it has for the last four decades. There are houses in the hills—but not too many—and if the surf is sounding loudly, it drowns out the sound of the traffic.

On days like this, it's possible to imagine it all as it once was.

Wally Froiseth 1950s "Hot Curl": Wally Froiseth was a pioneer big-wave rider, winning the 1957 Makaha contest. This streamlined hot curl was made of solid koa. (© Malcolm Wilson) SPECIFICATIONS: 11' 4" LONG; 20" WIDE; 100 POUNDS

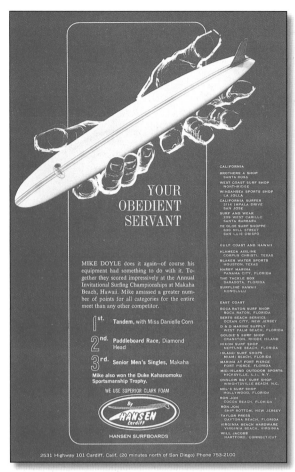
Vintage Surfboard Advertisements, 1950s–1970s

(Voyageur Press Archives)

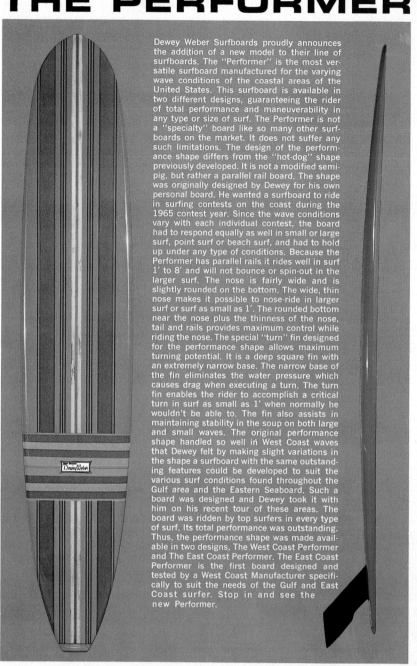

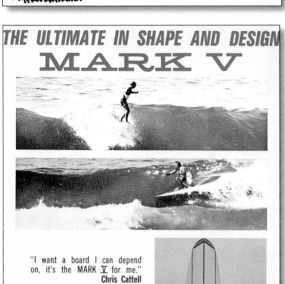

The Surfer Stomp

A Rock'n'Roll Soundtrack to the Waves • 1959 to 1967

Left, **Surf Music, 1960s:**
Dick Dale played music by
surfers, for surfers. Armed
with his trademark Fender
Stratocaster, aka *The Beast*,
Dale and the Del-Tones rocked

coastal ballrooms and school
gymnasiums. (Michael Ochs
Archives.com/Capitol Records)

Above, **Surf Anthem, 1961**
(Voyageur Press Archives)

When the sun set on the rolling surf, it was time for the music to rock. Teens throughout Southern California parked their boards and made a pilgrimage to a stately old oceanfront dancehall. Here, they did the Surfer Stomp to a band at the breakpoint of a new music that the surfers called their own.

The Rendezvous Ballroom looked out over the sea from the quiet town of Balboa. Opened in 1928, the dancehall spanned a full block between Palm and Washington streets, its twelve-thousand-square-foot dance floor easily hosting 1,500 couples with a sixty-four-foot-long soda fountain and a mezzanine

Let's go surfin' now,
Everybody's learning how—
Come on a safari with me!

— The Beach Boys, "Surfin' Safari," 1962

STOMPING "OUT OF CONTROL" IN DANCE CONTEST . . .

To Music of The
RHYTHM ROCKERS

THIS WEEKEND

FRI. MAY 18 AND SAT. MAY 19

At The

RENDEZVOUS

608 E. OCEAN FRONT, BALBOA
OR 5-0900

DANCING 8 to 12 P.M. ADMISSION $1.00

- MINIMUM AGE 15, MAXIMUM 20
- If Chaperoned by Parents, Minimum Age Limitations Do Not Apply

Rendezvous Ballroom Advertisements, 1960s
(Voyageur Press Archives)

Facing page, **Dick Dale and *The Beast*, 1960s:** With his lefty Stratocaster, Dale picked out country tunes, R&B melodies, and his own original compositions that became known as "surf music." The volume came courtesy of Leo Fender's hot-rodded Showman amp; "wave" sounds were thanks to the Fender reverb unit. (Voyageur Press Archives)

of intimate couches and banquettes. In the 1930s, teenagers flocked to "Bal Week" during Easter vacation as the Rendezvous was a headquarters for swing, the big bands of Harry James, Benny Goodman, Tommy and Jimmy Dorsey, and more broadcasting by radio from the dancehall and across the nation. Now, at the dawn of the 1960s, there was a new sound at the Rendezvous.

A guitarist named Dick Dale was rocking the Rendezvous with screaming licks backed by honking horns and tribal drumming from his Del-Tones band. And Dale played it loud.

The surf gang went crazy for the music—a cool blend of R&B, country western, and rock'n'roll. They stomped across the hardwood floor in their huaraches, lost themselves to the Frug, and filled the hall with primal energy.

It was the dawn of surf music.

Throughout the 1960s, surf music crested on several fronts. Dale was one of the best-known exponents of reverb-heavy instrumental rock—along with other bands like the Ventures, Belairs, Frogmen, Mar-Kets, Chantays, Surfaris, and many more. A vocal tradition also appeared, led by the doo-wop harmonizations of Jan & Dean and the Beach Boys. Much of the earliest surf music was made by surfers for surfers. But as the style caught a wave, others

hopped on, lured by the hot new sounds, the surfing chic, or simply to cash in on the fad.

Dick Dale was a surfer, so he's often credited as one of the founders of surf music. His bouncy tune "Let's Go Trippin'" was a Southern California regional hit in 1961, a year after the Ventures' nationwide success in 1960 with "Walk, Don't Run." The Ventures hailed from inland Tacoma, Washington; they had a big break in the music business, but wouldn't have known what to do on even a small break at the beach. And although Dale was perhaps not the coolest cat on a hot foam board, he certainly played his music for an audience of wave-riders at the Rendezvous.

He was christened Richard Monsour at birth in 1937 in Boston, Massachusetts, the son of a Leba-

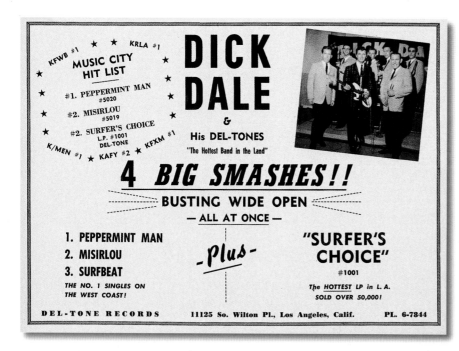

Above, **"Surfer's Choice" Advertisement, 1960s** (Voyageur Press Archives)

Facing page, **Dick Dale and the Del-Tones Albums, 1960s** (Voyageur Press Archives)

nese machinist father and Polish mother. As a youth, he taught himself to play Hank Williams songs on ukulele and guitar, but among his other influences was an uncle who played the oud, a Middle Eastern lute used to accompany belly dancers. Soon, the youngster could play anything that made noise.

When the family moved to El Segundo in the mid-1950s, Monsour started surfing along the South Bay beaches. He wrote country-western instrumentals, but like a lot of other guitar slingers—from Duane Eddy to Link Wray and Buddy Holly—he soon changed his tune to rock'n'roll, and in 1956 he won an Elvis Presley soundalike contest. He was Dick Dale and the Rhythm Wranglers on his debut album in 1958, but when he played his first concert at the Rendezvous in 1959, he was Dick Dale and the Del-Tones. As Dale said, this new music matched "the feeling I had while surfing; the vibration and pulsification, and the tremendous power."

It was the summer of 1959, *Gidget* was on the big screen, and Californians were going surfing. With its perfect weather, warm water, and white sand beaches, the strip from Long Beach to San Clemente quickly became the epicenter of California surfers. This was the first big wave of teenage baby boomers, and they all needed somewhere to go and something to do. Balboa was smack in the middle of the beach scenes, so surfers,

Valleys, greasers, hodads, and gremmies came to the Rendezvous to do the Surfer Stomp.

"Dick Dale was the surf guitar god and teen idol, and he was where it was at," remembers Pat McGee, the original skateboarding "It" girl of the 1960s. McGee won the Women's Division of the National Skateboard Championship in 1965 and appeared on the cover of *Life* magazine. A junior at San Diego's Point Loma High, she was drawn north by the siren call of the Surfer Stomp. "We drove all the way up from San Diego in my 1950 Mercury, because the Rendezvous was the scene. It was a big deal for a bunch of girls to drive from San Diego to Newport Beach. Anybody who had gas money could go, and gas was 35 cents a gallon. There were more really cute surfer guys in one place than a young surfer girl could dream of. And the music filled your body and mind. Back in San Diego we did the Surfer Stomp at our high school dance that year and we made the gym floor ripple. The principal made the band change the music."

Dale was riding a big wave. Because his Rendezvous gigs were attended by surfers, his sound was called "surf music." Dale didn't argue. He released "Let's Go Trippin'"/"Del-Tone Rock" followed by "Jungle Fever"/"Shake N' Stomp" on his own Deltone label in 1961. His debut album, *Surfer's Choice*, featured a photo of Dale surfing on the cover and quickly sold eighty thousand copies.

That LP included an exotic little track titled "Misirlou Twist" that opened with a ferocious guitar glissando like a breaking wall of water. The tune was part of Dale's Lebanese heritage, a traditional Mediterranean folk dance now hot-rodded with an electric guitar turned to 11 and run through a reverb unit and the biggest, baddest amplifier yet made. The surfers loved it, and "Misirlou Twist" rocketed to number one on Hollywood's KFWB.

In 1963, Dale appeared on the *Ed Sullivan Show* while *Life* hailed him with a two-page spread. He was picked up by Capitol Records and released four albums in quick succession—*King of the Surf Guitar* (featuring a stomp version of "Hava Nagila") and *Checkered Flag* in 1963, *Mr. Eliminator* and *Summer Surf* in 1964. Parts in movies also came, including 1960's *Let's Make Love*, 1963's *A Swinging Affair*, and two of the Frankie and Annette flicks, *Beach Party* and *Muscle Beach Party*. As goofy as those beach movies could be, they also had their moments,

Taking It to 11

Dick Dale and Leo Fender Rock the World

During his ascent to surf-music god, Dick Dale became friends with electric-guitar maverick Leo Fender, and together they innovated a long string of guitar and amplifier innovations that would push rock'n'roll to 11.

Fender was in the right place at the right time with the right skills. He started in the guitar business in the 1940s and although he himself was a stalwart country music fan, his inventions drove the rock'n'roll rage. Born in Fullerton, California, in 1909, Fender repaired radios as a hobby in high school, later partnering with Clayton "Doc" Kauffman in a radio repair business, Fender's Repair Service, which also sold and rented homemade PAs and musical instruments. During World War II, the market for Hawai'ian and western swing took off, so their K&F Manufacturing began making amplifiers and electric lap-steel guitars with a pickup designed by Fender. In 1946, Kauffman lost interest and Fender Electrical Instrument Co. emerged.

In 1950, Fender introduced his solid-body Esquire electric guitar, followed by the Broadcaster, which became the Telecaster due to trademark conflict. Fender followed with the electric Precision Bass and high-powered Bassman amp. In 1954, he introduced his Stratocaster, which remains the most popular electric guitar ever made. The increased power and sophistication of the Strat called for better amps, and Fender offered the Twin.

In the late 1950s, Fender and Dick Dale became friends and the inventor used the King of Surf Guitar to stress-test his new amps. As Dick Dale tells the tale (in the third person): "Leo Fender gave the Fender Stratocaster along with a Fender Amp to Dale and told him to beat it to death and tell him what he thought of it. Dale took the guitar and started to beat it to death, and he blew up Leo Fender's amp and blew out the speaker. Dale proceeded to blow up 49 amps and speakers; they would actually catch on fire. Leo would say, 'Dick, why do you have to play so loud?' Dale would explain that he wanted to create the sound of Gene Krupa the famous jazz drummer that created the sounds of the native dancers in the jungles along with the roar of mother nature's creatures and the roar of the ocean.

"Leo Fender kept giving Dale amps and Dale kept blowing them up! Till one night Leo and his right hand man Freddy T. went down to the Rendezvous Ballroom on the Balboa Peninsula in Balboa, California and stood in the middle of 4,000 screaming dancing Dick Dale fans and said to Freddy, I now know what Dick Dale is trying to tell me. Back to the drawing board. A special 85 watt output transformer was made that peaked 100 watts when Dale would pump up the volume of his amp; this transformer would create the sounds along with Dale's style of playing, the kind of sounds that Dale dreamed of. But! They now needed a speaker that would handle the power and not burn up from the volume that would come from Dale's guitar.

"Leo, Freddy and Dale went to the James B. Lansing speaker company, and they explained that they wanted a 15-inch speaker built to their specifications. That speaker would soon be known as the 15" JBL–D130 speaker. It made the complete package for Dale to play through and was named the Single Showman Amp. When Dale plugged his Fender Stratocaster guitar into the new Showman Amp and speaker cabinet, Dale became the first creature on earth to jump from the volume scale of a modest quiet guitar player on a scale of 4 to blasting up through the volume scale to TEN!"

With all that power at his fingertips, Dale unleashed classic surf music on the world.

Hawai'ian Noises

Singing to the Surf in Old Hawai'i

The first surf music was sung in ancient Polynesia on the islands of Tahiti and Hawai'i where the surf was as integral to life as air.

In ancient Hawai'i, the Islanders surfed for pleasure, for status, for gain and loss, surfers wagering lives, property, and freedom on wave-riding contests.

The *ali'i*—the chiefs and royalty like Kamehameha I, Prince Jonah Kuhio, and Queen Emma—proved their royalty with their surfing ability.

Before Captain Cook's arrival, Hawai'ians had gods for every occasion and their system of religious *kapu* ruled every aspect of daily life, from growing taro to riding waves. *Kahuna* were holy men, each of them with different skills: Some read the future, others blessed crops, and there were *kahuna* who specialized in the ocean and knew what the gods wanted to hear for bringing up the surf.

The Hawai'ians did not have a written language but some of their precontact chants survived long enough for *haole* scholars and missionaries to write them down. As Ben Finney and James D. Houston wrote in *Surfing: A History of the Ancient Hawaiian Sport*: "When the ocean was flat the Hawaiians took measures to address the return of rideable waves. If a group of surfers wanted to address the ocean, they might gather on the beach, find strands of *pōhuehue* (beach morning glory), swing them around their heads together and lash the surface of the water chanting in unison. One such surf chant has been recorded and translated as follows:

Kumai! Kumai! Ka nalu nui mai kahiki mai,
Alo poi pu! Ku mai ka pōhuehue,
Hu! Kaikoo Loa.

Arise! Arise, ye great surfs from Kahiki,
The powerful curling waves.
Arise with pōhuehue
Well up, long raging surf."

Other chants had to do with famous surfing feats and days of waves. Every important chief kept a chanter in his retinue to glorify the chief's bravery and skill on a board.

The Hawai'ian music we know today is an alchemy of those ancient chants combined with musical instruments introduced by the cultures that came to Hawai'i after Cook.

In the mid-1800s, sailors, missionaries, and other visitors arrived in Hawai'i, while Islanders who shipped out as able-bodied seamen began to see the world. Hawai'ians adapted and adopted outside musical influences into their own to create beautiful music. The ukulele, slack key guitar, and steel guitar all came from this mixing of Hawai'ian and *haole* culture.

One of the many stories tracing the ukulele's history goes back to a specific date—August 23, 1879—when the ship *Ravenscrag* arrived in Honolulu carrying Portuguese immigrants from Madeira to work the sugar cane fields. To celebrate their arrival, a passenger named Joao Fernandes broke into song on a small, four-stringed guitar called a *braguinha*. Hawai'ians on the dock were impressed at the speed of this musician's fingers as they danced across the fingerboard, and they called the instrument *ukulele*—"jumping flea."

Early Mexican *paniolo* cowboys brought their guitars to Hawai'i and taught Islanders to play in the Spanish style. The Hawai'ians soon were retuning the strings by "slacking" them. Slack key allowed Islanders to play bass on the loosened bass strings while maintaining the melody on the treble, and their fingerpicking was adapted to match the movements and mood of hula dancing.

Adapting the guitar to suit their own musical styles, Hawai'ians also often used a steel bar to slide along the strings, producing a unique crying tone. The origins of the steel-guitar style and its technical inventor are widely debated, but three individuals—James Hoa, Gabriel Davion, and Joseph Kekuku—may have discovered the technique independently of one another and are credited as its inventors. The steel guitar is featured on some of the earliest known recordings of Hawai'ian music.

When modern surf music arrived at the hands of Dick Dale, the Belairs, the Ventures, and others, it had more to do with African rather than Polynesian roots, but some of surf music's artists—particularly Don Wilson and Bob Bogle of the Ventures—were inspired by the slack key, ukulele, and steel guitar of Hawai'ian music. And here in the new century, Hawai'ian surfing-star-turned-pop-star Jack Johnson is as comfortable with a ukulele as he is with a traditional acoustic guitar.

What Hawai'ian music and surf music had in common is they were both inspired by the sound and feel of the ocean and waves.

Hawai'ian Steel Guitar Books, 1910s–1930s
(Voyageur Press Archives)

Required Listening, Surfer Style, 1960s (Voyageur Press Archives)

Facing page, **Surfer Stomp Directions, 1960s:** For surfing newcomers and hodads, Bruce Johnston and his Surf Stompers offered this handy step-by-step guide accompanying their 1960s Del-Fi single, "Do the Surfer Stomp." (Voyageur Press Archives)

Kids called it "surf music"; I didn't call it that. The kids called me "King of the Surf Guitar." I surfed sun up to sun down. I don't claim to be a musician, I didn't go to Julliard. I'm into just chopping, chopping at 60 gauge, 50 gauge strings. That's the sound, the sound of the waves chopping. The surfing sound is not the reverb . . . So when historians, so-called historians, say the reverb's the surf sound . . . they don't know what they're talking about. It's the heavy machine gun, staccato sound. The waves.

— *Dick D, 1994*

and one of the best was Dick Dale jamming with Little Stevie Wonder, then making his first appearance to the world. And it all began at the Rendezvous.

"I remember making the trek to the Rendezvous in the summer of '61 to see what all the fuss was about over Dick Dale," says Paul Johnson, guitarist for the Belairs who later had a classic surf hit with "Mr. Moto." "It was a powerful experience; his music was incredibly dynamic, louder and more sophisticated than the Belairs, and the energy between the Del-Tones and all of those surfers stomping on the hardwood floor in their sandals was extremely intense. The tone of Dale's guitar was bigger than any I had ever heard, and his blazing technique was something to behold."

The band that took surf music national didn't hail from Southern California—nor could its members even ride a board. Still, they knew how to play their guitars, and while the Ventures did not truly play "surf music," they certainly inspired most every true surf band on the beach.

Don Wilson and Bob Bogle came from similar musical backgrounds, Wilson learning ukulele at twelve, Bogle picking up a slack-key guitar at the same age. In 1958, they bought instructional books and began to practice on pawn-shop guitars. Wilson and Bogle soon graduated to Fender electrics bought on time payments and played club dates while keeping their day jobs. Their sound influenced by Les Paul, Chet Atkins, and Duane Eddy, they called themselves the Versatones at first, then the Ventures.

In April 1960, Wilson and Bogle cut their composition "Walk, Don't Run," the second release on the Blue Horizon label owned by Wilson's mother Josie. They proudly took their platter to Bob Reisdorff,

who ran the local Dolton label. Reisdorff passed, but the Ventures had faith. They next brought the single to Pat O'Day, who had a show on Seattle's KJR. O'Day played "Walk, Don't Run" after each news bulletin, catching Reisdorff's ear. Haggling with Josie Wilson, the band cut a deal naming Reisdorff and Wilson joint producers, but giving the Ventures and Blue Horizon artistic control. Released nationwide in August 1960 by Dolton, "Walk, Don't Run" became the number-two record in the country, held from number one by Elvis's "It's Now or Never," Brian Hyland's "Itsy Bitsy Teenie Weenie Yellow Polka-Dot Bikini," and Chubbie Checker's "The Twist."

Dolton was marketed nationally by Liberty Records, so the Ventures' recording operations moved to LA and Liberty's studios. Within a year after recording "Walk, Don't Run" and shopping it around town, the band cut an eponymous debut LP consisting mostly of covers. It hit number eleven in January 1962.

And from there, the hits just kept on coming—a combination of great music and clever marketing. From 1961 to the twenty-first century, the Ventures wrote more than a thousand tunes and recorded three thousand, with fourteen songs making it into the Billboard Top 100. They released more than 250 albums and at one point had five LPs in the Top 100 at the same time. Their *Play Guitar with the Ventures* LPs were the first and only instructional albums to make the album charts. Countless young guitarists learned to play from these albums—as well as play along to Ventures tunes.

In May 1969, the Ventures recorded the theme song for TV's *Hawaii Five-o*, which is a surf song, in a sense. The single hit number four and is probably their most recognized recording ever, even if most people don't realize it was the Ventures.

Remembering the Surfer Stomps

Hot Nights, Hot Music

Surfer Gordon McClelland grew up in Southern California attending surfer stomps all over Orange County and observing the origin of surf music with a critical eye: "In about 1961 the instrumental rock music that Dick Dale and Paul Johnson played was the first to be called 'surf music.' If you check it out deep you'll find it was the surfers at the dances in Newport, Anaheim, and Redondo Beach that came up with the idea of calling it surf music, not the players themselves, even if some of them claim otherwise.

"Dick Dale played mostly rhythm and blues, funky cowboy music, and just a bit of 'surf music' at the dances in Newport and Anaheim. The driving instrumentals were truly great and a real treat when he did play them, but they were few and far between in the early shows.

"The Belairs—Paul Johnson's band—played a bit more of what was called 'surf music,' but they too mixed in a lot of other rhythm and blues music and popular dance music of the era.

"The truth is that many surfers were really into other bands like the Righteous Brothers. They were a top draw whenever they performed and played at many surf stomps. In fact, 'Koko Joe' was one of the most popular surf stomp tunes, even though I don't think anyone called it 'surf music.'

"The Rhythm Rockers from Santa Ana, the Beach Boys, and many others soon followed. Players like the Ventures, Duane Eddy, and even Al Casey that played similar rock instrumental guitar music—all before Dale and Johnson—jumped on the wagon and began putting surf titles on their instrumental music and marketing it as 'surf music,' in spite of the fact that they had nothing to do with the surf culture."

"DO THE SURFER STOMP"
DONNA ≠1354

FEET SLIGHTLY APART, STRAIGHT AHEAD
PARTNERS STAND ABOUT 1½ FEET APART FACING EACH OTHER
BOTH PARTNERS AT SAME TIME:
Snap your fingers
A. SLIDE YOUR RIGHT FOOT BACK, THEN FORWARD STOMP, do it again

B. SLIDE YOUR LEFT FOOT BACK, THEN FORWARD STOMP, do it again

REPEAT A
Twice right foot
slide - STOMP
slide - STOMP

REPEAT B
Twice left foot
slide - STOMP
slide - STOMP

A.

B.

"You Won't Part With Yours Either," 1960s: Fender's ad series for its new Jazzmaster guitar included this surfer who refused to set his axe aside when riding the waves. Perhaps not surprisingly, the Jazzmaster—and its successor, the Jaguar—became prized surf music guitars. (Voyageur Press Archives)

Purists color the band "surf exploitation music."

And they're big in Japan. In fact, the Ventures invented Big in Japan. During the 1960s, the band's version of surf music outsold the Beatles in Japan two to one. In 1970 and 1971, they were the number-one composers in Japan—writing songs with vocals recorded in Japanese. Five of their compositions hit number one on the Japanese charts, and after surpassing forty million in record sales there, the Ventures became the first foreign members of Japan's Conservatory of Music.

As of 2004, the Ventures still hadn't been inducted into the Rock and Roll Hall of Fame.

While Dick Dale, the Ventures, and a long string of other instrumental bands were hammering out their Surfer Stomps, a new school of surf music was emerging. Jan Berry and Dean Torrence were surfers and singers. Together, they sounded good, harmonizing their doo-wop vocals on odes to teenage life—surfing, hot rods, and chicks. And they looked good, too. This was 1959, rock'n'roll was only a few years old, and Jan and Dean were on the cusp between the crew-cut, frat-pin look of the 1950s and something entirely new. Equally blond, tall, and handsome, they managed to be clean-cut and hip at the same time. They dressed nice, they could move onstage, and the surfer girls dug them.

Jan and Dean were native sons of the Golden West. At West Los Angeles' University High, Jan was a talented athlete and good student. He was also a rebel—much like *Gidget*'s Moondoggie, torn between the square and hip life. "When I was young I had all the advantages," Jan remembers. "My father worked for Howard Hughes, we lived in Bel Air. I went to the best schools, and got the best girls. My intelligence quotient was well above average; and yet I could be a rebellious, troublesome punk who brought more than a little anxiety to my parents. That sounds normal enough; but the truth is, nothing about my life has been ordinary."

After high school football practice, the echoey acoustics in the shower room benefited the harmonizing of Jan and several of his fellow football players, including Dean. Soon they created a singing group called the Barons with grand plans to play the school talent show. From the shower room, they moved into the Berry's garage, where Jan had a piano and state-of-the-art Ampex recorder, a present from his father. Jan became the arranger and producer, coaching his friends in multipart harmonies and capturing it all on tape.

The big day came, and with neighbor friends on piano and drums, the Barons belted out "Get a Job,"

In the fifties, you couldn't get a license to play in the high schools and junior highs—you could only dance to horn bands. They thought anybody who played guitar was evil. We said, "You want your kids out in the street or would you rather have them in one big place?" They said, "They gotta wear ties!" Who the hell ever heard of surfers wearing ties? They finally gave us a permit to reopen the Rendezvous Ballroom, which was a whole city block. Opening night we had 17 surfers in their bare feet—wearing ties. We had a box of 'em and handed 'em out to keep the city happy.
— *Dick Dale, 1995*

"Rock and Roll is Here to Stay," and "Short Shorts" for the talent show crowd. The girls loved it. Jan and Dean were hot to put together new tunes, but the other Barons were hot for hot rods and had no time for music. Suddenly the band was a duet.

One night while Jan and Dean were struggling to write their own song to record, one of the old Barons members, Arnie Ginsberg, showed up with an idea for a song titled "Jenny Lee" inspired by a local stripper. The boys worked on their harmonies for weeks with plans to debut the tune at a big party at Jan's house. And better yet, Jan wanted to show this song off with a demo record: He planned to take a finished tape to a recording studio to have a disc cut.

When they were finally ready to record, Jan rounded up his trio, but only Arnie was available as Dean was packing to leave for six months of Army Reserve duty. Jan and Arnie cut the song that night anyway, and the next day Jan took the tape to a Hollywood recording studio.

At the studio, an older man listened in as the engineers played Jan's homemade tape. Impressed by the doo-wop, he introduced himself as Joe Lubin, record producer for Arwin Records, owned by Doris Day and her husband, golf star Marty Melcher. If Jan would allow him to add instruments to the vocals and release it on Arwin, Lubin promised he would make Jan and his high school buddy bigger than the Everly Brothers. So while Dean was suffering through basic training, "Jenny Lee" became a national Top 10 hit—for Jan and Arnie.

Dean remembers: "Two months later while cleaning my M-1 after a day at the firing range . . . a high school buddy of mine runs up to me all excited and holds up his portable radio and says, 'Listen, "Jenny Lee" is on the radio!' I'm stunned! . . . Jan and Arnie are on *American Bandstand*, flirting with all the Bandstand Babes, and I am crawling through the putrid-smelling mud at the infiltration course. I tried to accept the fact that I blew it, the opportunity had passed me by, so I went to the base Dairy Queen and drowned my sorrows in a vanilla malt."

Meanwhile, Jan and Arnie were performing on the *Dick Clark Show*, then the *Jack Benny Show*. In August 1958, they were part of the first rock'n'roll concert at the Hollywood Bowl, alongside Bobby Darrin and the Champs. But "Jenny Lee" was the only hit for Jan and Arnie. Ginsburg lost interest and went off to study architecture. Dean now got a second chance.

"I finally completed active duty and returned home," he remembers. "Jan asked me if I wanted to come up to his house to work on some music. I accepted the offer but I did inquire about Arnie. Jan said Arnie was no longer interested in the music business. I was very surprised: what was there not to like about making billions of dollars, performing on *American Bandstand*, rubbing elbows with Elvis, Frankie Avalon, Sam Cooke, flirting with Annette Funicello, buying a new sports car right off the showroom floor, having dinner at Dick Clark's house and having chicks scream at you. What's there not to like? I wanted to get started before Jan or Arnie changed their minds."

From 1959 through 1962, Jan & Dean had hit after hit with singles and albums. They were essentially an R&B doo-wop band, and listeners who never saw them perform assumed they were African American.

In 1963, Jan & Dean heard the recordings of another Southern California harmonizing group called the Beach Boys who had a local hit with "Surfin'" followed by a national hit with "Surfin' Safari." Jan & Dean had just released a single called "Tennessee," but the success of this new surf music caught their

Ventures Single and Album, 1960s: Since they didn't actually surf, many aficionados never considered the Ventures' sound "surf music." Still, their recordings were all over the airwaves in the 1960s, influencing "true" surf bands. (Voyageur Press Archives)

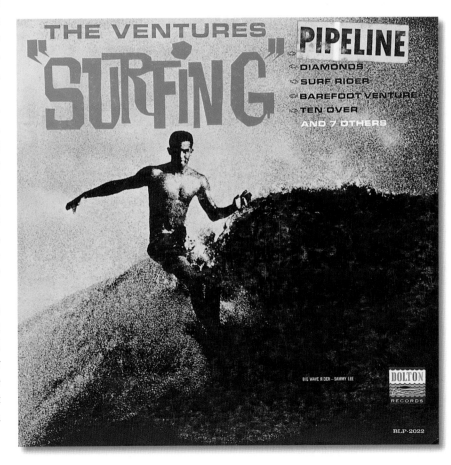

The Surfin' Bird is the Word

An Interview with Tony Andreason, Guitarist for the Trashmen

Is it such a shame to be a one-hit wonder when your one hit is so wonderful?

Surf music is all about having fun and getting crazy, and it's unlikely any surf band got crazier or had more fun than the Trashmen when they cut "Surfin' Bird." This song is berserk. It rocks, it makes no sense, and it probably scared parents to death—which is the Triple Crown for surf music.

"Surfin' Bird" hit the Top Five in 1964, and it was only the fresh emergence of the Beatles that kept this novelty song from taking the top slot.

"Surfin' Bird" was the hare-brained idea of the Trashmen, a quartet from the surf capital of Minneapolis, Minnesota—the land of ten thousand lakes and a thousand dances. The Trashmen—Jim Thaxter, Dal Winslow, Steve Wahrer, Tom Diehl, and Tony Andreason—became enormously popular as a "surf" band in the land of ice and snow, playing to teen clubs.

"Surfin' Bird" was a very strange song, a morphing of two other hits: the Rivingtons' doo-wop nonsense classic "Papa Oom Mow Mow" and the dance it inspired, the Bird. It was a gag, but it resonated.

Four decades later, Tony Andreason, original guitarist for the Trashmen, explained their immortal party song.

The Ramones' version of "Surfin' Bird" rocked, but your original is better. Edgier. Weirder.

Well, thanks.

"Surfin' Bird" is a truly strange song.

Yes.

But a great song, and it makes you wonder: What was going on in Minnesota in 1963 to produce it?

Well, we were playing gigs all around Minneapolis and the Midwest in the early Sixties. . . . We were playing college parties and roller rinks and Battles of the Bands against bands like the Underbeats. DJs for the radio stations would come up and do these shows too for money. They would throw records at the audience and have games and things like that between sets.

Where did the band name come from?

When I got out of the service, Steve Wahrer and I went over to Don Woody's house. He had a huge record collection and one of them was a song called "Trashman's Blues" by Tony Kiray. Steve thought that would be a great band name and we laughed about it, but then there it was on Steve's bass drum, and we became The Trashmen.

How did you become a surf band in Minneapolis?

We had heard surf music on the radio and we were intrigued. It just sounded good and we wanted to learn more about it, so we went to California.

Do you remember the year?

It was summer 1963. We drove all the way out in a brand-new Bonneville with a four-speed stick. We had a portable record player in the car, listening to Dick Dale records—"Dick Dale Stomp" and "Let's Go Trippin'."

So it was kind of a pilgrimage?

I think the first place we stayed was in Malibu.

A nice start.

I had never seen the ocean.

Get out!

Nope.

How old were you?

I was 19. I had never seen the ocean and had no clue what it was about. We sat on the beach and watched the surf come in. We were transfixed on it. Mesmerized. I thought, "Those guys are really getting a kick out of this," so I thought I would try it.

I got a surfboard and went out and absolutely got washed into shore. I basically wiped out. I was picking myself up and some surfers asked where I was from. I was dead white and obviously not from California. We told them we were the Trashmen and we were from Minnesota and we wanted to learn about surf. They told us about the surfer's life and playing music. They thought it was cool we had come all the way from Minnesota. They gave me a surfer medal to protect me in the surf.

You heard some music while you were out here?

We went to the Rendezvous Ballroom and heard the Chantays and Dick Dale. It was all a great experience and a unique experience and we wanted to take it back to our friends in Minnesota. We left California and drove straight back. It took us 32 hours.

Yikes.

Well, we had jobs. That is what they called them then—not gigs. We got back to Minnesota and learned as much surf music as we could. We did "Hava Nagila" and "Pipeline" and "Dick Dale Stomp." The kids in Minnesota had never heard it either and they liked it. They were making up their own dances.

Did you guys wear band suits?

We always wore matching suits.

What kind of crowd would be at these shows?

Like a thousand kids.

Wow. A thousand wound-up Minnesota farmkids all jacked on hormones and Everclear. That would be some energy.

Exactly. We loved it. We were backstage at Chubb's Ballroom in Minneapolis getting ready to go on and we were talking about "Papa Oom Mow Mow" and "The Bird is the Word" by the Rivingtons. Steve Wahrer said, "Maybe we could do it this way." He came up with a strange voice and did that *babababababa* thing. The song had three chords and he said, "When I shake my head, that is when you change the chord." We had never done the song before and I had never heard that strange voice, but we liked it. Just pulled "Surfin' Bird" out of the air, so to speak.

So not only was he singing like a madman, he was shaking his head like a madman.

Yep.

People went berserk.

They did—and they started doing the Bird dance.

Can you describe?

Flop your arms and move your feet and you are doing the bird dance beat.

So you made up "Surfin' Bird" in the dressing room of a ballroom, played it that night, and the crowd went nuts.

Yes, and DJ Bill Diehl—the Wizard of the Wax, the Deacon of the Disc—was there and he heard it. He said, "What is that song? Did you see the crowd? That is a hit. You have to record it."

When you guys first recorded "Surfin' Bird" didn't you think: "Man, this song is really strange?"

We thought it was weird, yes, but different. It sure was different.

How long from when you recorded it until it went to Number One? And how shocked were you?

We were shocked for sure. It went to Number One quickly. In just a few weeks.

Since then, "Surfin' Bird" has been covered by a lot of different bands—the Cramps, the Ramones.

Yeah. We thought it was pretty cool when they covered the "Bird."

You guys did it better.

Thanks.

"Surfin' Bird" Album, 1960s (Voyageur Press Archives)

Charlie don't surf
And we think he should
Charlie don't surf
And you know that it ain't no good
— The Clash, "Charlie Don't Surf," 1980

Jan & Dean Single and Albums, 1960s: Along with the Beach Boys, Jan and Dean launched the vocal style of doo-wop surf music. The duo's single "Surf City" was the first song with the word "surf" in the title to hit number one. (Voyageur Press Archives)

ears, and they began looking closer to home for inspiration.

"About the same time," Dean recollects, "Jan and I were booked to do a concert in the South Bay area of Los Angeles at Hermosa Beach High School, not far from the beach town of Hawthorne. Since Jan & Dean didn't have a live band (we used studio musicians to make all of our records), the promoter of the show had to hire a back-up band to play for us. For this one particular show, the promoter hired a local group who had just had their own hit record titled 'Surfin' Safari'—they called themselves the Beach Boys."

Jan & Dean and the Beach Boys met for the first time in a school classroom temporarily converted into their dressing room. "The Beach Boys then went on stage to do their own opening set," Dean says. "The crowd went crazy, they loved their hometown boys!" But after Jan & Dean performed their set, they still had to fill out their contracted time slot, so they joined forces on the Beach Boys' two big hits: "The two groups launched into 'Surfin'' and 'Surfin' Safari' and the audience flipped out, the guys on stage flipped out, and a lifelong friendship started on that high school stage, one warm California spring evening way back in 1963."

A couple days later, Jan called head Beach Boy Brian Wilson to say that Jan & Dean had decided to try their hand at making surf music. The idea was to cover "Surfin'" and "Surfin' Safari" and incorporate them into an upcoming album also featuring their new single, "Linda": the LP was to be retitled *Jan & Dean Take Linda Surfin'*. Brian not only gave his blessing, he offered to lend a hand in the studio.

In March 1963 at Hollywood's Western Recording Studios, Jan & Dean and the Beach Boys joined forces again. After the session was over, Brian offered a preview of his next record, belting out "Surfin' U.S.A." Jan & Dean sought to record the song, but Brian Wilson instead offered them a similar but unfinished tune. The title was "Surf City."

Jan & Dean collaborated with Brian Wilson in composing and recording "Surf City," and three months later it hit number one on the Billboard national charts. Among aficionados there is ongoing debate over what defines surf music, who was

the first true surf band, and what was the first surf song to top the charts. All agree, however, that Jan & Dean's "Surf City" was the first song with the word "surf" in the title to reach number one.

Jan & Dean Take Linda Surfin' was released soon after. On the cover, Jan and Dean were decked out in the uniform and weaponry of the West Coast: T-shirts, shorts, and purple and yellow surfboards, accessorized by a pretty young blonde. The West Coast now had a sound and a look—surfing was it.

Before they were the Beach Boys, they were Kenny and the Cadets, then Carl and the Passions, and finally the Pendletones. The musical push came from Brian Wilson, who was a fan of the Four Freshmen and Chuck Berry and who would later be declared a musical genius, which he most certainly was. Wilson shared a room with his brothers, Carl and Dennis, and late into the night coached them in the art of vocal harmonizing. Their cousin, Mike Love, sang along on Christmas carols and at birthday parties.

In 1959, Brian was supposed to pen a sonata for his Hawthorne High twelfth-grade piano composition class. He wrote a sweet melody that he called "Surfin'" and handed it in. Wilson earned a C for the semester.

In spring 1960, Brian and some friends performed the campaign song for student body president candidate Carol Hess. That led to further appearances, Brian singing alongside Carl and Mike. Carl had his doubts about the whole music thing, so Brian dubbed the combo Carl and the Passions. They cycled a number of friends and neighbors through the group, and their highlight was opening for the Four Preps at a high school assembly.

On Labor Day weekend 1961, their parents, Murray and Audree Wilson, vacationed in Mexico, leaving three hundred dollars in food money for their growing boys. The Wilson brothers instead went hungry and invested the money in band instruments. Then they began rehearsing Brian's "Surfin'" sonata. When mom and dad returned, they found their sons had an act. They called themselves the Pendletones, a play on the popular shirt of the day.

Murray pitched his sons to a friend, Hite Morgan, owner of Guild Music. On September 15, the Pendletones performed "Surfin'" in the Morgan's front room, and Brian and Mike signed a songwriting contract with Guild Music that same day.

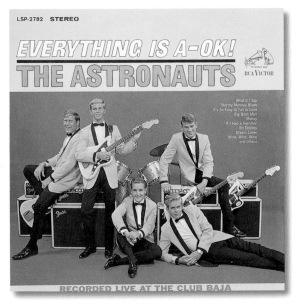

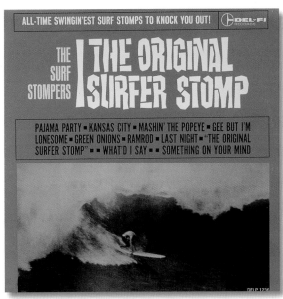

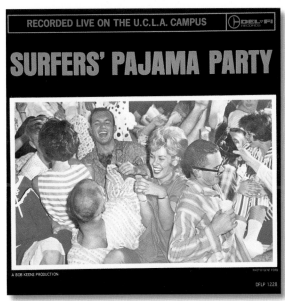

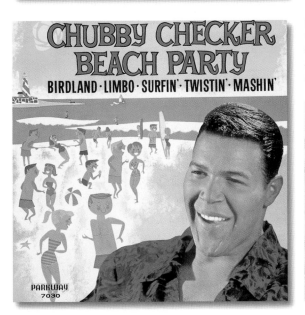

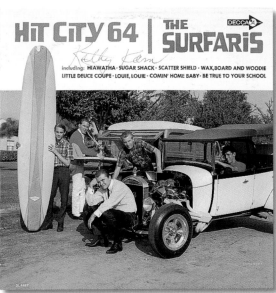

Surf Music Cool, 1960s

(Voyageur Press Archives)

The Honeys

The First All-Girl Surf Band

Early in the morning we'll be startin' out
Some Honeys will be comin' along . . .
— The Beach Boys, "Surfin' Safari," 1962

By 1963, just three years had passed since Brian Wilson got a C in high school for writing the song "Surfin'," but who was laughing now? The Beach Boys had signed with Capitol Records and everything they touched turned to solid gold. Brian Wilson was the budding producer extraordinaire behind the band and was always looking for new sounds and new projects. Wilson had long been a fan of the young Phil Spector's productions with the Crystals and the Ronettes. He was floored by Spector's new 1963 production of the Ronettes' "Be My Baby," a hit that inspired Wilson to arrange the first all-girl surf band, in 1963.

Wilson had produced a few non-surf girl-group records in 1962. But in October of that year, the Beach Boys were playing a Sunset Strip club called Pandora's Box. Songwriter Gary Usher brought some friends to see them, including singer Marilyn Rovell.

During a break, Brian was talking to Usher when he accidentally dumped a cup of hot chocolate all over Marilyn. It was love at first spill.

Marilyn would become the cornerstone of the Honeys, along with her sister Diane and Usher's girlfriend, Ginger Blake (Sandra Glauntz). Their first release was the "Surfin' Down the Swanee River"/ "Pray for Surf" 45, produced by Nick Venet and arranged by Brian Wilson. That was followed by "Pray for Surf"/ "Hide Go Seek," which prompted the use of the Honeys as backup singers for some of the biggest singles by the biggest West Coast acts of the time: Jan & Dean ("New Girl in School"), the Surfaris ("I Wanna Take a Trip to the Islands"), the Hondells ("My Buddy Seat") and the Beach Boys ("Be True to Your School").

The Honeys also sang background vocals on the entire *Muscle Beach Party* album by Annette Funicello (songs by Brian Wilson, Gary Usher, and Roger Christian).

Nineteen sixty-four saw the release of the Honey's coup de grace, a Brian Wilson masterpiece production titled "He's a Doll," featuring a scorching sax solo by Steve Douglas and released on Warner Brothers' records. Several Honeys sides came out

The Pendletones recorded their first songs—"Surfin'," "Luau," and "Lavender"—at Los Angeles' World Pacific Studios on October 3, 1961. The line-up included Brian on drums, Carl on guitar, and Al Jardine on acoustic bass; along with Dennis, they all shared vocal duties. Murray then took the demos to Herb Newman, owner of Candix and Era Records, and on December 8, the Pendletones were signed.

The name wasn't quite right, though. Era promotions man Russ Regan suggested they change to the Beach Boys. Candix wanted the Surfers, but someone already had that name. Regan won out, and in December 1961, "Surfin'" by the Beach Boys was released as a promo issue on X Records and commercially on Candix. The platter went straight to number three in Southern California and as high as number seventy-five on the national charts. Despite the success, Jardine left to study dentistry.

On February 8, 1962, Brian, Dennis, and Val Poliuto of the Jaguars recorded six songs for Morgan's Deck Records—"Surfin'," "Surfin' Safari," "Karate," "Little Surfin' Girl," "Luau," and "Judy." By May, Candix folded, and Murray was shopping their demos around Hollywood. Liberty, Dot, and Decca passed, but Capitol's Nick Venet heard something he liked and signed the boys in June. With new member David Marks, the Beach Boys overdubbed an existing master of "Surfin' Safari" and backed it with a hot rod song called "409." Their surf anthem soared to number fourteen and the hot rodder's ode raced to number seventy-six. Just like that, the Beach Boys were sitting on top of the world.

On New Year's Eve 1962, the Beach Boys did their first big live gig, a memorial concert for Ritchie Valens who died in the plane crash with Buddy Holly and the Big Bopper. Performing at Long Beach Mu-

under aliases during 1964/65 but the Honeys would not emerge again with another single until 1969's "Tonight You Belong to Me," backed with "Goodnight My Love," which was produced by Wilson during the same time as his psychedelic meditation album *Friends*.

On December 7, 1964, Wilson and Rovell married. Two weeks later, Wilson suffered his first nervous breakdown and dropped off the Beach Boys' tour. Wilson was replaced by future country superstar Glen Campbell for six months, then permanent bassist Bruce Johnston—who was a part of the first surf group, the Gamblers and later produced the hit single "Hey Little Cobra" for the Rip Cords. In 1966 Marilyn was used as a demo vocalist for Brian Wilson's "Vege-Tables" production for the aborted *Smile* masterpiece. Her vocals were later replaced by the Beach Boys in April of 1967—a session attended by Beatle Paul McCartney.

Ginger Blake left the Honeys during the early '70s to sing backup for the Supremes, Cheryl Dilcher, and Jimmie Webb, as well as to release several of her own quality singles under various aliases. Marilyn and Diane continued to record with Brian Wilson under the name Spring. In 1972, Brian and Spring

recorded vocals for an amazing version of "Vegetables," released by Jan & Dean on their album, *Gotta Take That One Last Ride*—with artwork by Rick Griffin. Spring recorded their own album, produced by Brian Wilson and David Sandler (engineered by sound genius Stephen Desper) in 1972 and released several strong singles thereafter as American Spring. Their 1973 Columbia single "Shyin' Away" failed to dent the charts, but several recognized underground writers praised the single and Brian Wilson went to promote it on FM radio in New York City.

The Honeys reunited to record for various releases in the 1970s and 1980s, did local popular Los Angeles shows, and maintained a fan club.

Despite never having a hit single, the saga of the Honeys is both important to the surf genre and the production career of musical genius Brian Wilson.

The Honeys are a gas, man, and their pioneering efforts paved the way for girl groups like the Go-Go's and the Bangles whose hit singles were often harmony-laden and surf-themed. The Honeys have stayed busy in the studio backing the Smithereens, Rodney Bingenheimer's the GTOs, and Carnie and Wendy Wilson of Wilson Phillips—the daughters of Brian and Marilyn.

nicipal Stadium, they earned a whopping three hundred dollars. Jardine saw the light, dropped dental school, and returned to the band.

The Beach Boys' next hit, "Surfin' U.S.A," was penned by Brian and Mike. But they may have allowed themselves to be a little too influenced by Chuck Berry, who threatened to sue as the melody was so close to Berry's "Sweet Little Sixteen." The threat was enough, and Berry got sole writing credit for the song. "Surfin' U.S.A" went to number three in the United States, number thirty-two in England, and number nine in Australia.

The Beach Boys' first album, *Surfin' Safari*, was equally weighted between surfing and car songs, including "The Shift," "Summertime Blues," "Moon Dawg," "Stoked," "The Lonely Sea," "Noble Surfer," and covers of Dick Dale's "Let's Go Trippin'" and "Miserlou." At the same time, they released a hot

rod album called *Little Deuce Coupe*, including a tribute to James Dean and the soon-to-be classic "Fun, Fun, Fun." The LP's "I Get Around" scored the Beach Boys' first number-one hit.

Brian Wilson's legendary problems began in 1964, even while the hits kept on coming. The pace and stress were overwhelming him; he retreated into drugs and suffered nervous breakdowns. Brian liked writing and recording more than touring and performing, so while the Beach Boys were on the road, he was home experimenting with sophisticated production techniques to create new sounds. Brian hired platoons of studio musicians to work on what he planned as his masterpiece, 1966's *Pet Sounds*, including "God Only Knows," "Wouldn't It Be Nice," "Caroline No," and "Sloop John B." Yet while the LP was an artistic success, sales were poor.

Above, **Beach Boys Single and Albums, 1960s** (Voyageur Press Archives)

Right, **Clean-Cut Beach Boys, 1960s:** The Beach Boys were smooth, slick, and stylish—and that applied to both their look and their music. (Voyageur Press Archives)

Disappointed but undaunted, Brian began working on the next Beach Boys album, *Smile*, which he declared would be nothing less than "a teenage symphony to God." With this as his goal, it's little wonder he faltered.

Smile was shelved, and Brian was off to fight his own personal and creative demons. Still, Capitol released a handful of tracks from the projected album— "Heroes and Villains" and Brian and Mike's feel-good tour de force "Good Vibrations." Brian spent six months recording "Good Vibrations" in four studios and seventeen sessions at the unprecedented cost of sixteen thousand dollars. The song is beautiful, complicated, and elaborate, and it went to number one.

Despite the success of "Good Vibrations," *Smile* lay in the can for decades, and by 1967, Jimi Hendrix was prophesizing the end of surf music. Brian's erratic behavior forced the Beach Boys to pull out of the Monterey International Pop Festival in June—the place where Jimi began his American reign.

Many surfers at the time rejected the Beach Boys and their music as fluff created by kuk outsiders. While they wrote songs about surfing, only Dennis Wilson actually surfed, and their sound was not the heavy-reverb, guitar-powered instrumentals to which the surfers loved to stomp. "I remember the first time we heard 'Surfer Girl,'" surfing legend Mike Doyle says. "We started hissing and hooting because we thought it was so dumb." Gordon McLelland agrees: "The surfers I knew in Orange County during the early 1960s were not hostile towards the Beach Boys, they just thought the music was corny and sort of wrote it off as commercial stuff for the hodad masses."

Still, there's no denying the genius of Brian Wilson and the music he created. Paul McCartney says the Beach Boys inspired *Rubber Soul* and *Sgt. Pepper's Lonely Hearts Club Band*; he praised *Pet Sounds* as "perhaps the album of the century." *Rolling Stone* magazine voted *Pet Sounds* number two

The End of Surf Music?

Dick Dale and Jimi Hendrix Trade Guitar Licks

And you'll never hear surf music again...
– Jimi Hendrix, "Third Stone from the Sun," 1967

Jimi Hendrix recorded "Third Stone from the Sun" in April 1967 while the rock'n'roll world was making love and war. Gearing up for the Summer of Love, hippies held love-ins on beaches and mountaintops while, at the same time, Brits and Americans were in the fiercest battle since the Revolutionary War. From across the Atlantic, the British were invading with the Beatles, the Who, the Kinks, the Animals, the Rolling Stones, Pink Floyd, and the Moody Blues. The English accent cannonaded the pop charts, wearing down America's defenses—Elvis Presley, Chuck Berry, the Monkees, Simon and Garfunkel, the Doors, and the Beach Boys.

The USA needed heavier metal to put down the onslaught, and Jimi Hendrix looked to be the musical cavalry.

Hendrix was actually behind enemy lines, in London, when he recorded "Third Stone from the Sun." The song ended with a psychedelic soliloquy in which Hendrix whispers the cryptic words: "And you'll never hear surf music again."

What did Jimi mean? Didn't he like surf music? Or was he bemoaning its demise?

Fast forward to summer 2004. Dick Dale was playing a gig at the Glendale Cruise Night with a power trio joined by his son, twelve-year-old prodigy Jimmy Dale. Dad and lad had a good act, doing shtick and putting out an impressive amount of sound. After the show, Dale was watching a parade of hot rods leaving town when someone queried him: "Any idea what Jimi was saying all those years ago?"

A longtime Hendrix fan, Dale did indeed: "As a matter of fact, 'You'll never hear surf music again' was a dedication to me from Jimi as he recorded 'Third Stone from the Sun.' What happened was, I had cancer [in 1967] and was told I only had three months to live. It was all kept pretty secret but it got so bad that for the first time I missed a gig—at Harmony Park—because I was rushed into surgery. Dave Meyers and the Surftones filled in. Hendrix was recording when he got the news, and someone told him I was dying. It wasn't true, but Jimi thought it was and that is why he said those words at the end of 'Third Stone.'

"And that is why I dedicated it back to him on my last CD. I said, 'Jimi, I'm still here. Wish you were.'"

on its Greatest Albums list; *Sgt. Pepper's* was number one. Like the Beatles, the Beach Boys evolved from simple pop roots to more sophisticated music, becoming one of the most influential and successful American bands of all time.

Even among surfers, taste has changed over time. In 1972, surf movie makers Greg MacGillivray and Jim Freeman used new songs–"Sail On Sailor" and "Water"–from the Beach Boys as the soundtrack to their movie *Five Summer Stories*. Rodney Sumpter also used the Beach Boys in his 1974 surf film *On Any Morning*. As the years passed, even die-hard detractors came around: "None of us much liked the Beach Boys when they first came out," says *Surfer* magazine founder John Severson in 1997. "Now I think their music is wonderful. Now I understand it and know why everyone thought they were so incredible."

Catch a wave and you're sitting on top of the world
— The Beach Boys, "Catch A Wave," 1964

A Surfing Anthem

The Long, Happy Life of "Wipe Out!"

The song starts with a bizarre crackle and then an even-more-bizarre voice chuckling the title—"Wipe Out!" An instant hit, the song has since become perhaps the single best-known surf music tune.

"Wipe Out!" was written and recorded by the Surfaris, a surf band from Glendale, California. Jim Fuller—the Surfaris' original guitarist and the surfer who cowrote the song—tells its story:

Happy Birthday to you and your hit song "Wipe Out!"

Thank you. Forty years. Eight million broadcasts.

Wow.

That is what I have been saying for forty years.

It wasn't planned this way?

Not even close. It was a fluke. We needed a B side.

A B side to what?

"Surfer Joe." It was a song that came to [Surfaris drummer] Ron Wilson in his sleep. We recorded it and it came out pretty good. We were so young and naïve we didn't know we needed a B side.

Who were "we" and how young were "you"?

We were the Surfaris. I was 15 and the others were around there: Ron Wilson, Bob Berryhill, and Ron Connolly. We were all from the Glendale area and we were still in high school. Our parents were driving us to gigs.

What kind of gigs?

Skating rinks. Teen clubs. We were lucky if we'd earn $10 to $15 a night, each.

Fun.

It was fun. It was 1963. We were a surf band.

Did you guys surf?

Sure. We were all from Glendale but we spent as much time at the beach as possible.

Where did "Wipe Out!" come from?

We had a manager named Ron Smallen and he thought if we recorded a song we could buy a van for the band and some new instruments.

And maybe some new surfboards.

And some new surfboards. We all went to a record-

ing studio in Cucamonga in December 1962 and recorded "Surfer Joe." It came out okay, and then someone noted that we needed a song for the *other* side of the 45.

Traditionally, yes. Where did it come from?

Well, Ron Wilson was in the high school marching band and he had this drum cadence that he speeded up.

Where do the sound effects at the start come from?

That was our manager Ron Smallen. He broke a board covered with plaster and then cackled "wipe out!" into the mic.

Where did your guitar riff come from?

It was just something I had in my head. Something I had been working on for a couple of weeks.

And it all gelled there in the recording studio.

It came together rather nicely.

What was your axe?

I had a Fender DuoSonic with a lot of reverb that night. I really liked that guitar and I wish I had held onto it, but who was to know what was coming? When "Wipe Out!" became a hit, the Surfaris cut a deal with Fender. We did some ads in music magazines and they gave us a lot of equipment. I got a brand-new Dakota Red Stratocaster. I've been playing Strats ever since, but I do wish I still had that DuoSonic.

So you got your new equipment?

That and a lot more.

"Wipe Out!" has to be the simplest song ever written.

Simple, but effective. We rehearsed it in six takes and then we nailed it.

WIPE OUT
by SURFARIS

Recorded by-
THE SUFARIS
THE CHALLENGERS
THE VENTURES

THE CHALLENGERS

THE VENTURES

KEYS
04754

MIRALESTE MUSIC & ROBIN HOOD MU

WIPE OUT
By THE SURFARIS

☆

Recorded
by

THE SURFARIS
on
LONDON
HLD 9751

☆ and ☆

THE SAINTS
on
PYE
7N 15548

GUITAR SOLO WITH PIANO ACCOMPANIMENT 3/-

☆ ☆ ☆ ☆ ☆ AMBASSADOR MUSIC LTD., 23-24, Greek Street, London, W. 1. ☆ ☆ ☆ ☆ ☆
Sole Selling Agents:-
Southern Music Publishing Co. Ltd., 8, Denmark Street, London, W.C. 2.

"Wipe Out" Sheet Music, 1963 (Voyageur Press Archives)

COLUMBIA PICTURES presents

GIDGET

CLIFF ROBERTSON   JAMES DARREN

ELL   with   MARY LaROCHE   and THE FOUR PREPS
JO MORROW

SCOPE   EASTMAN COLOR

Blue Screen

Hollywood Exploits Surfing—and Vise Versa • The 1920s to Today

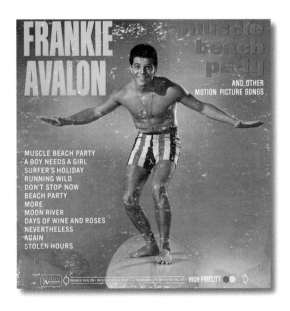

Left, Gidget Surfs, 1959: Practicing her board-riding moves in her bedroom, Gidget prepares to spread the good word about surfing around the globe. (Columbia Pictures)

Above, **Frankie "Surfs," 1960s** (Voyageur Press Archives)

SURFIN' all day...
SWINGIN' all night...
you are invited to a
"BEACH PARTY"
TONIGHT!

STARRING

BOB
CUMMINGS

DOROTHY
MALONE

FRANKIE
AVALON

ANNETTE
FUNICELLO

HARVEY
LEMBECK

JODY
McCREA

JOHN
ASHLEY

ALSO STARRING
MOREY
AMSTERDAM
AND
EVA SIX

And Featuring
DICK DALE
AND
THE DEL TONES

In AMERICAN
INTERNATIONAL'S

BEACH PARTY

Directed by   Written by   Produced by   Executive Producer   Music by
WILLIAM ASHER · LOU RUSOFF ... JAMES H. NICHOLSON ... LOU RUSOFF · SAMUEL Z. ARKOFF · LES BAXTER IN PATHECOLOR AND PANAVISION

COPYRIGHT © 1963 AMERICAN INTERNATIONAL PICTURES   PRINTED IN U.S.A.   5   Property of National Screen Service Corp. Licensed for display only in connection with   63/26
                                                                                                         the exhibition of this picture at your theatre. Must be returned immediately thereafter.

Beach Party, 1963:
"Surfin' all day, swingin'
all night," promised this
Beach Party lobby card.
(American International
Pictures)

Hollywood has mishandled, misrepresented, misinterpreted, and misaligned few other people, places, or sports more than surfing. Perhaps only the Nazi party has been worked over more. Perhaps, that is.

Most American sports boast classic movies—and some of these films have won Oscars. Hollywood has been good to baseball, football, basketball, golf, and even bicycle riding. There's an Oscar-winning movie about track and field—*Chariots of Fire*—and Robert De Niro won another for portraying a boxer in *Raging Bull*. Heck, Jackie Gleason was nominated for an Academy Award for playing an overweight pool shark in *The Hustler*.

Surfing? Bruce Brown's *The Endless Summer* from 1966 rocked the box office but wasn't nominated for diddly, although it is generally considered a classic, and is reputed to be the most commercially successful documentary film ever made. And Sean Penn should have been nominated for *something* for his surfer dude character Jeff Spicoli in *Fast Times at Ridgemont High*. Instead, he'll just have to be happy with creating one of the great comic icons of the twentieth century. Spicoli has the laugh power to reduce audiences to tears just by appearing on screen, putting him up there with the likes of Buster Keaton, Charlie Chaplin, the Marx Brothers, and John Belushi.

Surfing doesn't get much respect in the transition to the silver screen. When the Sport of Kings is portrayed by the Hollywood Squares, the result is almost always rated C for Corny, Crummy, Contrived, Commercial, and just altogether Crappy. Some of the worst movies ever made were waxploitation flicks: *Surf Nazis Must Die, Monster from the Surf*, and too many more. And then there were the *Beach Party* movies with the horrendous yin of Frankie crooning to Annette, countered a little by the yang of Eric Von Zipper and guest appearances by the likes of Dick Dale, Buster Keaton, Little Stevie Wonder, and Candy Johnson, the Perpetual Motion Dancer. Most surfing flicks from the late 1950s to today have latched on to stereotypes about surfing and packaged them for audiences around the world, all in search of the filthy lucre.

Hollywood has exploited surfing, and not always to the betterment of the pursuit. On the other hand, several generations of surfers have done well by Hollywood, going back to Duke Kahanamoku. Duke—and others from Tom Blake to Mickey Dora and Mickey Muñoz—exploited their own surfing and ocean skills to earn good money in front of and behind the camera. Sometimes they had to put on wigs and dress up like women, but they were being paid to go surfing.

Duke Kahanamoku could walk on water, and when Hollywood needed someone with those skills, they knew who to call. Over the years, Duke performed in some thirty movies, beginning with the role of Noah Noa in 1925's *Adventure* and ending with 1968's *I Sailed to Tahiti with an All Girl Crew* in which Duke played himself. In between, he was a pirate captain, devil-ape, wild-animal trapper, and a host of dusky natives and Indian chiefs with names like Tamb Itam, Jaffir, Kalita, and Manua. In 1948, Duke appeared as Ua Nuke alongside John "Duke" Wayne in *Wake of the Red Witch*. Yet Duke's Olympic status prevented him from surfing, swimming, or doing water stunts in any films except newsreels. According to Duke's biographer, Sandra Kimberley Hall, "The International Olympic Committee was adamant about athletes not being paid for pursuing their sporting activities outside of the Olympics. Look at what happened to Frank Beaurepaire, James Thorpe. To my knowledge, the only film he surfed in was Douglas Fairbanks's travelogue *Around the World in 80 Minutes*."

Duke's disciple, Tom Blake, was a national swimming champion and natural waterman, but because he was not an Olympian he wasn't prohibited from doing anything. Hollywood was waiting. Blake's first film stunt was in *Where the Pavement Ends* from 1923 where he wrestled a dead shark. Over the next eighteen years, Blake worked in dozens of Hollywood movies with the likes of Clark Gable on *Strange Cargo* in 1939 and John Wayne on *Wake Island* in 1942.

Hollywood paid Blake's bills for many years, but he soon tired of the life. "The shallowness of the film industry was what eventually caused Tom to leave the profession," notes biographer Gary Lynch. "He grew to fundamentally dislike the film industry centered at Hollywood and finally disassociated himself from it after World War II." When Hollywood saw that women dug Olympian-turned-movie-star Johnny Weissmuller in a loincloth, they all but ordered him to divorce his wife, and paid her off with ten thousand dollars. Blake saw what Tinseltown did to some of his contemporaries and he didn't like it: "It was embarrassing to see the writers and directors of Hollywood make an intelligent and gifted athlete like Johnny talk and act like an ape-man," says Lynch.

Yet while Blake held Hollywood in the same disdain as many surfers who followed in his wake, he wasn't afraid to milk the studios for traveling and bean-curd money.

Preston "Pete" Peterson was a contemporary of Tom Blake, competing against him in swimming and paddle races in the 1920s and 1930s. But while Blake's story is well known, Peterson remains a riddle wrapped in mystery with a side order of enigma. Born in 1913 in Texas, he was in California with his parents in time to buy his first board by the age of seven. Peterson went on to become one of the great watermen of the twentieth century: He dove deep, dived high, and swam, surfed, stroked, and sailed with the best. He won the Pacific Coast Championships in 1932, 1936, 1938, and 1941—four out of the ten years it was held. Peterson was the first to paddle to Catalina from the mainland and one of the first wave of

> Annette: *We got an early start.*
> Frankie: *We're gonna have a ball.*
> Annette: *We're gonna ride the surf.*
> Frankie: *And that ain't . . .*
> Frankie and Annette: *Allllll! Beach party tonight!*
> — Annette and Frankie, "Beach Party," 1963

Real Surfing Movies

Bud Browne Pioneers the Surf Film

As the popularity of surfing grew in America, entrepreneurs like Bud Browne, Greg Noll, Bruce Brown, and John Severson traveled up and down California to Mexico, Australia, and beyond, shooting the best surfers on the best waves. They edited the movies together, thought up a narration, and fed it all live to stoked surfers along the coast. The movies also had an ever-changing soundtrack of whatever music the auteur thought was appropriate.

Bud Browne was the first to make a real surf movie. Tall and angular, Browne learned to surf at Venice Beach in 1939 while working as an LA County lifeguard. After serving in the Navy during World War II, he taught school while taking classes at the USC Film School.

In 1953, Brown cut together forty-five minutes of surfing footage from Waikiki and packaged it as *Hawaiian Surfing Movies*. All at the same time, Browne would project the movie, do a live narration over the PA system, and play music from a reel-to-reel tape recorder in the projection booth.

Hawaiian Surfing Movies was a cult hit, inspiring Browne to make a film a year for the next eleven years, including *Locked In*, *Cat on a Hot Foam Board*, *Spinning Boards*, and *Cavalcade of Surf*. Browne toured California, showing his movies at civic auditoriums, women's clubs, high school auditoriums—anywhere they'd let him set up his gear. And as surfing began to flourish in the 1950s, his films became insanely popular.

In those days, Browne was a one-man show: setting up the projector, voicing a live narration, and DJ-ing a soundtrack that fit the action. Gordon McLelland now works with Browne packaging and distributing his films as well as selling footage to other surf moviemakers: "Remember, the pre-1960 surf movies had no soundtrack: the narration was live and the music was from records or a tape machine that would be turned on and off between talking. The narration often changed and it wouldn't have been unusual for different music to be used at different showings. My recollection is that Severson and Bruce Brown mostly used cool jazz, mixed with comedy ragtime, classical music and I believe John used 'Peter Gunn' in several films for the big-wave sections. John Severson didn't like 'surf music' at the time and thought it was mostly kooks trying to cash in on the culture. That said, he did take the picture of Dick Dale surfing below the San Clemente Pier that appeared on Dale's first album.

"The surf movie connection to 'surf music' was after the fact," McLelland continues. "The music came first at surf stomps, then later, due to popular demand the connection to films was made. Watching videos won't help much because all Bud's films and most of the others had the music changed when they went to video, to avoid lawsuits from record companies, music publishers, and the musicians. It seemed appropriate to use surf music so we all did it when the new soundtracks were created."

***Gun Ho!* 1963**
(Voyageur Press Archives)

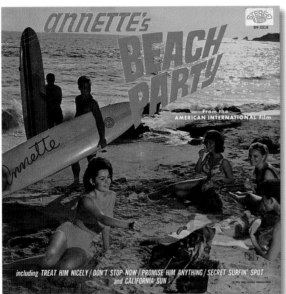

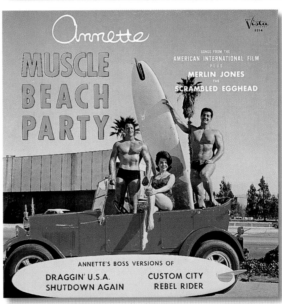

**Annette "Surfs,"
1960s:** She may never have gotten her incredible 'do wet, but she looked good doing it. (Voyageur Press Archives)

California *haole* to invade Hawai'i, going over with Lorrin Harrison and Gene Smith in 1932. Riding the South Shore reefs on heavy redwood boards, Peterson and his fellow adventurers were jazzed to find Hawai'ians on balsa boards weighing only thirty to forty pounds. When the Californians ran out of money, they stowed away on the USS *Republic*, posing as soldiers for a free trip home. From what he witnessed in Hawai'i, Peterson experimented with balsa and lighter materials, innovating lifesaving equipment that is still in use today: paddleboards, soft rescue tubes, all-fiberglass hollow boards, and foam/plywood/balsa sandwich surfboards. Peterson was also an expert tandem surfer, still winning contests into the 1960s.

Peterson worked as a stuntman, stunt coordinator, set designer, and shark wrangler on films and TV shows from the 1930s to the 1980s. Yet for all his legend, Peterson is nearly invisible; one has to rely on word of mouth and rusty memories to get an idea of what he did in Tinseltown. John Elwell surfed Makaha with Peterson in the 1950s and called him "a huge figure in surfing in the Thirties to the Fifties," and remembered him doing stunning surfing stunts in RKO specials.

Paul Stader was another old-time surfer who worked his way up from stuntman to stunt coordinator to second unit director on dozens of shows starting in 1937. In his first picture, he did a dive

Surfing's the source, man!
— *Surfer 15,* Point Break, *1991*

doubling for star Jon Hall in John Ford's *The Hurricane* and became an instant stuntman. Stader went on to perform all of Weissmuller's swings and dives in the *Tarzan* series, and worked with Peterson on *The Poseidon Adventure* and *The Towering Inferno* decades later.

Peterson and Stader did tens, if not hundreds, of stunts for Tinseltown, from wrestling sharks and falling to their "deaths" to riding waves. Their screen credits are mostly invisible, however. As Stader's motto went, "The only credit we get is at the bank."

The surf bums in the 1959 movie adaptation of *Gidget* spend most of their time lounging around the Malibu beach shack talking parties and chicks, then every once in a while they stand up on cue, grab their surfboards in a chorus line, charge into the water, and take off on the same wave en masse. Yet of all the actors in the cast, only one truly knew how to ride a wave: Doug McLure. As *Gidget* surfing stand-in Mickey Muñoz remembers, "He was a reasonably good surfer, but he was married to a high-maintenance lady who demanded he work constantly, so a lot of times it was up to me to drag him out of his house and go surfing. I also became pretty good friends with Cliff Robertson, who impressed me with all the work and research he did to get his part right. To play the part of the great Kahuna he learned to surf and hung out with all the characters so he could really be a surfer."

Behind the scenes, it was Muñoz, Mickey Dora, and a half-dozen other true surfers who made the charges against the rock at Secos. Dora doubled for the Moondoggie character played by James

Surf Party, 1964:
If Frankie and Fabian could surf, then surely Bobby Vinton could ride a board just as well. (Twentieth Century-Fox)

Darren—although the Great Kahoona character was closer to the real Dora. Dora stood in to hotdog the fun little Secos waves, until Gidget gets all moonie over Moondoggie. The closest they come to consummating their flirtation is riding tandem. Look close at the screen and you'll see it's Dora on the bottom, holding up an oddly muscular young woman named Mickey Muñoz.

Muñoz donned a blond wig and one-piece bathing suit to double for Sandra Dee, yet even four decades later he can't really remember why. Muñoz was small, but not nearly as petite as Dee, who looked like she would blow away in an offshore breeze. Surfer Linda Benson was Dee's main double, but for the tandem ride, Muñoz was called on. Muñoz was a regular foot and Benson was a goofy foot, and this was the first—but definitely not last—time that Hollywood didn't bother to know the difference.

for her at the time because she wasn't an outdoors type person."

Muñoz and a lot of the other real surfers were around the set most of the time it was on the beach as well as a bit at the studio. They tried to steer the movie away from corny and into reality, but they rarely succeeded. "Hollywood works in its ways and the director is king," Muñoz explains. "Whatever the director conceives of, that is what you try and do. But if he came up with something that was either not possible or too off the wall, everybody would go, 'Hey, that's not surfing.' I'm sure we put in our two cents. I've never been afraid to do that."

Muñoz got a full summer's work out of *Gidget* and earned enough screen time and money to get a coveted Screen Actors Guild card. "I think a SAG card cost $500 then, and that was a lot of money," Muñoz said. "Once I got my SAG card I got other stunt work in Hollywood. I kind of pursued it. I knew a lot of people in the business and so through those people I got work. Not a lot, but I did work as a stuntman and whatever I could do on set—usually water oriented."

Mickey Muñoz doubled for Mickey Rooney on a TV show called *Mickey.* He tandemed with a sturdy surfer named Marge Calhoun—on *her* shoulders—and nearly drowned doing a water-ski stunt. When the producers asked Muñoz if he could water-ski, Muñoz claimed he was an expert—even though he had only done it once. Like a lot of surfers before him, he came up with the skills to pull off a difficult stunt. "They dragged me off a pier on that ski and I ended up under water like 20 feet. There was no Water Safety then and there was only the driver in the boat and he was looking ahead, so I blew a few bubbles down there."

And like Tom Blake before him, Muñoz wrestled a shark. A live shark. "I teamed up with a character named Frank Donahue to film some stock footage of a man and woman fighting a shark. We went five miles out to sea from Santa Monica and caught a mako shark on a handline. Frank dressed me up as a woman, again, and had me fight the shark—live—and makos are bad-ass. I was in pretty good shape then from paddling

Ride the Wild Surf, 1964: The surf was wild—and so were the instant clichés. Color it "influential": Most every surf film that followed owed a debt to *Ride the Wild Surf.* (Columbia Pictures)

Muñoz does remember that the job came at a good time. "I was married at 19 and had a son by 20 and I needed money. I worked on *Gidget* for almost three months and it was pretty good money—like $65-$85 a day. I did the surfing but I was also lifeguarding on the set, and I tried to coach Sandra Dee. I tried to teach her how to hold a surfboard and walk down to the water's edge and even paddle, so they could get some of that on camera. But she was a skinny little Hollywood blonde and not a real athletic person. I don't know if I had much respect

***For Those Who Think Young*, 1964:** "Thinking young" meant surfing, dancing, and other beachside hijinks. (United Artists)

The King of the Beach Party

William Asher, the Man Who Bewitched the World

William Asher was a surfer, but he didn't become famous on a surfboard. Instead, he was the director of the movies that created an indelible picture of the surfing life—the Frankie and Annette *Beach Party* films.

Movie and TV director/producer Asher led an enviable life. Not only was he married to the bewitching Elizabeth Montgomery, it was Asher who produced Marilyn Monroe singing "Happy Birthday, Mr. President" to JFK and directed Sally Field in the *Gidget* TV series as well as numerous other movies. Yet surfers know him best as the director of *Beach Party*, *Bikini Beach*, *Beach Blanket Bingo*, *Muscle Beach Party*, and *How to Stuff a Wild Bikini*.

William Asher was interviewed by Terry, Tiffany, and Becky Dufoe.

How were Frankie and Annette cast for the Beach Party *films?*

They were not cast by me. Sam Arkoff did that. When I was brought in for *Beach Party* the picture was cast in so far as Frankie and Annette. It was a peculiar thing. They had a script when I came in, but it was the same old thing about mothers and fathers and teachers and school. They opened with a day in school and closed with them at home. I told Sam that kids got wild, but I wanted to make a picture about kids who weren't in trouble. I didn't want to see any parents, I didn't want to see any schools. I wanted to see them at the moment when freedom arrives and I wanted to see them have a good time. I didn't want to see them doing anything but having a good time without any supervision and that's pretty much what those pictures were.

Were the films based on your own experiences?

Yes, because I'm a surfer. That was something that I wanted to change. Surfers were considered to be pretty wild people—in trouble and all this. They were defined that way, but I surfed all the time with young people and I didn't see anybody in trouble for the most part. I told Sam, "You never see a film about that. About kids not being in trouble." And he said, "What would it be about if they weren't in trouble?" I said, "It would be about them having a good time." He was pretty shaky on it, but he has no trouble now claiming it was his idea from the beginning.

Before A.I.P., many times teenage roles were played by adult actors.

Yeah, right. I didn't use Central Casting for anything. I cast the pictures right off the beach and from a Union standpoint you're not allowed to do that.

Did the kids you approached on the beach believe you were legitimate?

It was so embarrassing because I knew all these kids from surfing, a little bit, and I had to start going around to the girls and the guys and asking them if they wanted to be in this picture! It sounded like some shabby thing when some sleazy guy comes up to a girl and says, "Do you want to be in a picture?"

Sam Arkoff assured me there was no casting couch.

No, there wasn't a casting couch. These kids we hired were not professionals who had been exposed to such a thing. They were hired because of their looks and their surfing, because they were surfers. There was no hanky panky.

While the majority of the cast were surfers, what about Frankie and Annette?

None of the main performers were really surfers, so I had a little difficulty with that, especially with Frankie. When we made the first picture, *Beach Party*, in 1963, there were no wetsuits and we were surfing with nine-foot boards made of redwood and fairly thick and they were heavy. It was all poor Frankie could do to lift one, let alone run and snatch it off the A frame where the boards were stacked up. You had to be pretty strong to do that. Frankie said, "I can't do that!" and I said, "Sure, you can do it."

Did you have problems with Annette?

We did everything we could to get Annette in the water.

Annette didn't like the water?

No, it was cold. It was cold as hell! When you first go in the water it is shocking and ice cold.

I take it the scenes with Annette surfing were done by the blue screen effect?

Yeah.

What kind of trickery did you use to get Annette into the water?

Oh, just cuts and shots of her running down to the water and then we used a stunt double with somebody else diving into the water. She would go as far as the edge of the water and that would be it. She would get her toesies wet.

What did you think of someone from the "Mickey Mouse Club" playing your lead character?

Well, the only way to get her was on loan out from Disney. And Walt gave me a real talking to when he found out who was directing this film. Not that he suspected that I would necessarily endanger her purity, but he had to be sure. . . .

He said, "The one thing that I insist upon, and if it's violated I'll take her right out of the picture, is she can't wear a bikini. She can't show her naval." So, it wasn't easy to try and make a bikini picture without showing naval! Of course she's quite large busted, so you can't go for any string effect up here. (Points to chest.) If you notice, most surfers that I know are very small breasted and she is not that, so you needed a big top and a big bottom and she was dressed to go to the library! She was certainly not dressed for surfing. That was the only interference he gave us.

Did you and Sam Arkoff have any private conversations about Walt Disney's interference?

Yeah. We couldn't do anything that would spoil her image in anyway. She was pure. No drinking. Surfers didn't drink, maybe beer, didn't smoke. The biker guys did the drinking and the smoking, in the movie and in real life.

My favorite character in your movies was Eric Von Zipper, played by Harvey Lembeck.

Frankie and Annette could not surf. How was Harvey Lembeck on a motorcycle?

He was great! He was a real rider and I got his motorcycle gang right out of the Hell's Angels bike club.

The Rat Pack were made up of real life members of The Hell's Angels?

Oh, yeah. I had to go to them and say, "Look, you should tell me now if you're willing to do this because we're going to make asses of you guys. You'll be the comedy relief in these films. We'll make real dunces out of you for comedy sake." A lot of them didn't like it. . . . [One Hell's Angel named Animal cornered Asher] and said, "We don't like the way you treated us in the beach pictures." I said, "I did a great thing for you guys. I made you popular, I made you fun, I made a good image of you." He said, "You made us stupid." And I didn't say it but I wanted to say, "You *are* stupid." But I said, "No, you guys play the role of stupid guys, but nobody questioned your real power." He said, "Well, you better not do another one!" I said, "I am doing another one." And he said, "Well, we'll be in to see you next time you do it!" I said, "Is that a threat?" He said, "Take it any way you want, but you're going to see us, a lot of us, if you try to do another one! You especially!"

Wow! Did this shake you up at all?

He scared me because those guys are rough and they are not above putting you some place where nobody would find you!

Did any of the Rat Pack or shall I say, The Hell's Angels, come after you?

No, they never did, they didn't show up. I think maybe Animal convinced the guys that they were actors and not playing real life.

In the movies Annette wouldn't dare do anything to mess her hair up.

(Laughs) Yeah, that's true! Another thing from the beach pictures that was interesting is that no one had a last name.

As the films seemed to be a series we were wondering why the character names would be different?

Oh, that was a mistake. That was me being careless.

The Beatles were supposed to appear in Bikini Beach?

Suddenly the Beatles came to America and Jim Nicholson got in touch with me and he said, "There's a group called the Beatles." Nobody had heard of them, and he said, "I want to get them in this next picture we're doing, this next beach picture." And I said, "Great!" I went over there to meet and he had some film on them. I said, "Oh, yeah! These guys are great!" So, I wrote the script for them for *Bikini Beach* and they came over here [but then they appeared on] *The Ed Sullivan Show*! They knocked everybody dead and the agents said, "Oh, no. We can't give them away for what you want to pay for them!" So, I had to take all of the stuff that I had written and throw it out because it had been written about four guys. I had to re-write the script to make it about one guy.

Do you remember what you had the Beatles doing in the script?

Yeah. They were from England and they wanted to see what it was like living on the beach in California. They had their traveling bus and they stopped off in Malibu sometime late in the night and when our kids woke up, this whole set up was there—the Beatles bus and a lot of equipment, tents, you know, and a big project there. They wondered who it was and they got to know them and there was a love story between Annette and one of the Beatles.

Was your wife Elizabeth Montgomery ever concerned about you working so closely with all those bikini girls?

Believe me, she stayed down there and watched me pretty close when I was working with all those beauties. She didn't worry. I was pretty good.

and surfing and the muscles in my back flared when I fought the shark. It wasn't very ladylike. Then we took the shark back to land, froze it, and they had me fight it again—not fresh, but frozen."

Like others who have surfed through Hollywood films, Muñoz isn't a great fan of the movies he was in: "*Gidget* was corny, but you know I've probably seen it three times since we made it; each time I see it I appreciate it more for a fairly honest attempt to capture what was going on in surfing at the time. They tried, but Hollywood can't seem to help Hollywoodizing everything they do."

In 1963, Samuel Z. Arkoff and James H. Nicholson of American International Pictures began producing a string of "surf" movies, directed by William Asher and starring Frankie Avalon and Annette Funicello. These waxploitation films—*Beach Party* (1963), *Muscle Beach Party* (1964), *Bikini Beach* (1964), *Beach Blanket Bingo* (1965), and *How to Stuff a Wild Bikini* (1965)—shamelessly cashed in on the surf craze, employed a lot of real surfers, launched some careers, revived others, and sunk a few.

The *Beach Party* flicks flip-flopped from phony to funny every few minutes. It's hard not to like

a series that revived Buster Keaton's career and launched Little Stevie Wonder, but there's also a lot that's hard to stomach—like Frankie Avalon, that short, dark, and handsome Italian guy from South Philly portraying a surfer who had an annoying habit of breaking into song in front of his girlfriend.

The ongoing theme of each of these movies was Annette fending off frisky Frankie, who is not yet ready to get married. Their breakup-to-makeup shenanigans resulted in a lot of love songs, heartbreak songs, and makeup songs—Frankie and Annette crooning in front of a projection screen with the full moon shimmering on the water and the lights of Point Dume twinkling in the background.

Musically, the *Beach Party* movies all had a similar motif. Frankie and Annette were joined by semi-regulars like chanteuse Donna Loren—borrowed from Dr. Pepper commercials—and a force of nature named Candy Johnson as the Perpetual Motion Dancer. Johnson shook that thing like few things have ever been shaken; there was so much mojo locked up in her booty she had the power to take out surfers on waves, bikers on their choppers, and any other male within a hundred yards. Each movie also boasted a regular house band, starting with Dick Dale for the first two movies. He was replaced by the Pyramids, the Exciters, and the Kingsmen. Love ballads, novelty songs, and some good rock'n'roll—these movies had it all.

Beach Party: The first of the series set the stage for the corny-to-cool scenario. The film begins with Frankie and Annette on spring break, driving a jalopy along PCH and singing a bongo-driven, jazzified "Beach Party" theme song. This song tests the assertion that it's hip to be square, but the music goes uphill from there.

After a quick charge through the surf, Dick Dale and his baby blue Stratocaster jump into "Secret Surfin' Spot" and the gang starts frugging. From a contemporary perspective, Dale's rocking scenes may not appear to be anything special. But this was 1963, pre-Scopitone, pre-*Hullabaloo*, pre-*Shindig*, pre-*MTV*; it was music video before music video. The close-ups of bikinied girls and baggied guys whooping it up in the sand probably had every teen in the theater ready to move to California and go surfing.

The actual plot of the movie was pretty painful. A frumpy anthropologist studies the kids, comparing their mating rituals to aboriginal tribes before he, too, catches the spirit. Surfing has that kind of effect.

Muscle Beach Party: This sequel again featured Frankie crooning for Annette and vice versa. Dale penned the theme song, "Surfer's Holiday," and in what is arguably the finest musical moment of the series, plays guitar for a blind, twelve-year-old musical sensation billed as Little Stevie Wonder.

Born Steveland Judkins Hardaway in Saginaw, Michigan, he signed with Motown and had a hit with "Fingertips (Part 2)." In *Muscle Beach Party*, Little Stevie rocks the house with "Happy Feeling." Candy Johnson does her perpetual motion thing to the tune and cracks the camera lens at the end.

Bikini Beach: Dick Dale did not appear in the third movie—nor did the Beatles, who were signed and scheduled, but dropped out after hitting it big on *The Ed Sullivan Show*. This left the producers to scramble and create a character called

Potato Bug, played by Frankie, and hire the Pyramids as house band. The gag with the Pyramids is they were bald—a slap to the mop tops of the British Invasion—and their wigs fly off when they flip into the hot-rod song "Midnight Run."

Pajama Party: Then things got really weird. *Pajama Party* seems like a rush job. Frankie Avalon didn't sing, Tommie Kirk played a Martian named Go Go, and Annette's character name changes from Dee Dee to Connie. Dressed in a nightie, she sings a love ballad called "Stuffed Animal" to a stuffed animal. Dorothy Lamour does a bizarre dance number called "Where Did I Go Wrong?" *Pajama Party* also witnessed the return of Buster Keaton and Frankenstein's monster's bride, Elsa Lanchester. Call it a greatest hits . . . of something.

Beach Blanket Bingo: Annette's back as Dee Dee and Frankie is singing to her again. Donna Loren roasts a hot dog (metaphor, anyone?) as she sings the lost-love ballad "It Only Hurts When I Cry." The Hondells are the house band, Linda Evans lip-synchs her way through a few numbers as Sugar Kane, and Harvey Lembeck does a musical number as biker Eric Von Zipper.

How to Stuff a Wild Bikini: This was the last of the series to star Frankie and Annette. Poor lovelorn Frankie is stationed in the South Pacific and spies on Dee Dee with the help of witch doctor Buster Keaton. Meanwhile, Dee Dee is back on the beach being tempted by various things, leading to more makeup and breakup songs. The highpoint here is the house band, Portland, Oregon's the Kingsmen, who became eternally famous for "Louie, Louie."

The Ghost in the Invisible Bikini: Released in 1966, Frankie and Annette were gone, replaced by Tommy Kirk and Deborah Walley. Just as surf music was going down, so were the surf movies.

Ride the Wild Surf had great potential. The film was shot first and acted later, bending a story around North Shore surfing footage captured during the winter of 1963-1964. The waves are howlers, which is where the potential lay—yet so, too, were many of the words that came out of the "surfers'" mouths. In the end, it was a serious but failed attempt to capture the mood of the North Shore at the time. *Ride the Wild Surf* launched a few careers—and a thousand surf-flick clichés.

The story begins with three mainland guys arriving fresh off the plane in Honolulu, then driving

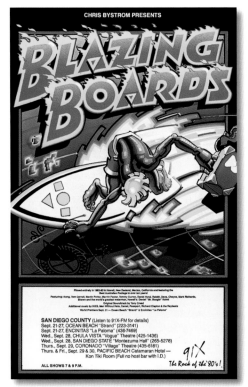

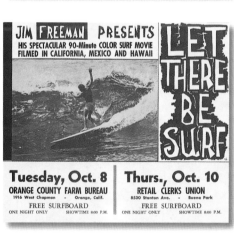

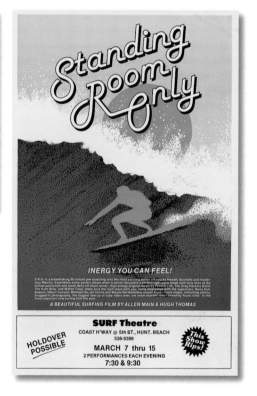

across the island to challenge the big stuff on Oahu's North Shore. Steamer Lane (Tab Hunter), Jody Wallis (Fabian), and Chase Colton (Peter Brown) dress in suits and ties accessorized with a variety of social, physical, and philosophical chips on their shoulders. They look groomed and groovy, but the North Shore ruffles their feathers. Our heroes meet chicks, fight fights, and are constantly challenged by the waves to prove their manhood.

The *wahines* are played by Barbara Eden, Shelley Fabares, and Susan Hart, setting a high standard for future surfer girls.

The supporting cast includes James Mitchum as Eskimo, a big, gruff, no-nonsense guy with a Roman nose who rides the biggest stuff wearing black-and-white striped trunks. Sound like someone we know? Greg Noll says he was a victim of circumstances. "Hey, I was just out there surfing, you know, because it was good Waimea that season," Da Bull snorts. "I kind of knew there was something going on because Mickey Dora was out surfing Waimea, and he had never done that. He didn't really like the big stuff, but I knew he was getting paid and so was Mike Hynson. Well, Mickey and I were friends and I wanted to see how he would do and maybe keep an eye on him. We rode a lot of fun Haleiwa and Sunset and 15-20-foot Waimea, and I caught so many waves in those black-and-white trunks, they created the Eskimo character and wrote him into the movie."

Real Surfers Don't Sing to Their Chicks!

Bruce Brown Keeps it Real with *The Endless Summer*

Brown was a real surfer in a world being taken over by poseurs. Like a lot of men and women who had been involved with surfing through the 1950s into the 1960s, he was appalled by Hollywood's interpretation of surfing on the big screen, from *Gidget* to the Frankie and Annette flicks. In all of these movies, the surfers were played by dark, slight actors—*jamocas* who could carry a light tune better than a heavy surfboard, and all had a nasty habit of breaking into song in front of their girlfriends.

Brown grew up in Long Beach, learned to surf there, and was one of thousands of stoked gremmies going nuts at the screenings of Bud Browne's surf movies. In 1955 he made an 8 mm surf movie while stationed on a submarine in Hawai'i, and three years after that, surfboard manufacturer Dale Velzy sponsored Brown to make his first surf movie, *Slippery When Wet*. That movie followed a group of surfers on a safari to Hawai'i, and the action was equally complemented by Brown's witty, near-perfect narration and a jazz soundtrack by West Coast jazz pioneer Bud Shank. According to Shank, "The soundtrack to [the film] *Barefoot Adventure* sold 10,000 records in 1961, which was unheard of for a jazz release."

In 1964, Brown set forth to conceive a surf movie about real surfers. He wanted to reassure us that surfers weren't red-eyed bums or google-eyed romancers, and he set out on an around-the-world quest with surfers Mike Hynson and Robert August to show just how cool surfing was, and that surfers were gentlemen and scholars who would go to great lengths to get their kicks.

The Endless Summer started as just another 16 mm surf movie, but after Brown took the movie to Salina, Kansas, and rocked the house, he blew it up to 35 mm, released it theatrically, and it blew up big time. The movie became a huge hit and the most successful documentary of its time.

Whether or not Bruce Brown got his message across to the world, the movies and music and commercializing stereotypes of surfers that he and other real surfers deplored just kept on rolling. What had been a secret thrill to a stoked elite through the 1940s and 1950s, was now a worldwide sensation. By 1965, everybody wanted to be surfing all across the USA.

Surfer Fred Van Dyke got some face time in *Ride the Wild Surf*, but that pales in his memory compared with the surf time: "That winter had the best Waimea and Sunset surf that I can remember," Uncle Fred says. "It would come up to 25, drop, and come up again, and that went on for about two months. We were totally surfed out, but forced ourselves to continue. We really did not get a break for a couple of months, and it was mostly glassy except for the mid-afternoons. The camera people didn't realize how special it was and they got fantastic footage."

The surfing was shot entirely from land, which was a shame as it didn't capture the danger of riding those waves. After two months, the producers had hours of surfing footage in the can—and a lot of what was in the can featured Noll's black-and-white striped can. Noll says he was briefly considered as the actor for the part of Eskimo, but he accents the *briefly*. "They called me up to LA to audition for the Eskimo part, I guess," Noll laughs. "I went up there and stood on a stage and they gave me a card to read. I think I said three words, 'The cat is . . .' and then the hook came out and they yanked me off the stage. I guess I had the shortest acting career ever."

Ride the Wild Surf is as corny as just about every other surf movie not made by surfers, but the entertainment value goes *way* up when you watch it forty years later with Da Bull. "Oh my God, look at these guys!" Noll roars at the sight of Fabian, Brown, and Hunter checking the Waimea lineup. "A suit and tie? At Waimea? Look at the hair. It's perfect! Look at the car. No rust! No wonder we didn't hang out with these guys. They're a bunch of Hollywood dorks. A bunch of phonies. I avoided them like the plague, and the other guys hung around because they were getting paid.

"That's Haleiwa there, and who's the guy in the stinkbug stance at Sunset? There's L. J. Richards on that wave and that's Ricky Grigg. The backside guy is Butch van Artsdalen. I remember that style. Check out Jeff Hakman! What is he, eight years old there? Here's a big wave. That's Mike Stange taking off behind me at Waimea and wiping out and there I go wiping out so maybe Mike wouldn't be lonely when he went over the falls. Oh and now I'm claiming it there on the shoulder. Guess I was ahead of my time, huh? Okay, it's starting to come back to me

now. I remember telling the camera guys that if they wanted some good wipeouts to keep an eye on me, because that's what I was good at."

Noll watches with one hand over his eyes, the other on the remote control. When the Hollywood phonies are on, he fast-forwards to get to Barbara Eden's parts (if you know what we mean) or the surfing. When Dora takes off at Waimea, Noll perks up like a proud father watching his fledgling son. This was Dora's first time at Waimea, and all he could find to ride was a crummy ten-foot four-inch hotcurl with a pointed tail and round bottom; on film you see him struggling to turn and trim the board at Sunset and Haleiwa. But Noll is proud of how his friend held up at Waimea. "Look at him take off on that wave, a little fade at the top and a big drop," Noll says. "This is his first time and he rode really well. Look at him there in front of me.

"I distinctly remember riding behind Dora on one wave at Waimea and he looked like he was slowing down and about to get creamed. I put my hand on the back of his shorts and gave him a shove and that got him through to the end standing up. Well, that was kind of like the guy pulling the thorn from the lion's paw. Dora never forgot that wave and it became one of the foundations of our friendship."

When Barbara Eden and Peter Brown buy New Year's Eve fireworks from Mr. Chin, Noll nods, "They got that part right, anyway. The North Shore on New Year's Eve has always been World War IV."

Ride the Wild Surf ends with a scenario that most surfers write off as hokey. Still, it has some basis in truth. There is a big day at Waimea with the surf escalating every fifteen minutes. The number of surfers in the water dwindles like ten little Indians, with all of them holding their ground and hoping to be the last man standing. That's not how most big days are—although there have been instances, notably a swell at Makaha in December 1969 when it was Noll himself who was the last man standing on one of the biggest days of the twentieth century. *Ride the Wild Surf* didn't let truth get in the way of a good story, though. The movie launched the Life or Death in the Big Wave ending that would appear in surf movies seemingly forever.

"So, they got a few things right in this *Ride the Wild Surf*," Noll harrumphs. "But holy shit, did you see that guy's hair?"

Philly Cheese

How Three Guys from Philly Went Surfing on the Blue Screen

When Hollywood first thought "surfer," directors saw short, dark, and handsome. At least they got the handsome part right.

The silver screen's first surfers included three Italian guys from Philly—James Darren as Moondoggie in 1959's *Gidget*, Frankie Avalon as Frankie in 1963's *Beach Party*, and Fabian as Jody Wallis in 1964's *Ride the Wild Surf*. In the real world, they may not have known how to balance on a board, but they sure knew how to break into song to serenade their ladies.

To understand their wave-riding careers, you have to understand the wave they were all riding—the wave of popularity for a genre known as the "Philadelphia teen idol."

James Darren was named James William Ercolani upon birth in the City of Brotherly Love in 1936. He started out as a crooner and actor, playing bit roles in several films before catching the big one in *Gidget* and surfing through the sequels—1961's *Gidget Goes Hawaiian* and 1963's *Gidget Goes to Rome*. His Moondoggie days boosted his singing career as well, and by 1963 he boasted a hit with "Goodbye, Cruel World."

Darren set the Hollywood mold for "surfer" in *Gidget*, and when American International Pictures cast *Beach Party*, they looked to another Italian boy from Philly—Frankie Avalon.

It was Frankie who best defined the Philadelphia teen idol. Francis Thomas Avallone was born in 1940. His father taught him to play trumpet and Frankie performed from an early age, winning more than his share of talent shows and awards. When songster Al Martino signed with Capitol Records in 1952, he threw a neighborhood party with Frankie on trumpet, which caught a talent scout's attention and landed him a spot on *The Jackie Gleason Show*. More television followed, and at fourteen in 1954 he released an instrumental trumpet piece, "Trumpet Sorrento." Frankie was playing trumpet with local dance band Rocco and the Saints all over Philly, from the Sons of Italy Hall to Somers Point, a popular vacation retreat. The band's drummer was one Robert Ridarelli, who soon changed his name to Bobby Rydell and became a Philly teen idol of his own with hits like "Volare."

Between 1959 and 1965, Hollywood foisted films from *Gidget* and *Beach Party* to *Blue Hawaii* on a naïve public, while Bruce Brown tried to counter all the nonsense with *The Endless Summer*. Finally, by 1967, the waxploitation genre had exhausted itself, producers had run out of corny songs, and the surf movie went dormant, thankfully, until deep into the 1970s.

In 1975, American International Pictures, who was responsible for all of the Frankie and Annette flicks, took another stab at surfing with *Murph the Surf,* the Hollywood version of Jack Murphy, a well-known Florida surfer who attempted one of the biggest jewel heists ever—stealing the Star of India sapphire.

Then in 1978, surfer-turned-director John Milius stepped in and stole the show with *Big Wednesday*. The film was Milius's coming-of-age memoir, *American Graffiti* on a surfboard.

The film's surfing has Peter Townend doubling for William Katt, Ian Cairns for Gary Busey, and J. Riddle and Bill Hamilton for Jan-Michael Vincent, with Katt and Vincent doing some of their own wave-riding. Some of the surfing is beautiful—particularly PT in his prime, carving and soul arching at Malibu, Hollister Ranch, and Costa Rica. As Hamilton says of being paid to professionally wipe out, "Stunt work is a great way to get paid if you're into pushing the adrenaline button. The way the guys use science and technology these days to eliminate so much of

American Bandstand began as a local program on WFIL-TV in Philadelphia in 1952, providing a launching pad for local talent, including Frankie. When Peter DeAngelis and Robert Marucci started Chancellor Records, they began recording Frankie's trumpet as DeAngelis knew him from the old neighborhood where his sister babysat baby Avallone. Frankie's first releases didn't sell much outside of Philly, but did earn him a small role in the movie *Jamboree*.

Then, against his will, Frankie recorded a song called "De De Dinah," but held his nose while he sang to demonstrate what he thought of the song. Chancellor released the sinus-congested version in 1957 and it sold a million copies. His cut "Venus" was backed by an orchestra, female choir, and all the bells and whistles, and the song went giant. Frankie went on to record three more gold records—"Bobby Sox to Stockings," "Just Ask Your Heart," and "Why."

Suddenly, Frankie Avalon was a star, and soon he was riding the waves with reformed Mouseketeer Annette Funicello in *Beach Party*. The rest, as they say, is surfing history.

Frankie's success on a surfboard led to Fabian catching a wave. Christened Fabiano Anthony Forte in 1943, he grew up in Philly's South Side, within blocks of Frankie and Rydell.

Chancellor Records' DeAngelis and Marucci were scouring the neighborhoods in search of talent. At Frankie's suggestion, they went to the Forte home and found Fabiano sitting on the front porch. According to legend, he was crying, depressed about his father's health and the family's finances. They asked Fabiano if he knew anything about rock'n'roll. He didn't, but was game for anything.

Fabian got a makeover and voice lessons, and in June 1958, he released "I'm in Love" on Chancellor. He appeared on *American Bandstand*, caused a few heart attacks, and in November cut "I'm a Man" and made himself a name.

In almost every biography of Fabian, his movie career is written off as forgettable—and that would include *Ride the Wild Surf*, a semisincere attempt to capture the real drama and romance of surfing Hawai'i's North Shore. Befitting his heartthrob status, Fabian—as well as fellow "surfers" Peter Brown and Tab Hunter—show up on the beach like primped peacocks, perfectly coiffured and blow-dried, even sporting natty suits and skinny ties. Fabian soon gets his feathers ruffled by the surf, the Hawai'ians, tough guy James Mitchum, and his bubbly blond *wahine* Shelley Fabares.

James Darren, Frankie, and Fabian cast the early Hollywood mold of "surfer." Yet in each of their movies, they left the real surfing to the pros.

the deadly stuff is impressive, but you have to hand it to those guys in the Thirties and Forties who were going on balls and adrenaline alone."

Reinventing the *Ride the Wild Surf* cliché, *Big Wednesday* ends with a climactic day of surf where the three buddies are reunited for a session subtexted by all that Passage into Adulthood business. For the finale, the crew shot a big day at Sunset Beach, standing in for Malibu, and pushed reality a little bit: twelve-foot west peaks don't swing through Malibu all that often, but oh well, it's Hollywood.

Toward the end of *Big Wednesday*, the Vincent character wipes out bad, but survives. Apparently they didn't want Riddle or Hamilton to chance the wipeout and lose a double, so they looked else-where. Gerry Lopez was involved with the shoot in California and Hawai'i, and he saw firsthand what happened: "For *Big Wednesday*, Bruce Raymond and Jackie Dunn were paid $100 each to go out and eat shit as hard as they could. Bruce did his first at Sunset but looking at the dailies, Milius decided it wasn't gruesome enough, so had Jackie do his thing at the Pipe. Jackie took off on about a 10-foot wave, stalled at the top, and let himself get pitched, swam in, got the board, and went back out and did it three more times—for a hundred dollars. I wouldn't do it for ten thousand. In the editing, they turned the negative upside down and that little cut of Jackie, who looked even more like Jan-Michael than either Billy or Jay, really made the wipeout sequence work."

Big Wednesday cost twelve million dollars to make only to be released in the shadow of *Saturday Night Fever*. The movie was savaged in the media. "I was devastated," Milius remembers. "I wanted to join the French Foreign Legion."

And oddly enough, this was one movie most surfers applauded.

North Shore was a surf movie by the numbers. The plot was *Ride the Wild Surf* born again in the 1980s with an equal dose of laughable lines and silly scenarios. Still, the movie remains a flawed classic.

Rick Kane is a *haole* from Arizona who wins a wave-pool contest that gets him to Hawai'i to compete in the Pipeline Masters. Ridiculous, yes. *North Shore* was another surf film mishandled by the Hollywood Squares, but it wasn't for lack of horses. They had natural comedians the likes of Robbie Page and Mark Occhilupo; they had great surfers the likes of Laird Hamilton, John Philbin and Gerry Lopez; they had righteous babes like Nia Peeples. And they still managed to make a clumsy, very 1980s movie.

Lopez acted the role of bad-ass Vince, and in retrospect he says *North Shore* could have been better if they'd had more—more time, more money, and more surf. "Hey, they had six weeks to shoot that movie and not a lot of money and the surf was terrible. I think if they had gotten good waves at the Pipe like they did for *Blue Crush*, then *North Shore* would have been better," Lopez says. "Like most surf movies, *North Shore* has aged a little with time, and while it is still something of a howler, it is also a time capsule looking back to the Eighties on the North Shore, in all its day-glo glory."

Point Break was half surfing flick, half California crime thriller. Eager, young FBI agent Johnny Utah (Keanu Reeves) tracks down a gang of seasonal bank robbers who hide behind masks of the presidents of the United States. As the robbers leave wax residue behind and the tan lines show on their real behinds, the FBI figures they're surfers gone bad—or at least worse than your typical surfers. Reeves finds the gang, who is lead by New Age ringleader-surfer Bodhisattva, played by Patrick Swayze.

The chase is on, and *Point Break* has its moments—both great and cringy. A lot of the metaphysical babble coming out of Bodhi's mouth makes real surfers howl with derisive laughter. And the editing of some surf scenes is off, as the producers didn't bother to differentiate between regular and goofy foot.

For the surfing, Matt Archbold doubled for Swayze with Jodie Cooper standing in for femme fatale surfing moll Tyler Endicott, played by Lori Petty. Surfer Vince Klyn has a cameo as a bad-ass bad guy, along with Anthony Kiedis of the Red Hot Chili Peppers.

For the ending, *Point Break* stuck to the cliché launched by *Ride the Wild Surf*. Take a poll of just about every surfing movie and you'll find they end with a day of giant surf and a brush with death: *Big Wednesday*? Jan-Michael Vincent almost buys it. *In God's Hands*? Matt George rocks off into the deep. *Blue Crush*? Anne Marie takes a licking at Pipe but keeps on ticking. *North Shore*? Same deal. Sticking to this formula, *Point Break* ends with Utah tracking Bodhisattva around the globe for two years, finally getting his man at Bell's Beach, where Swayze shows up to surf the "fifty-year storm" he long predicted. Ludicrous, yes, but that's Hollywood.

Utah slips the bracelets on Bodhi in the middle of a water fight. Bodhi is busted, but in one of the finest bro gestures ever caught on film, Utah lets Bodhi go to ride the wild surf one last time. Bodhi paddles out as the guy with the bad Australian accent screeches, "You leeeeet heeeeem gieeeoooo!" Bodhi takes off on a monster and eats the Mortal Doughnut.

That's not Matt Archbold as Bodhi in the finale; it's none other than for-real wild-eyed adrenal-junkie hairball-hellman Darrick Doerner wiping out at Waimea accidentally on purpose and bodysurfing to the bottom of a gaping, twenty-foot barrel. No special effects or CGI here. It was one guy putting his neck on the line for real to keep it real. That was, as they say in Hollywood, a hell of a trick.

Doerner is now best known as being the dance partner to Laird Hamilton, the man at the helm of the PWC who dragged Laird into that giant death wave at Tahiti's Teahupoo and many other monsters at Jaws and around the world. But in 1988, all of this tow surfing was off in the future, and surfers had to catch giant waves with their bare hands.

The *Point Break* stunt started with a photo of Doerner taking off on one of the biggest waves ever ridden, on Super Bowl Sunday 1988. "The *Point*

The Sport of the King

Elvis Surfs *Blue Hawaii*

Night and you
And blue Hawaii.
The night is heavenly
And you are heaven to me . . .

— Elvis Presley, *Blue Hawaii*, 1961

O f all the waxploitation films starring short, dark, and handsome guys from Philly as surfers, it was a tall, dark, and handsome guy from Mississippi who actually did a decent job portraying a true surf bum. In *Blue Hawaii*, Elvis Presley is Chad Gates, a *kamaaina* kid who gets out of the Army and returns to his little grass shack at Haunama Bay to take up the easy life. Elvis is believable as a guy who is content to surf, hang out, and play the ukulele until family pressures force him to consider the rest of his life.

Elvis does his best to juggle his responsibilities and future, and manages to sing a dozen songs to the tourist chicks he squires around Hawai'i—including the title song, "Aloha Oe," and one of his greatest hits, "Can't Help Falling in Love." The *Blue Hawaii* soundtrack was Elvis's most successful album, spending twenty consecutive weeks at the top of Billboard's LP chart in 1961–1962. Yes, this is a surfer singing to his girlfriend, but it's Elvis, and somehow you forgive him.

Elvis is the star of *Blue Hawaii* but Hawai'i itself is the costar, more glamorous and naturally blessed than any of the starlets Elvis woos. This was Hawai'i at the end of the 1950s when the first passenger jets were turning a long haul into a short hop and Waikiki rang with the sound of jackhammers and cranes for the next decade. This was old Hawai'i, and it nearly steals the scene from Elvis in what many consider to be his most entertaining movie.

The King Surfs
(Paramount Studios)

Fast Times

Surfing Genius

As with *Gidget*, *Fast Times at Ridgemont High* was the movie version of a novel written by an older man spying on youth culture. In this case, the older man was Cameron Crowe, a twenty-something *Rolling Stone* reporter who went underground at a typical, middle-class Los Angeles high school.

Fast Times began the 1980s with a bong. Filmed in November and December 1981 and released in 1982, it was directed by Amy Heckerling from Crowe's own screenplay. And it did some business, edging into thirty million dollars in box office receipts.

Fast Times launched many careers, including Judge Reinhold, Jennifer Jason Leigh, Phoebe Cates, Nicholas Cage (he is Nicholas Coppola in the credits), Anthony Edwards, and Forest Whitaker. And Sean Penn.

This was Penn's second screen role, after *Taps*, and he stole the show. As Jeff Spicoli, Penn plays a stoner surfer that is true to the times. As a fellow student states of Spicoli, "That guy has been stoned since the third grade."

Fast Times didn't include any actual surf scenes, but then it didn't need to. With his scraggly, scraggly blond hairdo, loud aloha shirts, Vans shoes, and quotes like "All I need are some tasty waves and a cool buzz and I'm fine," Spicoli was true to the surfer of the 1980s. In the Mount Rushmore of Hollywood surfers, Spicoli is right up there, blowing pot smoke in the faces of Turtle from *North Shore*, Colonel Kilgore from *Apocalypse Now*, and Mick from *Big Wednesday*.

There are a few people around Hollywood who grew up surfing with Sean Penn who say that Sean is now embarrassed by Spicoli and wishes he had never done the role. Whether he is embarrassed as a surfer or an actor is unclear, but either way it's a shame. Penn's Spicoli is one of the comic icons of the twentieth century.

Break producers came to Hawai'i and they were auditioning in town," Doerner remembers. "Mark Foo and Ken Bradshaw and all these guys drove in to audition, and I didn't know about it because I was lifeguarding. Well, Patrick Swayze whipped out that picture of me from Super Bowl Sunday and he said, 'Hey I want to meet this guy.' So they tracked me down and we had a rendezvous at Chun's Reef. I paddled out and there he was in the lineup.

"I said, 'Howzit, I'm Darrick.'

"He said, 'I'm Patrick Swayze, and I want you to die for me.'

"I said, 'I don't die for anyone.'

"And boom, I got the job."

Doerner surfed in *North Shore* and *Big Wednesday*, but *Point Break* was his big show. Since then he has worked on *In God's Hands* and *Die Another Day*, and he knows the business much better. Looking back on *Point Break* with a lot more movie experience tucked next to the flippers under his belt,

Doerner would do things a lot differently if he had it to do again. "*Point Break* was hard because they didn't know exactly what they wanted," Doerner says. "There was no storyboard, and so I had to wipe out over and over again. Six times I did it, broke seven boards, and perforated my eardrum on the second try. That one hurt. And they tried to dye my hair blond and it came out pink and orange and it burned my scalp and people were laughing at me. I went over to Makaha side one time and Mel Pu'u tried to chase me out of the water because he didn't think I was me. Well, the producers left and then came back and said, 'We want you to do the Iron Cross when you take off.'"

That was then and this is now, and many of the high-tech luxuries that North Shore surfers take for granted now didn't exist then. The buoy and satellite reports weren't refined and there weren't six WaveRunners in every lineup. Doerner felt the pressure and he didn't like it. "The producers were like, 'When's it going to happen?' and I'm saying, 'Hey, I'm just a surfer. I don't control the ocean. It does what it wants.' I didn't have any Water Safety hovering around on WaveRunners and no one was blocking for me. It was just me out there in a wetsuit with orange hair. The other times I had done the wipeout all the braddahs in the water didn't care that I was shooting a Hollywood movie. Booby Jones and Ricardo Pomar and some other guys were out there and the pecking order was in place and I had to hustle for waves with the rest of them and it was hard to focus on what I needed to do.

"Well, when they wanted me to do it again I called Laird and I said, 'Hey I want you to be my friend and be out in the water with me when I have to do this.' You know? Because I wasn't sleeping so good, knowing I had to jump off a four-story building again. Laird said he'd do it and he didn't ask for a dollar. Well, the day came and Laird played traffic cop for me and that helped, but I still had to go through the pecking order. When my turn came Laird said, 'Okay, everyone just stop,' and I pulled that one really cool Iron Cross at the top, then jumped and got down the face. It was like, splash, bounce, bounce, *oh woohoo* barrel ride. I bodysurfed right into a giant right barrel and it was really cool. I looked across Waimea Bay and could see the cliff and the cars and people and the hills, looking out of this giant barrel."

On film, the wipeout is nuts, and you have to wonder how much control even the most experienced surfer has in a situation like this, bodysurfing to the bottom of a twenty-foot pit. But Doerner was absolutely in his prime and he pulled it off. He came right out the back of that thing, and when he bobbed to the surface he was a legend. "I popped up and I could hear all these car horns honking and people were hooting and screaming and someone was yelling, 'That's a wrap!'"

Perhaps the biggest crime of *In God's Hands* is that it managed to be fairly humorless. Surfers are funny people. Hang around with Tom Carroll or Brad Gerlach for a few minutes when they're on and you'll see. *In God's Hands* took a natural comedian like Shane Dorian and turned him into an insular, thousand-yard-staring sourpuss.

Still, Dorian's surfing is worth the price of admission alone, and there are other surfing highlights from the likes of Todd Chesser and Brian Keaulana who both pulled into career tube-rides at Backdoor

and Jaws. *In God's Hands* had the talent and the chance to make history, but missed the drop and earned another C rating.

The story behind the story of *In God's Hands* could be a movie itself. Naturally, the film ends with a life-or-death day of giant surf in which Dorian's character faces his fears and lives while Matt George's character faces the future and dies. And so the producers needed to stage an epic wipeout, except this time the wave was Jaws.

Going over the falls in the worst possible place at Jaws is not something anyone is willing to do for any amount of money; some consider it suicide, others consider it disrespectful of the spot. Chesser was doubling for George, but when the big day came, he was AWOL. Buzzy Kerbox was pulled from the sidelines. "I wasn't working on *In God's Hands* with all the guys and I was a little bummed I didn't get any part of it," Kerbox remembers. "But I was there on Maui and I was picked to do the wipeout. We negotiated pretty much on the spot. I think it was $2,500 for the day and a per-wipeout adjustment which was like a few hundred dollars per wipeout."

A few hundred dollars per wipeout adds up when you do fifteen reshoots, the number of times Kerbox ate it on purpose at Jaws over two days in February 1995. The producers knew what they wanted, they just weren't exactly sure how to get it. "The biggest day was the first day we shot," Kerbox says. "The scariest part for me was knowing I was going to wipe out on whatever came in and whatever came in I was going. I don't wipe out at Jaws that often. I've had some bad ones, but the bigger it gets the more cautious I get. Wiping out on purpose didn't appeal to me too much because you never know what is going to happen there. You could wipe out not too bad and then the next wave is a monster and it gets you on the head. It's just weird. You spend all your time out there trying not to wipe out and then the next thing you know you're doing it on purpose."

When asked if he would ever wipe out in the pit at Jaws, Brian Keaulana lays it down like a true pro: "I think there are very few people in the world that have the skill and knowledge to survive a huge wipeout like that." Darrick Doerner echoes this, but in a more straightforward way: "Hell no. Do you think I'm crazy?"

Kerbox was crazy enough to try it, and like everything else in Hollywood it took multiple takes. "What they wanted was me coming unglued on the

Surfing the Apocalypse

Cinema's Most Famous Waves

Apocalypse Now was adapted and directed by Francis Ford Coppola from John Milius's original screenplay. Milius wrote the first version while still a film student at USC. He considered directing it, but handed it off to Coppola, who went on to create one of the most important American movies ever.

You'd have to get Milius and Coppola in a room under bright lights to figure which lines and scenes were whose, but there is no question that the famous surfing scene came from a surfer, and the surfer was Milius.

The "Charlie Don't Surf" scene is one of the most evocative scenes in the movie—and in all of American cinema. Milius explains his inspiration: "I wrote that scene because I saw Vietnam as a California war. World War II movies always had guys from the East Coast with accents, but Vietnam was a rock and roll war. A California war."

The producers and actors were all for the scene, and while Robert Duvall was preparing for the role of Air Cavalry Colonel William Kilgore, he went down to the beach at Malibu with Milius. "I showed Robert what a cutback was, let him listen to surfers talk," Milius says. "He was very good at preparing, and of course he nailed the role."

The "Charlie Don't Surf" scene burned lines and images into the world's consciousness. People who had never heard Wagner's "Ride of the Valkyries" now hum it in traffic because of Apocalypse Now. And like Spicoli before him, Colonel Kilgore barked out quotes that will live forever:

"I love the smell of napalm in the morning."

"Soldier, you either surf or you fight!"

"Charlie don't surf!"

"Someday this war's gonna end!"

"What the hell do you know about surfing? You're from goddamned New Jersey!"

Milius was shooting his own Big Wednesday while the surfing scenes for Apocalypse Now were going in the can, but he heard bits and pieces. "I guess the surf was really good at that beach just before the crew got there, and they had to settle for pretty small surf for the shoot," Milius said. "It looked nice, but I thought the mortar explosions going off in the surfline were kind of silly."

John Milius was nominated with Francis Ford Coppola for an Academy Award for Best Writing, Screenplay Based on Material from Another Medium, but lost to Kramer vs. Kramer.

Robert Duvall was nominated for Best Actor in a Supporting Role, but lost to Melvyn Douglas for Being There.

And Apocalypse Now was nominated for Best Picture, but lost to Kramer vs. Kramer.

In the fullness of time, you have to wonder: Is that fair? How many songs by the Clash did Kramer vs. Kramer inspire?

face," he says. "They wanted it to be as dramatic as possible but they didn't necessarily want me going over with the lip. In the movie the wipeout isn't supposed to kill the Mickey character. It just takes him to the bottom where he grabs a rock and runs off with it. They wanted dramatic."

Out of the fifteen wipeouts Kerbox did, the money shot came early on the first day. "The shot we used I was on the shoulder and it was no big deal. I was warming up and ready for more. They called no sets for a while and they called it off for the day. And the next day was smaller. So what could have happened was more scary than what did happen."

The irony behind all of this is that on the same day Todd Chesser was supposed to pretend to wipe out at Jaws and drown, he flew back to Oahu, got caught inside a giant wave at a place called Outside Alligators and drowned for real. *In God's Hands* was all about the ethics of using Personal Watercraft in giant waves. Todd Chesser hated them, but if there had been one on hand at Outside Alligators, he might still be alive.

Of all the stunts done by surfers going back to Duke Kahanamoku and Tom Blake, it was Rochelle Ballard who came the closest to eating it. More than forty years after Mickey Muñoz and Linda Benson redoubled for Sandra Dee in *Gidget,* Ballard was chosen as a surfing and body double for actress Kate Bosworth playing Anne Marie Chadwick in *Blue Crush.*

From small days at Haleiwa to medium days at Laniakea to big days at Backdoor, Pipeline, and Avalanche, Ballard made Bosworth look good. When Anne Marie tows into a monster at Avalanche, that was Ballard on the board. "That was also me going head-first over the falls at Pipe a few times. Not on purpose, but it still hurt," she remembers.

To set the record straight, there is one large Pipeline wave in *Blue Crush* that is pig-dogged by Noah Johnson, doubling as Anne Marie in a bikini and wig, much like Muñoz for Dee. That wave is epic, but it came about only because Ballard was sitting on the beach, recovering from near-paralysis due to a collision with another surfer at Laniakea just four days earlier.

Ballard was jazzed to be a part of *Blue Crush.* Producer Brian Grazer and director John Stockwell came to Hawai'i to tell the story of young women surfers struggling for courage, money, and respect, and the more she hung out with them, the more she realized they wanted to get it right. Grazer and Stockwell were surfers, and they listened to what the girls had to say and hired the right people—Don King, Sonny Miller, Brian Keaulana, Brock Little, Terry Ahue, Sanoe Lake. It was all good, as they say, and the money wasn't so bad, either.

Ballard was there to surf and duck-dive and get caught inside and paddle through heaving lineups, and she did it all. While working on the show, she knew she was going to have a shot at surfing big, perfect Pipeline with only a couple of others in the water, and that meant a lot to her. "You know, Anne Marie's story in the movie is close to my own story," she says. "Many years ago I hit my head on the bottom while surfing Cannon's, and I've been afraid of that place ever since. I'm comfortable with Backdoor up to eight feet but I'll tell you that there have been many, many days where I've sat on the beach looking at big Pipeline. I'll put my leash on and take it off and put it back on but then finally not go out. I'd go home seeing myself getting pitched over and hitting the rocks and it was scary. Just like Anne Marie. I thought I didn't have the guts to do it. I'd never made the drop at Big Pipe, and I was really looking forward to surfing a big Pipe day with no one else out, so I could have a chance."

The crew of *Blue Crush* got along well, but the ocean was the difficult star. Winter 2001-2002 wasn't cooperative and for most of the shoot, Pipeline was a sleeping giant that refused to awaken. The Second Unit shot surfing whenever it could. "I was having a blast working on the movie and surfing good waves with all these gnarly guys blocking for me and getting paid for it and eating too much Craft Services," Rochelle said. "It was so much fun, and it was good to be working with guys like John Stockwell and Brian Grazer who listened and cared." Rochelle was at Laniakea with Don King and Chris Taloa and the Second Unit crew, to shoot a scene where the local mok Drew character drops in on Anne Marie and breaks her board. Before the cameras were rolling, Rochelle Ballard took off in front of Chris Taloa for a warmup and the two collided. You've heard of a headbutt? Well this was a butthead, but it wasn't funny. Chris Taloa's big, hard Hawai'ian *okole* connected with Rochelle Ballard's head, and nearly paralyzed her. "That was a heavy, heavy thing," Ballard said, referring to the situation, not the thing that hit her. "I went from the most excruciating pain to total numbness. They took me out on the Ski and then Med Evaced me to the hospital and for a while there I thought I was paralyzed and would never surf again."

Ballard was out of commission for two and a half weeks, but the show went on. "Well I knew they had a permit to shoot for an hour at Pipe and I was really looking forward to that: surfing perfect Pipe almost alone."

Ballard's big chance on Pipeline came four days after she was injured. The crew had exactly one hour of perfect waves to capture the climactic last ride of the movie where Anne Marie charges Pipeline for death or glory. But for Ballard, discretion was the better part of valor after her crash: "I was on the beach with John Stockwell and Brian Keaulana and Pipeline was going *off*. This was

the best day in like three years and they had it for an hour, but I felt sick inside. John and Brian asked how I was feeling and I had to say that I didn't think I could do it. That was the worst feeling of my life, but I was too messed up physically to go charge giant Pipe backside. Well at that point they grabbed Noah and put him in wig and said, 'Let's do this thing.'"

Just like that, a starlet was born. Like Mickey Muñoz in 1959, Noah Johnson put on a wig and bikini and paddled out into an empty Pipeline lineup to bag the epic wave. He made a cute surfer girl.

Noah figures he rode about ten waves and made most of them, while on others he wiped out accidentally on purpose. "They wanted some wipeouts so I did the best I could. I dove the lip on one and jumped out of the lip on another and got super deep on a couple and ran into the closeout. You go where there's no choice but to eat it and then just use instinct to get through it safely. Your mind will only allow so much intentional stupidity so to a certain extent you have to put things beyond your control. Brian Keaulana was right there with the ski giving me rides back out to the lineup. Don King was shooting from the water and Sonny Miller was on the back of a ski with Kai Garcia driving. I remember being way deep in the barrel and waving at them. Ha ha, it was killer. That hour at Pipe was great, but somewhat balanced by the fact that I was dressed as a girl, and I couldn't go right. As a testimonial to my commitment to the job, I passed up a couple silly Backdoor waves that to this day I wish I had gone on. A scary brush with conformity."

There were also some shots that couldn't be used, the result of being a boy dressed liked a girl: "They had some epic footage of me from that hour at Pipe," Noah says, "but in all of the close-up shots, you can see my package hanging out from that bikini and it's obvious the surfer is a man, man!"

Going Vertical

The Parallel Ascent of Kelly Slater and the Surf Industrial Complex • The 1980s and 1990s

Left, **Kelly Slater:** The champ bends around the falling lip of a South Pacific reef-pass wave. (Photo © Jeff Divine)

Above, **U.S. Surfing Association Decal, 1962** (Voyageur Press Archives)

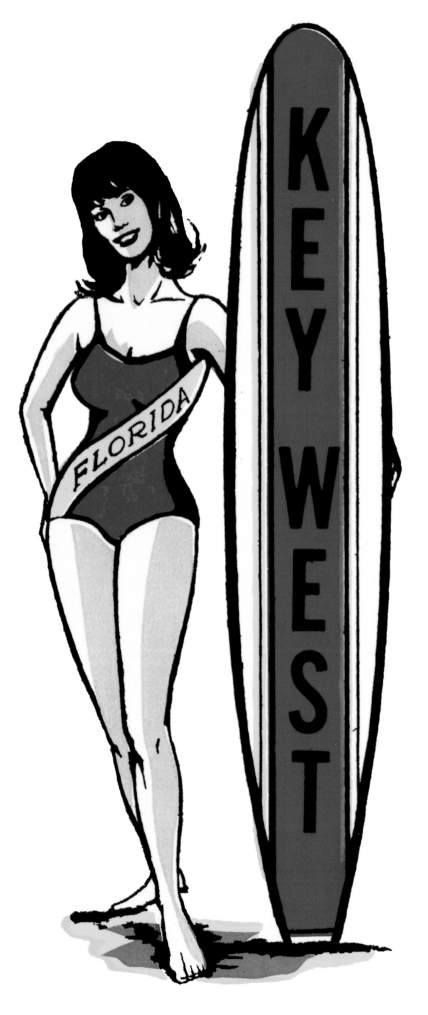

In the past, surfers rode waves in a variety of ways. Long, smooth turns cut across glorious green walls. Hanging ten and hotdogging it. Muscular drives down ever-bigger waves.

Then, at the dawn of the 1990s, Kelly Slater went vertical.

Within pro surfing, several performance schools emerged in the late 1980s and into the 1990s. Surfers such as Tom Curren represented the Power School of grand, flowing turns with lots of splash but less flash. Meanwhile, Martin Potter and Christian Fletcher were the very visible leaders of the Aerial School, turning the old Jan & Dean skateboarding song "Sidewalk Surfin'" on its head. The golden duo sang, "You can do the tricks the surfers do." Now Fletcher, Potter, and a slippery squad of surfers were doing the tricks the skaters could do—ollies, kick flips, lien airs, 360s.

In fall 1989, Fletcher's aerial surfing won him $31,725 at the Body Glove Surf Bout II at Lower Trestles. Interviewed in *Surfer*, Fletcher said he practiced by skating a half-pipe in San Juan Capistrano and playing *Skate or Die* on Nintendo. Soon after, he appeared on the cover of the skaters' bible, *Thrasher* magazine, and made the covers of *Surfer* and *Surfing*. All in the same month.

Kelly Slater was inspired by both the Power School *and* the Aerial School, and he sought to take the best of both and meld them into his own: "There were two surfers whose styles impacted me the most: Tom Curren and Martin Potter," he wrote in his 2003 autobiography *Pipe Dreams*. Slater admired the smooth, powerful rides of Curren: "He had the ideal mix of flow, radical moves, and a perfect style honed on long, California pointbreaks." Slater was also stoked by Potter, and wrote simply that "Seeing Martin Potter blasting an aerial on the cover of *Surfing* magazine in 1984 when I was 12 changed my life. . . . He was someone I could relate to, and right away, I wanted to fly."

In 1992, a twenty-one-year-old Slater solidified all the hype by claiming the World Pro Tour—the youngest surfer ever to do so.

But more than that, Kelly ignited a revolution. Combining Curren's flow with Potter's flair and exposed to the world by videographer Taylor Steele's *Momentum* flicks, Slater ushered in the New School of surfing.

Gone were the days of letting the wave dictate the ride. Kelly Slater drew lines never before imagined—not even in the drawings scribbled on your high-school notebooks.

Kelly's ascent came in a new era, and he rose higher than any other surfer before him. His ride paralleled the rise of the modern surf industrial complex of competition, media, and marketing that reached full speed during the 1980s and 1990s. Competitive pro surfing tours and companies like Ocean Pacific, Rip Curl, O'Neill, Body Glove, Billabong, Gotcha, Quiksilver, and more reaped hundreds of millions of dollars in sales and profits. Their marketing forces launched Kelly Slater as the poster boy of the New School.

Between the competitive pro tours, major sponsorship dollars, and huge hype, surfing would never be the same.

My beach! My wave! My chicks! Go home!

— The Surf Punks, "My Beach," 1980

Surfing Travel Decals, 1960s–1970s (Voyageur Press Archives)

Kelly Slater and the surf industrial complex were born the same year: 1972. Kelly was born in Cocoa Beach, Florida, to Judy and Stephen Slater, while the surf industry was multicultural and had many parents—American, Australian, South African, South American, Hawai'ian.

According to Judy Slater, her second son, Kelly, arrived pretty much as the world came to know him: brown and light and strong, broad-shouldered and determined.

Cocoa Beach was a small town on the Space Coast, dubiously semifamous as the setting for *I Dream of Jeannie.* It was best known around the state for being Partyville, where long-haired youngsters rubbed elbows with buzz-cut Apollo astronauts. While it wasn't much of a surf town by California standards, during the 1960s a hot crew of East Coast surfers hung out there,

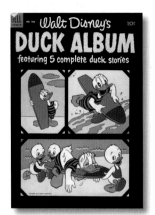

including Gary Propper, Dick Catri, Claude Codgen, and Mike Tabeling.

Stephen Slater moved to Cocoa Beach to surf and party and work construction and in 1967, he was serving as a bouncer in a bar when he rescued Judy from an unruly date. They soon married, and Robert Kelly Slater was born five years later.

Kelly had a normal Florida childhood, competing relentlessly with his older brother Sean, nearly getting killed numerous times by alligators and his own wiles. He rode a skateboard, then a bike, then a minibike. At five, he began riding waves on a Styrofoam bellyboard. "The waves in Florida suck," he

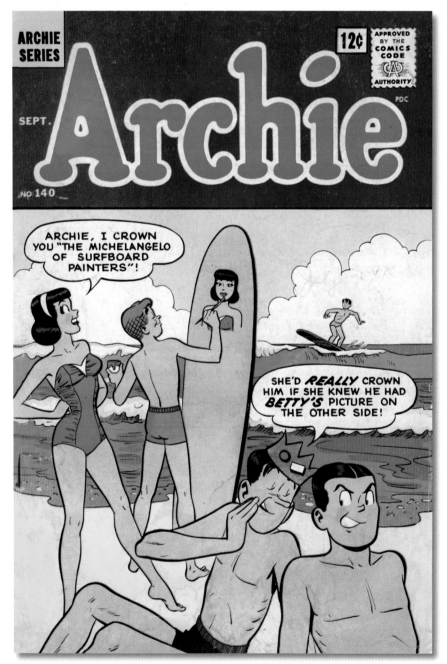

wrote in *Pipe Dreams*. "I hate to put it so bluntly, but compared to most places around the world, it's true." Still, they were all the waves he had.

His ambition was to get off that bellyboard everyone teased him about and onto something serious. In 1973, Malibu surfer Tom Morey trademarked a sophisticated bodyboard design called the Morey Boogie, which started a slew of copycats and a sub-craze for people who wanted to get in the ocean but not go through the rigamarole of buying a surfboard and having to learn to stand up. The Morey Boogie helped fuel the second surf explosion by putting more people in the water. Some surfers resented the intrusion, looking down—literally and figuratively—on "boogers" as second-class citizens. Kelly didn't care. A bodyboard was a step up from that Styrofoam thing, and he took it. On his skateboard, he was spinning 360s and doing other tricks; now he tried those tricks in the ocean, standing on his bodyboard. And he got a lot of opportunity to do it, because his mom loved the beach and taking her kids surfing was a good excuse to do some bronzing.

Kelly and his brother spent a lot of time at a burger joint called the Islander Hut, listening to the jukebox. The number one song in 1977 was Queen's "We Are the Champions"; Slater must have heard it a zillion times, and who knows what impression that left on his psyche. And then there was the sight of all those spaceships launching into the stratosphere from Cape Canaveral—visions of vertical freedom.

Surfing was fueling Kelly's dreams. He and his brother rode waves all day, read all the magazines, and watched all the movies: "The surfers in those movies were even better than the guys at home, and my favorite was Buttons Kaluhiokalani," he remembers. "He and fellow Hawaiian Larry Bertlemann could do anything on a wave—doing 360s in the barrel, sliding the tail, even hitting the lip and switching their stance—tricks that guys are still trying to do today. There was no limit to their imagination. I swear I saw Buttons go upside down and make a complete flip in one of the movies." Hawai'ian surfers Ben Aipa, Mark Liddell, and Larry Bertlemannn were also pushing the limits of performance surfing with their skateboarding-influenced, anything-is-possible style of super-loose hotdogging. Kelly was still just a kid, but it all left an impression.

He entered his first surf contest in 1980–the Salick Brothers Surf Contest held in front of the Islander Hut at Cocoa Beach. There were four other kids in his division and he was still riding his bodyboard, but Islander Hut was his turf, he knew the wave inside out and backwards, and he blew everyone away, doing standup, backside 360s. He attracted attention, including catching the eye of the Salick brothers and local surfboard shaper Matt Kechele, who was about to turn pro and would become one of Kelly's mentors.

Kelly was eight when his parents broke down and finally bought him his own, real surfboard. Yet even this new, albeit dangerous, single-fin was behind the times, as Australian Simon Anderson was winning three world tour events in 1981 on a new-fangled three-finned innovation he called the Thruster. Kelly's first board was exactly five feet long and airbrushed with an image from the film *Jaws* of a shark lurking for the attack.

In 1981, nine-year-old Kelly took his first trip out of Brevard County to compete in the Eastern Surfing Association Menehune Division Championships. He had never confronted anything other than the placid, continental shelf-protected breaks of Cocoa, and Cape Hatteras was a brave new world. Kelly couldn't make it past the shorebreak and finished seventh out of seven.

That same year, he was the youngest and smallest of a Menehune group organized by Dick Catri to tour Brevard County. Kelly was there because he was Sean's little brother, but by 1982 he was winning most events and earning prize surfboards and free stickers. Catri then took his wards to a Florida trade show, where Kelly shyly said hello to Tom Curren, and also met Quiksilver's Danny Kwock and Jeff Hakman, who gave him a pair of Quiksilver shorts. Catri picked up sponsorship for his Menehunes from Arena, a maker of sweat suits, and also Sundek, a Florida manufacturer of beach clothing. Now, Kelly had all the free gear he could handle. It was the shape of things to come.

Meanwhile back at the ranch, Kelly watched his family fall apart due to his father's drinking: "Many of the greatest athletes, artists, and overachievers of any kind come from imperfect families," he wrote in *Pipe Dreams*. "It creates character. We can't choose

Surfing, Comic Book Style, 1960s (Voyageur Press Archives)

what sort of home life we are given as a child, but it plays a big part in making us who we become. The more difficult things are, the more likely we are to latch on to something outside the home. My something was surfing. . . ."

Some people let personal problems drag them down; others use it as fuel. In 1982, Kelly was back to win the Eastern Surfing Association Menehune Division Championships, but family problems forced him to give up his slot in the United States Amateur Championships. Kelly and his brothers

The Surfer's Surfer

John Severson and the Birth of Surf Culture

Scrape away all the layers of experience that time has laid on John Severson—father, husband, painter, golfer, sailboarder, traveler, architect, environmentalist, writer, editor, moralist, publisher, filmmaker, square, hipster, baseball player, surfer—and on the bare canvas, you will find an artist.

John enriched the world by introducing it to the pursuit of surfing—first with paintings, then film, and then, in 1960, with his magazine *The Surfer*. He took surfing public with a combination of talent, commitment, courage, and pure surf stoke that laid a firm foundation for this thing we call the surf industry.

John was in love with art, and by tracing the course of his life, it's obvious that luck was in love with John Severson. His life has seen a number of turning points, some self-induced, some caused by forces that, in retrospect, can only be called fate.

The first was a move when he was twelve from Pasadena to San Clemente. Orange County was pristine, and so was the act of riding waves. Severson graduated from mats at San Clemente pier, to paddleboards at San Onofre, to ten-foot six-inch Malibu chips at Cottons Point.

A first-grade teacher, Mrs. Lane, encouraged young John's artistic talent. His mother also helped, enrolling him in correspondence art courses and buying him cameras. In high school, teacher Doug Hammond guided him on the school newspaper and other art projects. But as he explored all the facets of art, he kept coming back to the ocean, and surfing was his muse.

He received a degree in art education from Chico State, then a masters in art from Long Beach. In 1956, he was drafted into the Army, and in a twist of fate he now recognizes as a turning point, he was stationed in Hawai'i. "All these other guys were saying, 'Oh no, the worst duty in the world.' Everything was expensive. The locals hated the *haole*, but I was just delivered to heaven."

John lived in Haleiwa, often surfing the North Shore alone. Then he was ordered to join the Army surf team and practice at Makaha.

Fred Van Dyke was another who spent time in Hawai'i, and would later become a partner in John's first surf movie. An accomplished big-wave rider himself, Van Dyke had good things to say about Severson the surfer: "Regardless of what anyone else says, John Severson was the first person to hotdog big waves," Van Dyke says. "John touched me very deeply one day at Haleiwa. It was about 10 to 12 feet, almost bigger than you want to ride Haleiwa, and he went out and did turns and climbs and kick outs and things of that nature that took my breath away.

"John went on to ride bigger waves and he was able to do the hot dog maneuvers on them. John was just voraciously in love with surfing and he wanted to do something to move it ahead. He was extremely well-coordinated and an outstanding representative of what surfing could be. Most of us dreamed of climbing and hotdogging on a wave. He went out and actually did it."

In January 1959, John nearly died—blacking out twice—after getting creamed by the Makaha Bowl on a big day. Adventures like this in Hawai'i inspired his paintings—whimsical renderings of small, fearless men riding huge, fearsome Hawai'ian waves. John sold his paintings on Waikiki Beach, and with the proceeds invested in film for his Keystone 16 mm movie camera. What began as a hobby turned into a semi-career as his first film, *Surf*, played to hungry audiences in Hawai'i and California.

Released from the Army in 1958, John made more movies—*Surf Safari*, *Surf Fever*, *Big Wednesday*, *Going My Wave*. Unfortunately, time and overuse have worn away these movies, and they no longer exist—except in many a surfer's memory.

While touring his movies, John found an audience with an appetite for any surfing image. He sold photographic prints for a dollar, inspiring the idea for a pamphlet for his third release, *Surf Fever*. "People tried to talk me out of it," John says. "But I'm a surfer, you know. Sometimes I'll see an opportunity and I'll just go for it: forget the consequences. We printed up 10,000 copies of *The Surfer*

The Surfer **First Annual Photo Book, 1960** (Voyageur Press Archives)

and it all looked good, but when I went to the printer and loaded all those magazines into my VW van, I thought: 'What have I done?' I was going to charge $1.50 for these things, and I didn't know if I would sell a hundred. Well, the first place I went to there was a riot going on and I thought, 'Just my luck.' But they were all there for the magazine."

The Surfer was originally a quarterly canvas in which he could express himself through cartoons, words, and photos. But the demand turned *The Surfer* into a full-time magazine, blossoming from a quarterly to a bimonthly. John had the good taste to hire the likes of Rick Griffin, Hyatt Moore, Drew Kampion, and Ron Stoner—young, talented, stoked surfers who added their energy to one of the most unusual magazines in America. As Kampion, who came on as *The Surfer* editor in 1967, remembers John: "He's a great artist. Not just on canvas, but in whatever he touches."

How to describe the sixties? How to describe the changes surfing underwent? How to describe what it was like to be the shepherd and policeman of those changes? John had transitioned from a square, golf-playing country-club guy to angry counterculture spokesman. America was at war with Vietnam, and

with itself. Orange County was being transformed from rural paradise to suburban jungle. And to top it all off, fate gave John an interesting new neighbor—Richard Nixon, one of the most paranoid presidents in American politics.

Living next door to Nixon was the ten-ton weight that broke John's will. In 1970, he made one last movie, an environmental statement called *Pacific Vibrations*, and then he was gone, off to Maui.

Since John left *The Surfer* in 1971, he has been involved in projects at his leisure—painting, helping launch other magazines, publishing books, traveling, designing textiles, and of course, surfing. But still, at heart and at the canvas, John Severson is an artist: "Sometimes when an artist gets successful he gets trapped into a certain kind of art, like landscapes, or portraits, or clowns with big eyes. Well, I started off painting surf scenes and all along I've wondered if maybe I should do something else, maybe landscapes or portraits or clowns with big eyes. But you know I would have trouble painting cows in meadows or something and I think I've finally come to terms with the fact that I'm a painter of surf scenes. It's taken me a while, but I've come to terms with it.

"I paint surf scenes, and I'm stoked."

Bing 1966 Foam Surfboard: Bing Copeland was one of the pioneers of the isophthalic foam board, ushering in a new era in lightweight, high-performance boards. Bing collaborated with Donald Takayama in building this triple-rail model. (© Malcolm Wilson) SPECIFICATIONS: 10' 6" LONG; 24" WIDE; 3¼" THICK

were being raised by their mom. Money was tight and got tighter, but Kelly had his surfboards and the ocean and enough support to keep it rolling. He was not the first champion surfer to drown his problems in the ocean, and he wouldn't be the last.

Due to his 1982 ESA Championship and with help from U.S. Surfing Federation Director Colin Couture as well as Kelly's sponsors Sundek and O'Neill, he now had a travel fund allowing him to jet to the best competitions and get back to school on time. In 1984, he competed in his first pro event, the Sundek Classic, held during spring break party time in Melbourne Beach, Florida. The surf was small, so twelve-year-old Kelly took out an Australian pro nearly twice his age and weight, only to lose his next heat.

He traveled to California that summer to compete for a slot on the national team heading for the World Amateur Championships in Huntington Beach. This was Slater's first time in California; he didn't weigh much more than a wet wetsuit, and the waves of Salt Creek were more than he could handle. Kelly and Sean both missed out on the team, but they got to surf a lot of good waves from Orange County to Ventura County and had their eyes opened wide to the possibilities.

A few months later, Kelly won a ticket to Hawai'i in a Florida event and in December 1984, he really got his eyes opened. After watching countless movies of Pipeline, reading about it in magazines, and staring at posters on his bedroom wall, he paddled over to Pipe on a small day. He caught a few waves and started to get cocky, then got caught inside and got pounded.

Still, if he'd learned anything from his family problems, it was how to pull himself back up. A week after getting trounced by Pipeline, Kelly competed against the likes of future friends and foes Shane Dorian and Keoni Watson in the U.S. Amateur Surfing Championships at Makaha. The surf was small but powerful, and Kelly was as shocked as anyone to find himself the U.S. Menehune Champion.

In 1986, *Time* magazine reported that total retail surfwear sales hit one billion dollars for the first time, with Hobie Sportswear and Ocean Pacific the market leaders. The new Association of Surfing Pro-

fessionals (ASP) Tour was thriving, with ten events in Hawai'i, South Africa, Australia, and California. In California, wetsuit-maker Body Glove was doing good enough business to underwrite the Professional Surfing Association of America (PSAA) Tour, a training ground for young pros intent on making it to the ASP. Down Under wonders like Simon Anderson and Mark Richards ruled the waves, while young Santa Barbara surfer Tom Curren became amateur champion and looked to be the one to regain the momentum American surfing had lost to the Australians and South Africans.

These were the roaring 1980s for surf contests, as a combustible mix of rowdy surfers joined forces with bikini contests at big-buck events. The combination of hot surfing and hot chicks overheated at Huntington Beach's 1986 Op Pro. Thousands of contest-goers fueled by sun, sex, and booze went berserk, overturning cars, setting fires, threatening the overwhelmed police and lifeguards, and running wild through the streets. No one was killed but many were arrested and there was thousands of dollars in damage to beach facilities. The real damage was to the public image of pro surfing.

Kelly continued to compete as an amateur, yet during the Easter Surfing Festival 1986, he made it to a pro event final. He was now fourteen and still a pint-size kid, but his surfing was fast becoming a threat to other pros on the East Coast. Gaining confidence as a competitor, he still lacked experience in big waves. Hawai'i was too far away from school for quick trips, so Kelly and Sean traveled to Barbados and Puerto Rico to get used to size—and coral reefs. By the ripe old age of fifteen, Kelly was a seasoned traveler.

For all his later success, Kelly never really had a good result at the World Amateur Surfing Championships, held every two years. In 1986, he went to Newquay, England, and was the second youngest in the hyper-competitive Open Division. Despite the cold water and big waves, he made it to the final and came up against fearsome competition in the form of Australian Nicky Wood, Tahitian Vetea "Poto" David, and Hawai'ian John Shimooka. Kelly fell on two waves and finished third in the world. An accomplishment for most, for Kelly, it felt like failure.

In 1987, *North Shore* hit national movie screens, telling the tall tale of a surfer named Rick Kane who wins an Arizona wavepool contest, sending him

Below, **Dale Velzy 1960 "7-11":** Several years before the arrival of the short-board "revolution," Dale Velzy crafted his high-performance "7-11." "Kinda ugly—but not!" he remembers. "These were fun . . . cherry-red rails, they floated good, they rode the nose, they spun out pretty bad, but . . ." (© Malcolm Wilson) SPECIFICATIONS: 7' 11" LONG; 23½" WIDE; 3½" THICK; 35 POUNDS

Left, **The Adventures of Mike, the Malibu Surf King, 1969** (Voyageur Press Archives)

CHANNEL ISLANDS
surfboards

VENTURA·SANTA BARBARA

SURFBOARDS
BY
ERNIE TANAKA

GREG NOLL
SURFBOARDS AND FILM PRODUCTIONS

the Only way to travel

Gordie
SURF·BOARDS

Huntington Beach, Calif.

Jack's
SURF SHOP
Anaheim

Hobie
SURFBOARDS
DANA POINT, CALIF.

CON
SURFBOARDS

CUSTOM
GORDON and SMITH
SURFBOARDS

BING
SURFBOARDS

GREG NOLL
SURFBOARDS AND FILM PRODUCTIONS

SEA
CROSS
BURBANK
CALIF.
SURFBOARDS

Surfboards
by
HARBOUR
SEAL BEACH

GREG NOLL
SURF BOARDS

OLYMPIC
SURFBOARDS

SURFBOARDS
Joe Quigg

SANTA CRUZ   CALIFORNIA
SCOFIELD
SURFBOARDS

Surfboard and Surf Shop Decals, 1950s–1970s (Maynard Eshelman Collection/ Voyageur Press Archives)

SANTA BARBARA SURF SHOP
surfboards
by
Yater

By
HANSEN
Cardiff

the Only way to travel
Gordie
SURF-BOARDS
Huntington Beach, Calif.

VAGABOND
custom
SURFBOARDS

SURF BOARDS
BY
Jack Haley
SEAL BEACH, CALIF.

SURFBOARDS
by
TUCKER
BALBOA ISLAND

Surfboards
Hawaii
HALEIWA, HAWAII

Custom
BOARDS
by
HAUT

COMPLETELY
CUSTOM
Islander
SURFBOARDS

SURF BOARDS
by
JACOBS

Hobie
SURFBOARDS
DANA POINT. CALIF.

Hobie
DANA POINT, CALIFORNIA

to Oahu's North Shore to battle villainous locals, huge surf, pretty Hawai'ian girls, and treacherous surfboard shapers. As corny as the movie was, it remains a timepiece of 1980s surfing, and the fiction of that film mirrored Kelly Slater's reality.

That same year, Kelly won a wavepool event on the PSAA circuit in Irvine, California. That victory got him on the cover of *Surfing* and the buzz grew. "The magazines started calling me the future world champion," Slater says in *Pipe Dreams.* "Since I had won six East Coast Titles, four U.S. Championships, and two NSSA Nationals, all eyes were focused on me. While the attention and faith in me was nice, I still had to prove I could do it. Before I could even think of turning pro, I had to win as an amateur at the highest level."

So, just like in *North Shore*, he went to Hawai'i. There, Kelly tucked under the wing of surfboard shaper/big-wave guru Ken Bradshaw. Originally from Texas, Bradshaw had made a name for himself as one of the best at Sunset and Waimea Bay. Now, he showed Kelly the ropes along the Seven Mile Miracle.

Still, 1988 was a disaster for Kelly. Determined to win all there was left for him to win—the World Amateur Title, held on familiar turf in Puerto Rick—he bombed out of the qualifying team trials. The water was cold, the surf was bad, Kelly was wearing a thick wetsuit, and he couldn't get his freak on.

Despite his jinx, the buzz continued to build. *Surfer* did a nine-page feature in 1989 calling him the Next Big Thing, the Great American Hope. Heady stuff for a seventeen-year-old, but Kelly ate it up: "After that, I was no longer thinking of surfing as mere recreation," he writes. "I was beginning to realize it could be my career. It was my opportunity to set myself up for life, and I wasn't going to blow it."

In 1989, Kelly finally got to surf in the Op Pro, an event he had admired from land for many years. He rode in the amateur Op Junior against friend and foe Rob Machado. Injuring his hip doing the splits on a blown turn, Kelly still won in a rousing finale, giving the world a taste of the epic Slater-Machado heats to come.

Kelly also had new deals to surf for Rip Curl wetsuits and Ocean Pacific clothing, all part of the promotion machine of the blossoming surf industrial complex. "I was still an amateur but must have made at least as much as my high school teachers," he remembers. He had the juice to buy his family

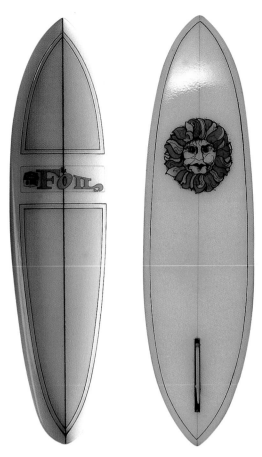

a house in Cocoa Beach, and for the first time in a long time, the Slater family had a permanent base. He spent some time in France with Tom Curren, learning the secrets of his sensei. Back at Cocoa Beach High, he resumed the abnormal life of a teenager, but as soon as the bell rang for winter break, he was off to Hawai'i, determined to make his way farther outside and deeper into the lineup of those giant waves.

Kelly's World Amateur Surfing Championships jinx continued in 1990, when he was jumped by three Brazilians in the semifinal and failed to advance. In July 1990, he surfed his first pro event as a true pro, the Life's a Beach Klassic in Oceanside, California. He made it to the second round, where he met his hero Martin Potter in a man-on-man heat. Kelly lost and Potter won, but on the podium, Potter gave the upstart his highest accolades: "I knew after I beat Kelly that I could win this contest."

With more success came more interest from the surf industry. Kelly was represented by agent Bryan Taylor, who stuck him in a bidding war between Op, Gotcha, and Quiksilver. As things got intense, Kelly famously escaped to Mexico, surfing the tip of Baja with the words "I Don't Even Care" stenciled to the butt of his trunks.

Left, **Bing 1968 Foil:** The short board "revolution" arrived in the late 1960s, characterized by surfboard's such as Bing Copeland's Foil. (© Malcolm Wilson) SPECIFICATIONS: 7' 8" LONG; 22½" WIDE; 2¾" THICK

Right, **Dewey Weber 1969 Pig:** Dewey Weber's Pig short board was innovative, fast, and an ideal hotdogger. (© Malcolm Wilson) SPECIFICATIONS: 5' 9" LONG; 20" WIDE

Facing page, **Tom Curren:** The son of accomplished big-wave surfer and board shaper Pat Curren, Tom Curren went prodigal during the Bad Old Eighties. His mellow reticence on land belied the fact that he was a competitive buzzsaw, and he became the Great California Hope, taking the world title from the Australians and South Africans and bringing it on home. Curren's surfing was solid, pure, and just about perfect. His style influenced Kelly Slater—and continues to influence today's new generation of surfers. (Photo © Jeff Divine)

When Kelly returned home, he began a beautiful relationship with Quiksilver, signing a multiyear agreement for six figures annually.

Kelly picks out one day and one wave—December 3, 1991, at Pipeline—as the turning point in his life. He was just nineteen, fresh out of Cocoa Beach High, and a freshman on the ASP Tour. He was the only rookie remaining in the Pipe Masters, where he'd made it to the quarter finals to face Australians Damien Hardman, Simon Law, and Mike Rommelse. Only two guys would go on to the semis, and Kelly wanted to be one of them.

Seven years had passed since punk-kid Kelly had paddled into Pipe and got worked. Now, he had grown into himself and was the very model of a modern surfer. If you took the top forty-four pros at the time and averaged their height and weight, it was Kelly exactly: five foot nine and 165 pounds. He was the mold of the New School surfer—short, light, built like an Olympic gymnast, riding incredibly thin, light surfboards at new speeds and in new places on waves.

He had proven a lot in other venues but had everything to prove at Pipe, in serious surf, in serious competition, in front of the world. As the clock ticked, Kelly could hear the judges and knew he was behind. He was sitting away from the competitively voracious Australians and was in position for a mean, wedging, inside wave that everyone but he could see was evil incarnate. This thing was black and mean, even by Pipeline standards—the kind of wave that can pitch a surfer headfirst into a deadly coral reef only a few feet under the surface. This wave needed an exorcist, and Kelly went for it.

"From the top of the wave, I dropped about 15 feet straight down," he remembers. "I barely stayed upright through the drop but somehow managed to redirect my momentum back up the face under the thickest pitching lip that came through all day. . . . One second I was staring out of a massive cave swirling around me, and the next I came shooting out in a cloud of spray. I raised my arm in a victory salute for a split second, before a cross chop separated me from my board."

Tom Carroll won the Pipeline Masters that year and Damien Hardman took the 1991 ASP World Title, Kelly finishing forty-sixth. Yet, as he wrote in retrospect, his ride at Pipe delivered him from his demons: "Up until that moment, I had spent my surfing career

Christian Fletcher: Out of the 1980s and into the 1990s, a tattooed, shaved-head, nose-pierced surfer from San Clemente shocked everyone with his look on land and his antics in the water. Christian Fletcher and his skateboard-influenced aerial surfing were reviled by many, but he proved to be ahead of his time with his look and his moves, which are now standard in the twenty-first century. (Photo © Jeff Divine)

Facing page, **Shea Lopez:** Surfers from Florida are forced to make mountains out of molehills. Shea Lopez is from the Gulf Coast, a place that only gets surf when the Civil Defense is telling homeowners to finish putting up hurricane windows and move inland. Lopez has learned to do a lot with a little and he was in the wave of hot East Coasters to follow the trail blazed by Slater. (Photo © Jeff Divine)

Right, **Surfing Championship Posters, 1960s–1990s** (Voyageur Press Archives)

Illustrated Man

From the 1960s to the 1970s as Drawn by Rick Griffin

From the 1960s to the 1970s, Rick Griffin's surfboard shrunk by three feet while his hair grew twelve inches and his art morphed from pen-and-ink sketches of surf-stoked gremmies to full-color psychedelic explosions of mystic eyes and flesh-colored Jesuses.

Griffin was a surfer and survivor in those potent, transitional years. He doodled and drew his way through youth, adolescence, and maturity, his life's arc following the same trajectory as surfing, but shooting him into the stratosphere of not just surf culture but popular culture. Griffin nearly didn't survive—but he still thrived, drawing all that he saw, and in the process, becoming one of the most influential artists of the twentieth century.

Surfing went from jazzed in the 1940s to rock'n'roll-stoked in the 1950s and 1960s. Then, in the 1970s, it went psychedelic. Shorter boards and expanded minds were the new wave, and many pioneering surfers who were prominent in the early years did not survive the transition.

Greg Noll, for one, went out with a bang. On December 4, 1969, Noll was the last man standing during the biggest swell anyone had ever witnessed at Makaha. Against all odds, he stroked into a monster wave, made it to the bottom, and then got destroyed. After that, Noll saw the writing on the wall—the dawn of the shorter boards and younger guys and drugs and revolution. He came in from that giant wave, returned to California, gathered up his family and, like Odysseus, moved as far north in California as he could, retiring from surfing to become a commercial fisherman.

Rick Griffin was to surfing what Michelangelo was to Renaissance Italy. Starting as a gremmie in LA's South Bay, he hooked into this surfing thing young, his artwork vibrating with surf energy and the stoke of the young men and women who were challenging the waves. His early work was subtle and funny, and true to the lifestyle as it progressed from the innocent days of *Gidget* and the Beach Boys through the complexities of the Vietnam War and the sex, drugs, and rock'n'roll of a new era.

Richard Griffin was a war baby, born in Los Angeles on June 18, 1944 to a Southern California mother and a Navy father, who was also an amateur archaeologist. Boy Griffin accompanied his dad on digs, and Native American art and other western motifs sublimated into his psyche to surface in his art decades later.

Griffin grew up on a Palos Verdes peninsula still rural amidst a Southern California smaller and quieter than now. From certain spots on Palos Verdes, he could see almost all of the beaches of Los Angeles County and it was at Torrance Beach that he started surfing. As junior high buddy Randy Nauert remembers, "We were all basically beach kids, dressed alike in tennis shoes and white shirts, who were bussed inland to this school. Rick, however, had just moved into Palos Verdes from Lakewood and he had this totally different style from anybody else. Griffin was this rockabilly greaser with French-toed, spit-shined shoes and a waterfall pompadour haircut. Man, I was just amazed by those shoes, so I walked over to him and said, 'Hey, you've got to teach me how to shine shoes like that.' Rick looked at me, kinda surprised and said, 'Well, what will you do for me in exchange?' I thought for a second and I said, 'Well, I'll teach you how to surf.' From that point on, we were best friends."

Griffin was also a natural-born doodler. He scribbled surf scenes on Pee Chee folders, school desktops, and any other available surface. But unlike most kids his age, Griffin showed real wit, talent, even genius. From copying *Mad* magazine cartoons, Griffin went pro, sketching custom cartoons on his friends' T-shirts for fifty cents a shot.

Griffin became a local legend, catching the eye of Greg Noll, then running his Manhattan Beach surf shop. Noll has always recognized talent, and he became Griffin's first mentor. Griffin drew up a pricelist for Noll's surfboards that was a fun little masterpiece, and it led to a free board and bigger things.

During a screening of *Surf Fever* at Narbonne High School, Griffin was introduced to John Severson, the original surf artist whose surfing movies were insanely popular. Severson had just started *The Surfer* magazine, and now he hired Griffin straight out of high school.

In the third issue of *The Surfer*, Griffin introduced the cartoon character Murphy, and an institution was born. Murphy was every-surfer, a stoked gremmie who went through life equally brave and puzzled, enjoying victories and suffering defeats with every other step. Based on Griffin's own experiences as a young Californian wave-rider during the boom years—getting scared by Hawai'ian waves, dodging Marine patrols at Trestles—Murphy tapped into the common experience of tens of thousands of young surf gremmies. Murphy became the surfer's mascot for the 1960s, an essential ingredient of every issue and even gracing the cover in 1962. As Severson told *The Surfer's Journal*, "He absolutely captured the surf stoke of that era." Looking back, the *The Surfer's Journal* publisher Steve Pezman agrees: "The surf stoke in his drawings was incredible. He drew waves that you could feel sucking out, the *whoosh* and *awooo!*—you could just feel the surfing sensation of those waves—those renditions of perfect, peeling tubes. No one had drawn them with such feeling before."

Griffin and Murphy had a great ride until 1964, when the cartoonist and cartoon began to run out of wave. While hitchhiking to San Francisco to hop a freighter for the South Pacific, Griffin just barely jumped out of James Dean's footsteps when he was involved in a car crash near King City. Griffin was nearly killed in the crash, which dislocated his eye and permanently scarred his face.

A new Griffin emerged. He covered his ruined eye and scarred face with an eye patch and beard. His art changed as well. From 1964 to 1967, Griffin drew a series of adventure cartoons in which he and photographer Ron Stoner spanned the globe, looking for waves and women and whatever else the road could throw at them.

Griffin then fell in with the Haight-Ashbury hippie crowd, and his art went psychedelic. Where Murphy had been a square, well-meaning gremmie who ran on natural energy, Griffin's new strips included the Zig Zag Man and the Grateful Dead, hookah pipes and magic mushrooms. His new symbols let the world know the times were a changin'.

Griffin created the poster for the 1967 Human Be-In at San Francisco's Golden Gate Park, making him *the* artist for the Summer of Love. From there, he was hired to draw posters for Jimi Hendrix, Cream, the Doors, the Jefferson Airplane, Iron Butterfly, concerts at Avalon Ballroom and Fillmore Auditorium, the original logo for *Rolling Stone* magazine, cartoons for R. Crumb's *Zap Comix*, and album covers for the Dead's *Aoxomoxoa*, the Eagles' *On the Border*, and much more. In 1968, Griffin joined Stanley Mouse, Alton Kelly, Victor Moscoso, and Wes Wilson as the Big Five poster artists, founding the Berkeley-Bonaparte Gallery. Griffin explained, "In San Francisco, doing posters on a regular basis was like going to my own art school." His work found fans, such as head Deadhead Jerry Garcia: "Rick, like the rest of us, was on a mission to turn on the

Tales From the Tube, 1972: Rick Griffin's artwork perfectly captured the vibe of the emerging 1970s surf scene. (Used by permission of Ida Griffin/Steve Pezman Collection)

world. It was like, 'If you like that, you're gonna love this!' I dug Rick's stuff because it related so well to my own psychedelic experiences. Everything he ever submitted to us always nailed it—boom!—like it grew out of the center of the earth."

Through it all, Griffin never forgot his surfing roots. To return the favor for launching his career, Griffin penned the poster for John Severson's *Pacific Vibrations* in 1969. His poster for MacGillivray/ Freeman's *Five Summer Stories* showed a changed, 1970s version of Murphy sporting sunglasses, long hair, and a turned-on vibe. Murphy was obviously now experienced.

In 1972, Griffin introduced some of his Haight-Ashbury friends to surfing. The result was *Tales from the Tube*, a comic book insert in *Surfer* magazine featuring Griffin, R. Crumb, S. Clay Wilson, Bill Ogden, Jim Evans, and Glenn Chase. With its psychedelic stoke, *Tales from the Tube* perfectly captured the 1970s surf scene.

Like a lot of others who overindulged in the 1960s, Griffin began searching for salvation in the 1970s. He found it in Jesus Christ, and his work, from *Surfer* to music, took a spiritual turn. As R. Crumb remembers, "Rick Griffin was always one of those real dreamers. He made up his own hybrid mythology. Even when he was a Jesus freak, it was his own crazy romantic version. He wasn't a jerk about it. If you look at his Jesus stuff, it has that kind of pure, beautiful rendering of the Catholic bleeding heart, all those dark warnings about the murkiness of the world, the archetypal religious symbols but he didn't dwell on them very much."

In 1991 Rick was riding his Harley-Davidson Softail when he had a fatal collision with a van. He donated his kidneys, heart, and good eye, and his ashes were taken to his favorite surf spot near Fort Ross, Mystos. Ever since, it has been known among the faithful as El Griffos.

running from big waves, but making it through that one gave me the confidence to ride anything."

The next year, Kelly won the Pipe Masters and his first world title. Hawai'ian Derek Ho won the 1993 title, but Kelly took it back in 1994–and won the world title every year until 1998, six overall. He also won the Pipe Masters in 1994, 1995, 1996, and 1999, inspiring a grateful Quiksilver to raise his salary to a rumored one million dollars annually. And along the way, he was voted to the top of the *Surfer* Readers Poll for eight years going.

While dominating pro surfing from 1991 to 1998, Kelly was deified as one of *People* magazine's "50 Most Beautiful People in the World" in 1991. That odd honor had something do with him guest-starring on *Baywatch* in 1992. And that lead to an on-again, off-again relationship with Pamela Anderson, who was on the beach at Waimea in 1999 when Kelly competed in the Quiksilver Big Wave Event in Memory of Eddie Aikau—an event he won in 2002.

One of the challenges of early success is what you do for a second act. In a young man's game—where a lot of guys are washed up by the time they reach their late 20s—Kelly Slater was going strong well into his 30s. In fact, he was just a few months shy of his 40th birthday when he sewed up his record 11th ASP World Title, in 2011. Slater also holds the record as the youngest champion (at age 20) and the record as the oldest (39). Beyond the 11 titles, his astonishing record of success includes close to 50 world tour victories and evolutionary performances at waves across the globe, from the small stuff at Lower Trestles to the grinding maw of Pipeline and Teahupoo.

Slater has had his share of trauma, drama, triumph, and tragedy. But by age 40 he was settled and straight and utilizing a unique combination of emotional maturity, sharply honed physical skills, and wave knowledge to regularly wax surfers who hadn't even been born when Slater began competing as a pro. There's never been anything like him in surfing, and there probably never will be again. When Slater was asked if he planned to retire sometime in the second decade of the 21st century, he replied: "You're tripping. I'm going to be winning world titles when I'm fifty."

Wouldn't that be a trip?

Kelly Slater: Born in 1972 and growing up as a surfer in the 1980s, Kelly Slater was equally influenced by the aerial surfing of Martin Potter and the smooth flow of Tom Curren. His brilliant alchemy of class and post-modern was a part of his brilliance into the 1990s and now. (Photo © Jeff Divine)

The Sport of Queens

Gidget Kicks Ass • From Ancient Hawai'i to *Blue Crush* and Beyond

Left, **Keala Kennelly:** Keala Kennelly was one of the hot surfers to come out of Kauai during the 1990s. She grew up surfing the reefs of the Garden Island, and lead the women's push at Pipeline, Teahupoo, and other dangerous waves. She also played a key role in *Blue Crush*, inspiring a new generation of surfer grrls. (Photo © Jeff Divine)

Above, **Surf Queen, 1950s** (Voyageur Press Archives)

On Oahu at Waikiki, there is a break called *Ke-kai-o-Mamala*, named after Mamala, a legendary Hawai'ian queen from the mists of Islander history. Mamala boasted supernatural powers. She could take the form of a beautiful woman, a gigantic lizard, or a great shark. Hawai'ian tales tell that Mamala hooked up with the shark-man Ouha, and they were a happy couple, drinking *awa* together and playing pebble games on the beach.

Mamala was also a supernatural surfer. She liked to paddle way outside and surf the big waves in Kou Bay. Her beauty—and her wave-riding ability—attracted Honoka'upu, a coconut grove chief who

All for the love of a beautiful surfing girl.

Surfing might be the Sport of Kings, but ladies like it, too. Traveling back in time to ancient Hawai'i and forward to 2002's *Blue Crush*, women have not always been riding the waves in the same numbers as men, but always with equal fervor.

The oldest surviving surfboard in Hawai'i's Bishop Museum is a small "floater" or *paipo* board that was the personal property of another, sixteenth-century Hawai'ian queen. The board was found in a burial cave at Ho'okena, and its story was told in the December 8, 1905, issue of the *Hawaiian Gazette*: "It is said that the oldest Kamaainas of Ho'okena have heard from their parents and grandparents that sometime in the reign of King Keawenuiaumi, about

> ## All things considered—maybe I was just a woman in love with a surfboard. It's as simple as that.
> — *Gidget in Frederick Kohner's* Gidget, 1957

250 or 300 years ago, a high chiefess named Kane-aumuna was then living at Ho'okena. Her principal amusement was *he'e holua* (coasting on a sled) and *he'enalu* (surfing)."

When Captain Cook came to the island of Owhyhee, he found men and women cavorting together in the surf, which didn't bother him much. But in his aftermath, such naked frolicking between the sexes bothered the missionaries very much indeed. In the nineteenth century, the invading religious zealots forbid the sport of *he'enalu*. And as the Hawai'ians died off by the tens of thousands, so did the sport of surfing.

By the nineteenth century's demise, women surfers were mostly the stuff of legend. Thomas Thrum wrote about surfing in the past tense in 1896's *Hawaiian Surf Riding*: "Native legends abound with the exploits of those who attained distinction among their fellows by their skill and daring in this sport, indulged in alike by both sexes; and frequently too—as in these days of intellectual development—the gentler sex carried off the highest honors."

It was a combination of modesty, morality, and the unbearable heaviness of hardwood that kept the majority of women out

Hawai'ian Surfer Girls, 1870s: "I watched the surf-swimmers for some time, charmed with the spectacle," wrote Charles Warren Stoddard in his 1873 *Summer Cruising in the South Seas*. His accompanying illustration of naked surfer girls left little doubt about what so "charmed" him. (Bishop Museum)

took a shine to the surfing demigoddess and stole her away from Ouha.

If you imagine a shark-man has a temper, you are correct. Ouha tried and failed to kill Honoka'upu, and the local women scorned his powers. Ouha cast off his human half and became a full shark—the great shark god of the coast between Waikiki and Koko Head.

of the water from the 1800s into the 1900s. There were few surfers in Hawai'i and of that minority an even smaller minority were women. One exception was Princess Kaiulaini who "was an expert surfrider around 1895 to 1900," recalls early-twentieth-century surfer Knute Cottrell: "She rode a long *olo* board made of *wili wili.*" And yet Kaiulani was the last of the legendary Hawai'ian women wave-riders of her day.

A new wave of surfing *wahine* arrived with the twentieth century—young women inspired by Jack London's writings, Alexander Hume Ford's promotion, and especially Duke Kahanamoku's charisma and fame.

When the homegrown *Hui Nalu* surfing club became official in 1911, two charter members were outstanding women surfers—Mildred "Ladybird" Turner and Josephine "Jo" Pratt. No less than Tom Blake in his 1935 book *Hawaiian Surfriders* recalls Pratt as "the best woman surfboard rider in the Islands." Blake also remembers Kahanamoku as the first modern tandem surfer. "Leslie Lemon was the first to stand on Duke's shoulders," he writes. "Miss Marion 'Baby' Dowsett and Beatrice Dowsett were the two girls who first rode with Duke, three on the same board...."

In winter 1914, Duke ventured to Australia, where he found good surf going to waste. He fashioned some surfboards from Australian sugar pine and gave exhibitions at Sydney's Freshwater Beach. Duke rode alone until the finale, when he hoisted a local girl, Isabel Letham, onto his shoulders. Miss Letham was already a hero for her swimming and bodysurfing, but after riding just four waves, she proclaimed surfing "the most thrilling sport of all."

Letham kept on surfing while Duke toured Australia, but when he returned, they rode together on separate boards in an exhibition that became legend. Isabel Letham was later inducted into the Australian Surfing Hall of Fame for her session with Duke—and her inspiration to future generations of Australian women surfers.

In California, Mary Ann Hawkins was also inspired by Duke's prowess. As a girl and then a teenager, Hawkins left a trench behind her as she swam to national records and championships. In 1934, Hawkins moved with her mother to Corona del Mar to be closer to the ocean so she could work on her endurance as an ocean swimmer. Here, she began surfing with the likes of Gene "Tarzan" Smith and

Lorrin "Whitey" Harrison. "Tarzan was the lifeguard down there at Corona del Mar," Hawkins remembers, "and in the course of my training and bodysurfing, he got to know me and started taking me tandem." Board shaper Joe Quigg remembers, "There were women who could get to their feet on a board that their boyfriend built for them. But, as far as just going out and being a surfer on their own, Mary Ann stands out in my mind. She was one of the best bodysurfers, man or woman. She could get across [waves] at Malibu bodysurfing that most people couldn't get across on a surfboard."

In 1941, Hawkins married Los Angeles surfer and board-builder Bud Morrissey. They had a daughter the next year, Kathy Morrissey, who remembers growing up on the sand: "I used to surf with Peter Lawford, Debbie Reynolds, and Robin Grigg. They were my babysitters on the beach while my mother was working in Hollywood." During the 1940s, there was demand in Tinseltown for talented water people in front of and behind the camera, and Mary Ann got regular work doing stunts.

By 1956, she was back in Hawai'i working on a movie—and renewing her love affair with the Waikiki surf. She headlined the water show at the Hilton Hawai'ian Village, sometimes joined by Esther Williams. She later founded a swimming school, teaching thousands of Hawai'ian visitors how to love the ocean.

When she passed away in 1992, her memorial at the Outrigger Canoe Club brought together hundreds of surfers. Mary Ann Hawkins could have gone through life with an Olympic laurel wreath around her head, but as the first great California waterwoman of the twentieth century, she chose instead a wreath of plumeria intertwined with seaweed.

Marilyn Monroe was a surfer after many a man's heart. Back in the 1940s, when she was still Norma Jeane Baker, she was just one of many young, beautiful starlets

Facing page, **Proto-Surfer Grrl, 1940s:** Synchronized swimming starlet Esther Williams styles as a surfer grrl for a Hollywood photo shoot in a time when navels were still a naughty no-no. (Surfing Heritage Foundation Archives)

Mary Ann Hawkins, 1939 and 1990: Inspired by Duke Kahanamoku, Mary Ann Hawkins became one of the first women surfers in California. Here she is in 1939 about to charge Hermosa Beach with a longboard; and in 1990, standing before one of the oldest surviving *alaia* boards, from 1933. (Photos © Doc Ball and Gary Lynch)

Aloha to
the surfriders
of the future

Mary Ann Hawkins-Medkiff

Right, **Pineapple Princess, 1950s:** Riding a wave into the 1950s, surfing sold pineapples with this Hawai'ian surf diva standing tall and proud. (Voyageur Press Archives)

Facing page, **Hawai'i and California Surfing Postcards, 1950s–1960s** (Voyageur Press Archives)

hanging around and having fun at Malibu, where she tandem-surfed with pioneering waterman Tommy Zahn. "She was in prime condition," Zahn remembers in Anthony Summers's book *Goddess: The Secret Lives of Marilyn Monroe.* "Tremendously fit. I used to take her surfing up at Malibu—tandem surfing, you know, two riders on the same surfboard. I'd take her later, in the dead of winter when it was cold, and it didn't faze her in the least; she'd lay in the cold water, waiting for the waves. She was very good in the water, very robust, so healthy, a really fine attitude towards life."

Marilyn and other women surfers *had* to be in fine shape as the heavy weight of the surfboards

held back many early female wave-riders. Most women surfers didn't have their own boards—and might have had trouble carrying them if they did. This was a time when surfing was a manly pursuit, because surfers were riding gargantuan Pacific System Homes redwood-balsa planks that were eleven feet long and weighed eighty to one hundred pounds. Or more. There were many men who couldn't handle these boards—and few women who could muscle them around on their own. "Most of the women who got into surfing then had a boyfriend in it, and they'd come down and eventually they'd say, 'Hey, let's get out in the water together,'" photographer John "Doc" Ball writes. "So, they'd have a tandem ride and finally started to get in the real deal."

Among Marilyn's beach crowd was Darrylin Zanuck, daughter of powerful studio head Darryl F. Zanuck. Darrylin liked to surf Malibu, but she too struggled with those monster boards. At some point, she stole Tommy Zahn away from Marilyn, and it was their surfing relationship that accidentally lead to the creation of the modern shortboard.

In summer 1947, Joe Quigg crafted what he called a "novice girl's board" for Darrylin. He trekked to five lumberyards searching for the lightest timber available, then fashioned a ten-foot two-inch redwood-balsa plank and sealed it with fiberglass and resin. Quigg made the board to satisfy Darrylin's need for a shorter, lighter, more-manageable ride that was easy for her to carry. It also had to fit in the back of her glamorous Chrysler Town and Country convertible.

Darrylin barely got a chance to ride her special board. On an August 1947 surfari to San Onofre, first Tommy Zahn took it for a test. Then Dave Rochlen went out and hotdogged it. And then Pete Peterson banked and swooped it, doing things atop waves that were impossible on their longer, heavier

Annette Don't Surf!

Hollywood's Mistreatment of Women Surfers

The very first major Hollywood motion picture about surfing was about a girl surfer—and then it all went downhill from there for the next three decades until the Hollywood image of the surfer girl was rescued by Lori Petty in *Point Break* and Kate Bosworth in *Blue Crush*.

Gidget told the tale of a teenage girl won over by the romance of the sea and the romance of romance. Gidget's teenage delirium motivated her to grab a board that was taller and heavier than her and made her cross that line in the sand separating the poser from the surfer.

Gidget surfed, and while she was maybe motivated more by her crush on Moondoggie than her love of the surf and sea, at least she did more than hold her man's towel, wringing her hands with worry as her beau risked his neck in the heavies.

After 1959, women were taken off the big-screen waves and left barefoot and worried on the beach. Screenwriter William Goldman once said "women are a problem in action films," and that proved a problem for Barbara Eden and Shelley Fabares, Annette Funicello, Nia Peeples, Patti D'Arbanville, Maylin Pultar, Catherine Zeta-Jones, and so many other surf-movie females in the next three decades of surfing movies.

Marilyn Monroe boasted more than a few roles as clueless, breathless, boy-crazy blondes, yet *Gidget* would have been a very different movie if Marilyn had played the role instead of Sandra Dee. At least Marilyn could have done her own stunts—she spent many a day wave-riding at Malibu—and it would have been easier to believe her as a naïve, love-struck bombshell causing so much havoc among the surf bums.

At least Gidget surfed in *Gidget*, and while she may have done so to get a guy more than for the pure surf stoke of sitting on top of the world, her image was better for women than how they were portrayed in the waxploitation that came with the surfing sensation that swept the nation in the 1960s.

The beach babes in 1964's *Ride the Wild Surf*—blond Barbie bombshell Shelley Fabares, perky and spunky Barbara Eden, and smoldering brunette Susan Hart—don't surf, and the most empowering moment for any of them is when Eden turns out to be a martial arts expert who kicks the *okole* of Peter Brown's character, Chase Colton. Women are accessories for the most part in *Ride the Wild Surf*, and their roles provoke howls from even the least feminist among us.

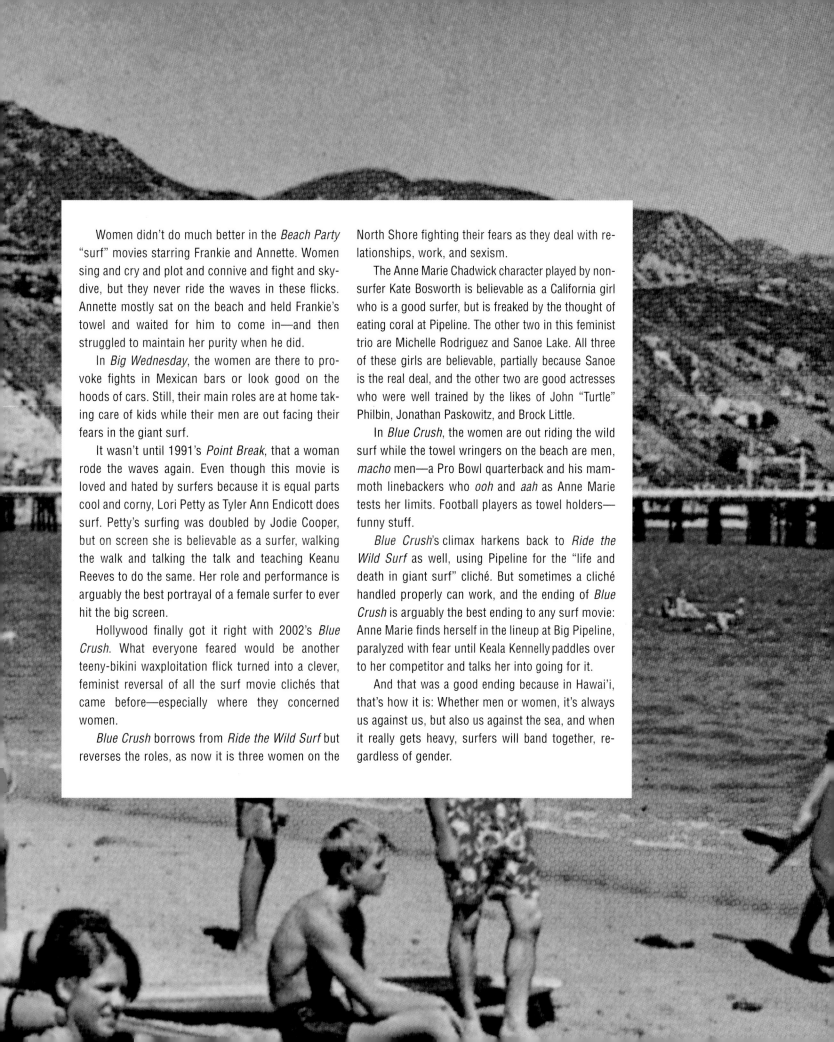

Women didn't do much better in the *Beach Party* "surf" movies starring Frankie and Annette. Women sing and cry and plot and connive and fight and sky-dive, but they never ride the waves in these flicks. Annette mostly sat on the beach and held Frankie's towel and waited for him to come in—and then struggled to maintain her purity when he did.

In *Big Wednesday*, the women are there to provoke fights in Mexican bars or look good on the hoods of cars. Still, their main roles are at home taking care of kids while their men are out facing their fears in the giant surf.

It wasn't until 1991's *Point Break*, that a woman rode the waves again. Even though this movie is loved and hated by surfers because it is equal parts cool and corny, Lori Petty as Tyler Ann Endicott does surf. Petty's surfing was doubled by Jodie Cooper, but on screen she is believable as a surfer, walking the walk and talking the talk and teaching Keanu Reeves to do the same. Her role and performance is arguably the best portrayal of a female surfer to ever hit the big screen.

Hollywood finally got it right with 2002's *Blue Crush*. What everyone feared would be another teeny-bikini waxploitation flick turned into a clever, feminist reversal of all the surf movie clichés that came before—especially where they concerned women.

Blue Crush borrows from *Ride the Wild Surf* but reverses the roles, as now it is three women on the North Shore fighting their fears as they deal with relationships, work, and sexism.

The Anne Marie Chadwick character played by non-surfer Kate Bosworth is believable as a California girl who is a good surfer, but is freaked by the thought of eating coral at Pipeline. The other two in this feminist trio are Michelle Rodriguez and Sanoe Lake. All three of these girls are believable, partially because Sanoe is the real deal, and the other two are good actresses who were well trained by the likes of John "Turtle" Philbin, Jonathan Paskowitz, and Brock Little.

In *Blue Crush*, the women are out riding the wild surf while the towel wringers on the beach are men, *macho* men—a Pro Bowl quarterback and his mammoth linebackers who *ooh* and *aah* as Anne Marie tests her limits. Football players as towel holders—funny stuff.

Blue Crush's climax harkens back to *Ride the Wild Surf* as well, using Pipeline for the "life and death in giant surf" cliché. But sometimes a cliché handled properly can work, and the ending of *Blue Crush* is arguably the best ending to any surf movie: Anne Marie finds herself in the lineup at Big Pipeline, paralyzed with fear until Keala Kennelly paddles over to her competitor and talks her into going for it.

And that was a good ending because in Hawai'i, that's how it is: Whether men or women, it's always us against us, but also us against the sea, and when it really gets heavy, surfers will band together, regardless of gender.

The Calhoun Clan, 1960s: The grrls get ready to charge Makaha: Marge is in the center, surrounded by daughters Robin and Candy. One of the coolest things a woman can do is surf. The second coolest is to produce hot daughters who also surf. (Photo © LeRoy Grannis)

boards. The new plank was voted the Loosest Board on the West Coast.

Quigg christened his creation the Easy Rider, but history knows it as the Darrilyn Board. It was the first Malibu board, it was inspired by a surfing girl, and it changed the world.

In many ways, Darrylin Zanuck was the original Gidget. As Quigg remembers, "She was at Malibu, really the first girl to buy a surfboard and buy a convertible and stick the surfboard in the back and drive up to Malibu and drive up and down the coast and learn to surf. She was the first Malibu girl to really do it."

By the 1950s, there still weren't a lot of women surfing because there just weren't all that many surfers. In California, surfers who passed each other on the road would wave, stop, and chat; they were members of an elite tribe, sharing a secret thrill.

Among the women surfers in the 1950s, Marge Calhoun stood tall. You can see her in Bud Browne's surf movies like *Gun Ho!* and *Locked In*; Marge appears here and there, and then gets a moment of glory, standing next to Peter Cole holding onto the women's Makaha Championship plaque. She had been surfing only three years and went to Hawai'i on a lark with friend Eve Fletcher. They had a Thelma and Louise thing going: Two women on the run from conventional lives, sleeping oceanside in a dilapidated panel van, and just surfing, surfing, surfing. They went places few surfers dared go—and almost no women.

Born in 1926 in Hollywood, Calhoun was one of those lucky few to grow up in Los Angeles when it was one of the best places in the world: "My parents would drive from Hollywood to the beach every weekend, even in winter," Calhoun said. "As soon as they showed me the ocean, I was a goner." Married in 1946, she was soon tending a home with two infants. Then, when she was thirty, she first saw someone on a surfboard, and her life was forever altered. "Once I saw that, I had to do it," she states simply.

Calhoun benefited from the Darrylin Board revolution. Her first ride was also crafted by Quigg—ten-feet two-inches long and made of balsa, weighing in at just twenty-seven pounds. When she got her hands on the board she went "berserk," as she put it. She took it down to Malibu where she found another surfer girl on the beach—Darrylin herself. "She was

As a female I've ridden the biggest wave in the world, which stood at about 30 feet, which is about 55 feet high, so for a little 5-foot person like me, going down a wave that big was an extraordinary amount of adrenaline. God, it was like, 'Ohhhhhh! Do it again! Let's do it again!' I mean, it was incredible. Oh, I'm an adrenaline junkie, yeah, definitely.

— *Layne Beachley, 2003*

this tiny little blond girl, but Darrylin was very nice. She showed me which way to point the board and when to take off and, man, I was gone," Calhoun says. "I had never fallen in love with a sport like I had with surfing."

Marge Calhoun became part of the stellar Santa Monica crew of the 1950s that included Peter Cole, Ricky Grigg, and Buzzy Trent. These men all helped Calhoun with her surfing, and in three years she felt she was ready to take it all to Hawai'i and

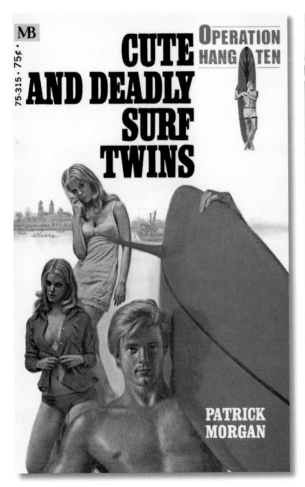

Surf " Literature," 1960s–1970s (Voyageur Press Archives)

Previous pages, **Layne Beachley:** Australian Layne Beachley took charge of women's pro surfing from the 1990s into the twenty-first century—and boldly went places on waves where no woman had gone before. (Photo © Jeff Divine)

Below, **Rochelle Ballard:** Rochelle Ballard pushed the limits of where women could go in big, gnarly Hawaiian surf. She took her lickings and kept on ticking. (Photo © Jeff Divine)

challenge the heavies. "Eve Fletcher was going for a one-month vacation, and I told Buzzy Trent I wanted to go with her. He told me I had to surf Ventura Overhead because that wave casts out like Hawai'i, and he also told me to surf Windansea because it breaks like an Island wave. Buzzy was a great mentor and taught me a lot in Hawai'i and California, although he would try to scare me at times. He was a tough guy with an iron body, but he had a great sense of humor."

Marge and Eve took what was known as the "rubber band shot" to the far-off Hawai'ian Islands—a grueling, twelve-hour flight out of Burbank operated by an outfit nicknamed "Wing and a Prayer Airlines." They arrived in a Hawai'i that was still small, quiet, romantic. Each got a lei around her neck, a hula greeting, and then went searching for surf. "We would spend days at Makaha with only a couple

of people in the water," Marge recalls. "At first, Eve and I lived in Waikiki, but there wasn't much surf there so we rented Peter Cole's panel truck for $80 a month. Eve and I lived in that truck and followed every swell. We would sleep wherever we wanted and eat at all the hole in the wall places and it was just fantastic. I consider myself very lucky to have experienced Hawai'i at that time."

As everybody went surfing across the USA in the 1960s, a young athlete from Southern California was in the right place at the right time to become the first female surf star. Joyce Hoffman was the stepdaughter of surfing fanatic Walter Hoffman, scion of the prosperous LA family who owned Hoffman Fabrics and helped popularize the aloha shirt around the globe. Under Walter's influence, Joyce developed a keen interest in surfing. She learned

at Poche and fondly remembers surfing Killer Dana with Walter before Orange County paved paradise and put up a yacht harbor. Joyce entered her first contest at Doheny when she was thirteen. She won, and en route to victory discovered she had an intense appetite for competition. As Matt Warshaw described her in his *Encyclopedia of Surfing*: "She later acknowledged that 'soulfulness' wasn't part of her surfing experience, and that her satisfaction came from being 'the best prepared,' which lead to winning contests."

Joyce began competing all around San Clemente, then California, then the world. Her connections combined with her ability shot her up the ladder fast. She became part of the Hobie Surf Team, won the Makaha International in 1964 and 1966, the U.S. Championships in 1965, 1966, and 1967, and the Laguna Masters in 1965 and 1967. When she won the 1965 World Championships in Peru, the globe took notice. *Sports Illustrated* profiled her under the title, "An Odd Sport, and an Unusual Champion."

The 1966 World Championships in San Diego changed the world of surfing when Nat Young cut high-performance turns on a short board to defeat David Nuuhiwa riding the nose on a traditional long board. Joyce won the women's division, launching her ever higher—the cover of *Life* magazine and features in *Seventeen*, *Look*, *Teen*, and *Vogue*. She was a competitive dynamo when everyone across the United States was wishing they had an ocean.

Joyce was defeated in 1968 by a tinsel-toothed fifteen-year-old from La Jolla named Margo Godfrey. Hoffman once told *Sports Illustrated*, "If I didn't think I was considered the best, I would quit," and she was as good as her word. She competed for another three years, but her results began to descend—except for winning the 1971 U.S. Championships. Then she dropped out. A decade later, she admitted to *Longboard Magazine* that her ambition to be number one was "horrible . . . the bane of my life."

Joyce Hoffman was one of many surfers who didn't survive the transition from the nose-riding longboards to the high-performance shortboard style. Now, Margo Godfrey took over.

As a child, Margo was skinny and awkward on land, but in the water she caught fire, beating all the boys to win the twelve-and-under division of the Windansea Surf Club *menehune* contest. Her drive and talent attracted the attention of surfers Corky Carroll and Mike Doyle, who coached her into the

final of the 1965 Makaha Championships and second at the U.S. Championships.

As a ninth-grader in 1968, Margo took the world by storm, winning three of the seven AAAA-rated events on the California amateur circuit and placing first in the Makaha Championships and the East Coast Surfing Championships. The next year, she became the first woman to earn a competitive paycheck, taking home $150 for winning the Santa Cruz Pro-Am.

By 1975, it was finally time for women to form a league of their own. On March 8—International Women's Day—Jericho Poppler and Mary Setter-

> I think if you fall in love with something, like surfing, and you find that's what you want to do, then go for your dreams. For me, I went for it, and luckily I met the right people and fell in love with the wrong people, and just lived my life the way I wanted to. I experienced the best times of my life through surfing. I would advise anybody to just follow your dreams.
> — *Lisa Andersen, 2004*

holm launched the Women's International Surfing Association (WISA). "Surfing does not demand aggressive strength," Setterholm explained. "Waves treat everyone equally; men and women are on the same terms as far as nature is concerned." Now married, Margo Oberg was living on Kaua'i and running her own surfing school, but she was lured back into competing by a lucrative performance contract from Lightning Bolt. WISA ran amateur events at San Onofre, Huntington, and Newport Beach capped by the $8,000 Hang Ten Women's International Professional Surfing Championships at Malibu. Some men refused to clear the water, forcing the women to surf around them, but Margo took home the $1,500 first prize.

WISA had a short run usurped by the 1976 formation of International Professional Surfers (IPS), which sparked a women's division in 1977. Margo quickly won two of the four women's events and became the 1977 IPS women's champion. She lost the 1978 pro title to another intense

competitor, Lynn Boyer, by the slimmest margin in history, but won the championship again in 1980 and 1981 just as a new generation was taking over.

Margo Godfrey-Oberg had a great competitive run in surfing. But perhaps her greatest accomplishment was validating the idea that women could not only ride big surf, but do it with style.

Lisa Andersen was the surfing girl for the 1990s. She learned from all the women who had come before—Kim Mearig, Debbie Beacham, Frieda Zamba, Jodie Cooper, Pam Burridge, Wendy Botha, Pauline Menczer. Andersen learned, then turned herself into perhaps the biggest woman surf star of all time.

At fifteen, Lisa Andersen saved up summer-job money to buy a one-way plane ticket from Florida to California, leaving a note for her mom saying she was going to become a surfing champion. "I didn't even know if such a thing really existed," Andersen explained later. "But I went to California on my own to find out."

And then, by God, she did exactly that. California for Lisa Andersen was Huntington Beach, where she worked as a waitress and slept on the beach. At seventeen, she won the girl's division of the U.S. Championships, took third in the World Championships, and then turned pro. As Matt Warshaw aptly summed up her style, "Andersen often said she wanted to 'surf like a guy,' and to a degree she did. She directed and focused her speed better than any woman before her and was therefore able to put maximum power into her turns; she also maintained a balletic line through her head and body."

Andersen ran away from home, yet she did not run away with the world surfing title—at least not right away. Up until 1992, she struggled with self-doubt and inconsistent performances, her head getting in the way of her talent. And then motherhood turned it all around. In 1993, she married Brazilian surfing judge Renato Hickel. She competed while pregnant, and missed only the last event of the year. Five weeks after giving birth she made a final and went on to win three of eleven events in 1994 to take her first world title. As she explained afterward: "[Childbirth] was the worst, most painful thing ever. Everything's easy after having a baby."

Andersen was the first woman featured on the cover of *Surfer* magazine, her image was accompanied by the teasing tagline, "Lisa Andersen Surfs Better Than You." And, man or woman, it was most likely true.

In 1992, she signed a lucrative contract with Roxy, an offshoot of Quiksilver that was mining a huge market in the fast-growing world of women's surfing. Three years later, Andersen designed a new kind of women's surf trunk that stressed function over form, and it took off. Through the 1990s, she was women's surfing's "It Girl"—blond, fit, tan, pretty. She was hot—and a hot surfer. She was also a mom who challenged the men—the complete surfer for women. As former world champion Pauline Menczer complained in 1996: "Women's surfing right now is Lisa Andersen. The rest of us might as well not even be here."

Andersen won the women's world title again in 1995, 1996, and 1997. Then it all came to a painful halt when her back failed on her and she missed the second half of the 1998 season. She was back in 2000, but finished fifth, then skipped the tour in 2001 to give birth to a son. She is now mostly retired from competitive surfing, but keeps running as a mother.

It is not known if Lisa Andersen's own mother kept that original runaway note, but the teenage prophecy about the women's world surfing title was a fairy tale come true.

At the dawn of the twentieth century, women surfers were proving they had the guts and skill on a level approaching the men. At places like Pipeline and Backdoor Pipeline, Sunset Beach and Todos Santos, Layne Beachley, Rochelle Ballard, and Keala Kennelly were pushing the limits of surfing. And it was that reality that lead to the fiction of *Blue Crush*.

This 2002 movie did for women's surfing what 1959's *Gidget* did for surfing in general. *Blue Crush* was produced by Hollywood super-mogul Brian

Facing page, **Jodie Cooper:** Australia's Jodie Cooper stunt-doubled the surfing for Lori Petty in *Point Break*. She had a great run as a pro surfer through the 1980s and into the 1990s, excelling in Hawai'ian surf and becoming almost unbeatable on the North Shore. (Photo © Jeff Divine)

Grazer, and did a better-than-expected job of telling the tale of Anne Marie Chadwick, a young blond surfer girl who faces her fears at the Pipe Masters. *Blue Crush* cost thirty million dollars to make and was helped along by a massive advertising campaign to gross fourteen million dollars on the opening weekend, continuing on to earn a nice dollar. The movie propelled Kate Bosworth to stardom, and best yet, inspired millions of women to catch a wave.

Guy surfers are awestruck by her. On the beach, the most amazing thing happens. You see all these guys hanging around, staring at her. They're afraid to come up and talk. She's really beautiful and she really loves to surf. And so when she paddles out, they're looking at her with a funny variety of feelings—appreciation mixed with respect. She's the ultimate surf chick.

— Surfer *editor Steve Hawk on Lisa Andersen, 1996*

Facing page, **Lisa Andersen:** Florida native Lisa Andersen ran away from home as a teenager, determined to become the women's surfing champion—if there was such a thing. There was, and she achieved her dream. (Photo © Jeff Divine)

After *Blue Crush*, there were many more female surfers in the water, buying clothes, and going to surf schools. By 2002, the female surfwear line Roxy had been in business for just over ten years; propelled by the charisma and talent of Lisa Andersen, Roxy sales skyrocketed from $1.1 million in 1990 into the hundreds of millions by 2002. By 2005, women surfers had several magazines—*Surfer Girl, Foam, Surf Life for Women.* And there were several surf camps set up especially for women, including Surf Diva in San Diego County and Las Olas in Mexico.

Now when you look out at the ocean in California or Hawai'i, Australia or Indonesia, there are women surfers everywhere, on longboards, shortboards, in the tube and off the lip, girls in the curl or hanging ten on a wall. And in all of them, whether they know it or not, you can find the legacy of Joyce Hoffman, Margo Godfrey-Oberg, Marge Calhoun, Mary Ann Hawkins, and the other pioneering women of surfing, traveling back in time to the Hawai'ian surf-friding queens of legend.

8

Monster

Surfing's Twenty-First-Century Man • The 1990s to Today

Left, **Laird Hamilton Rides Peahi:** Laird Hamilton's wife Gabby told *People* magazine her husband was "beautiful when he's in motion," and she wasn't just blowing smoke. Laird is a big man who manages to look right at home in the tremendous power of the wave called Jaws off the island of Maui. (Photo © Ron Dahlquist)

Above, **Big-Wave Riding, 1930s** (Voyageur Press Archives)

Dick Brewer 1970s Big Gun: This big-gun surfboard is a replica of a big-wave board made for Hawai'ian surfer Reno Abelliro. (© Malcolm Wilson) SPECIFICATIONS: 10' 10" LONG; 20" WIDE; 3½" THICK; 25 POUNDS

People had ridden big waves before. Way back in 1957, Greg Noll, Mickey Muñoz, and gang overcame the *kapu* and surfed Waimea Bay for the first time. Noll became the crowned king amongst pioneering big-wave riders, braving waves around Hawai'i of which others could only dream,

passes, a wave that is as impossibly powerful as Jaws, but in a different way.

In the summer, big swells generated deep in the Antarctic Ocean are sent across the Pacific with great energy. Even after they are slowed by the gradual rise of the continental shelf, these

> It's less about the one big wave than about your performances. It's about your body of work. It's about art.
> — *Laird Hamilton,* Outside *magazine, 2004*

such as his mind-blowing cruise at Makaha during the Great Swell of 1969. Sam Hawk, riding a giant at Oahu's Pipeline on "Huge Monday" in 1972, was duly immortalized in *Five Summer Stories.*

Fast Forward to Hawai'i and 1985, where Mark Foo, James Jones, and Ken Bradshaw confronted what Foo shakily termed "the Unridden Realm" in the form of a giant closeout wave at Waimea. Foo tried to take off, wiped out, and nearly drowned. All three were rescued by a helicopter.

That same winter, Alec Cooke, who called himself Ace Cool, brought his own helicopter. He and his big gun surfboard were lowered into the water at an Outer Reef to catch a big wave before he was mowed down by an even bigger wave. He too had to be rescued by chopper.

In 1998, Taylor Knox topped them all at Killers on Baja's Isla Todos Santos, during the K2 Challenge, offering a "biggest wave" bounty of a cool fifty thousand dollars. The old measure of halving a wave's height suddenly seemed ludicrous as Knox's wave towered sixty-two actual feet.

Soon there were more big waves discovered and big rides made at Maui's Jaws, Maverick's in northern California's Half Moon Bay, Sunset Beach's Backyards, Cortes Bank far off San Diego, and others around the globe. The fear factor had been taken over the top.

And then along came Laird Hamilton.

Tahiti's Teahupoo is the Tyrannosaurus Rex of waves. It's big, it's mean, and it would eat you alive for dinner with nothing but a burp to signal your passing.

Teahupoo is what is known as a "reef pass" wave, meaning it's formed by a break in a coral reef caused by fresh water flowing from the tops of mountains and out to sea. Teahupoo is the mother of all reef

swells can hit the California coast—and as far north as Alaska—with significant muscle. On the south side of the equator, these swells are at full strength, rolling through the ocean, minding their own business when all of a sudden they trip over the reef at Teahupoo, letting out a tremendous roar as they expend all that surprised, angry, ferocious energy at once.

In a word, Teahupoo is nuts.

This is the wave Laird Hamilton went to challenge. Surfing Teahupoo in 2001, he rode a line finer than any surfer had ever done before, getting towed and whipped into a monster slab of water by buddy Darrick Doerner, then using his beautiful motion and instinctive ocean knowledge to carve an incredibly thin path between death and glory.

Because if Laird had not made that wave, he would have died.

Laird Hamilton had made *People* magazine's "50 Most Beautiful People in the World" list in 1996. It was one of his more dubious distinctions, but a pat on his broad back nonetheless—and few other surfers had gained such mainstream visibility before. At that time, Laird was hanging with Gabrielle Reece, an Amazonian death-spiker who had gone from modeling to pro volleyball to acting. Laird and Gabby—all twelve and a half feet of them—were pitching woo at the time, and when *People* asked her what she

thought about Laird, she intoned just about the nicest thing any surfer's girlfriend has ever said about a surfer, or indeed, any woman has ever said about a man.

"He's beautiful when he's in motion."

She was right. Laird Hamilton *is* beautiful when he's in motion, and his beauty is unique, because there never has been another surfer who can ride big waves like Laird rides them. At forty years of age, standing six foot three inches, and tipping the Toledos at 215 pounds, Laird is twelve years older, half a foot taller, and 50 pounds heavier than the typical super middleweight pro surfer. Still, Laird looks like Mother Nature's prodigal son. He's impossibly fit, impossibly tall, impossibly blond, and impossibly tan; he's almost a caricature of a surfer, like something straight from the pulp pages of a Marvel comic.

Big Gun: One of the most famous surfing photos of all time: Greg Noll with his elephant gun times the sets at the Banzai Pipeline and prepares to paddle out. (Photo © John Severson/surferart.com)

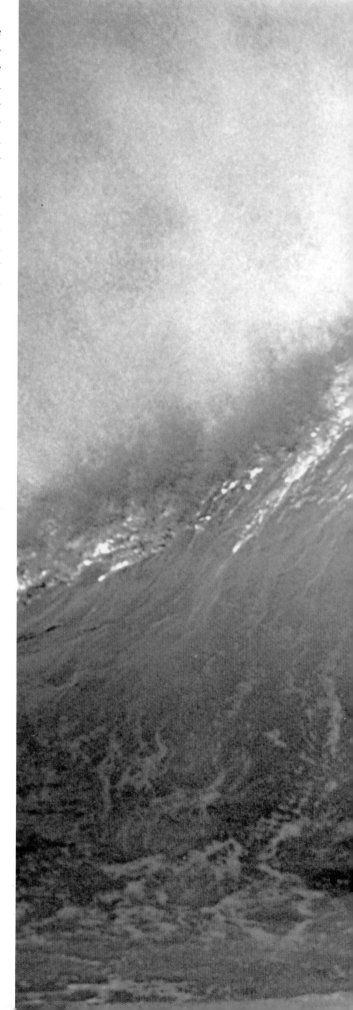

That superhero status also applies when he surfs, because when Laird dances around in thirty-foot surf at Jaws, toying with waves that few people want anything to do with . . . it just doesn't look real. If Laird in person is like the Jessica Rabbit of surfing, then Laird in motion looks like a special effect—somewhere between a stoned-out fantasy animation from a 1970s surf movie and a state-of-the-art modern Hollywood computer-aided stunt spectacular.

And even when you do believe that a man can actually ride waves that big and that well, you still can't believe the speed. More than a few people watching Laird surfing Jaws on the big screen in Stacy Peralta's stellar *Riding Giants* wondered why those helicopter shots—which do real justice to the

Surfing's a trip—you better have your bags packed.
— *Surfer Herbie Fletcher, quoted in Allan C. Weisbecker's* In Search of Captain Zero, *2001*

Falling Giants, 1950s:
As World Champion Martin Potter once said, "If you can't have a spectacular ride, have a spectacular wipeout. It's good for the sport." Good for the sport, good for your head, good for your mind—maybe even good for your back, if you land right. This unknown surfer is getting launched by the infamous Makaha shorebreak, sometime in the Good Old Fifties. (Photo © LeRoy Grannis)

size and speed of the waves—were sped up. And when they realize that Laird really is going as fast as forty miles an hour on those waves, they have the same reaction that Captain Cook did when he saw the Polynesians in their canoes and surfboards, being borne along so smoothly and swiftly by the sea: "It is scarcely to be credited."

Here in the twenty-first century, Laird stands alone. He is to big-wave surfing what Shaq is to playing center, Tiger Woods to golfing, Lance Armstrong to bike racing, and Barry Bonds to hitting home runs. There have been a lot of waves ridden by a lot of fine surfers before him, but no one else can boast such a combination of brawn and brains, innovation and intensity. Laird may or may not be the greatest surfer of all time, but there is no doubt he is the greatest big-wave surfer.

Get to know Laird Hamilton's story and it's easy to get all mysto about things. What supernatural power transplanted this small child to Hawai'i and placed him in the path of ace surfer Billy Hamilton, and what charm did he work on Billy to uncover a dad that gave him a classical education in all facets of surfing from small waves to big? Neither Greek mythology nor modern American superhero legendry have anything on this guy.

Laird Zerfas came into the world in 1964 to a beautiful mother, Joan, and a father who must have

been built with a physique like a Roman god. Laird was born in the water in an experimental reduced-gravity bathysphere at San Francisco's University of California Medical Center. Laird's biological father left the family to join the merchant marines when Laird was five months old, leaving mother and son adrift.

Providence took four-year-old Laird to Hawai'i, then guided him toward Billy Hamilton. Laird and

> There has been much hoopla and controversy surrounding the question of who has ridden the largest wave ever. The answer? Nobody. Several men hold the record and have successfully made truly huge waves, the type you could safely call 30 or 35 feet. Now that I have seen even larger waves firsthand, I do not believe it is possible to ride them. There have only been rare times when such waves, the ones above all the rest, have even been seen, let alone attempted. Those waves remain in another realm . . . the Unridden Realm.
>
> — *Mark Foo, "Occurrence at Waimea Bay," 1985*

Previous pages, **Maui Waves:** Surfing at Maui remains a ride back in time to the source. (Photo © Jeff Divine)

his mother were on a rare vacation, but he was in truth seeking something more: "After my dad left my mom and before I could even remember, I was in search of a masculine figure in my life," Laird says in *Riding Giants.* "My mom needed a husband, but I needed a *dad.*"

And there stood Billy Hamilton: "Here's this little kid playing around in the ocean, so I dove in," Hamilton remembers. "I said, 'What's your name?'

"'My name's Laird.'

"I said, 'What're you doing?'

"'Bodysurfing. You wanna bodysurf?'

"I said, 'Sure. Why don't you hang onto my neck? We'll bodysurf.'

"It was love at first sight with him and I . . . When we finished he grabbed my hand. He says, 'I want you to come and meet my mom.'"

With Hamilton and Joan hooked up via this minuscule Cupid, Laird grew up on Oahu. Banzai Pipeline was his backyard, and he was constantly waiting at the feet of two or three generations of great

Hawai'ian surfers, from Jose Angel to Eddie Aikau to Gerry Lopez.

Laird was five years old when the legendary Giant Swell of December 1969 ransacked Oahu's North Shore, driving many residents from their homes as unbelievable waves from a Pacific "Perfect Storm" lifted houses off their foundations and boats from the harbor, scattering them far inland. That '69 Swell closed out the North Shore, driving Greg Noll and a small group of valiant men around the bend to Makaha to challenge the largest waves ever encountered—and live to talk about it. The Swell was truly the end of an era. At the time, Noll was a bit like Odysseus. He saw the writing on the wall, witnessed younger men with shorter boards and different ideas, so he picked up his oar and began walking inland. Laird remembers the days and the changes: "I was young and impressionable in 1969," he says in *Riding Giants,* "so I understood the volume of what was possible. I understood there was stuff out there that hadn't been tapped and that the ocean was capable of producing places and things that no one had really done."

Billy Hamilton was one of that next generation of Hawai'ian surfers—smaller and more graceful, intent not just on lion-taming the Hawai'ian waves but in performing atop them. Billy was one of the better shapers around the North Shore, making boards of all kinds for some of the Old School surfers of the 1950s and 1960s, and some of the New School surfers of the 1970s. Laird grew up at the ankles, then the waists, of these guys. "I grew up with *men,*" Laird told *The Men's Journal.* "I was a kid surfing with hardcore guys, and they're dead serious. I screamed, yelled, just to make people conscious of me. They'd be like, 'Get out of my way, punk!' You got to be competitive with the men! Even my dad told me, 'When you can ride behind me, then I'll stop taking your waves.'"

Two years after the '69 Swell changed the zeitgeist of big-wave surfing, Laird began to challenge and prove himself any way he could. Too young and too small to paddle out on a big day, Laird showed that he loved the drop when he jumped off a forty-foot waterfall. "That was in me," he says. "That was my personality. A proving-yourself thing, too. Trying to outdo your dad."

Billy Hamilton was one of many surfers who led

an idyllic North Shore life through the 1970s, but grew sour at the ever-increasing hype and competition that encroached on the area. He moved his family to another island, looking to continue the old dream. By his teens, Laird was living on Kaua'i's North Shore, attending Kapaa High School. If you think he had a peaceful island upbringing, you'd be wrong. Kapaa was the third most violent school in the United States, dominated by massive Hawai'ian and Portuguese youths—and skinny, blond-haired Laird was at the bottom of the food chain: "Every day it was confrontations and fights," Laird remembers. "*Every* day."

These weren't just your typical teenage bullies; this was a race war, and Laird symbolized Archenemy No. 1. "Being a blond Caucasian, I kind of represented the stereotypical person that destroyed the culture of Hawai'i," he remembers. "A lot of people hated me, wanted to fight with me, just because of my skin color." As his future wife, Gabby Reece, explains, "He wanted to be Hawai'ian. He

used to dream of wishing he had brown skin, to be Hawai'ian because for him, that is what was beautiful and strong, because that is what was around him. Couldn't get girlfriends. Didn't have a lot of friends. What did he do? He spent and put all that energy into the water."

Laird was out of high school by sixteen, working as a mason, carpenter, and plumber before moving to California and finding a part-time stint as a model. In 1983, he was "discovered" by a photographer for Italian *Vogue*, leading to a photo shoot with Brooke Shields.

By the mid-1980s, Laird was back on more familiar territory on Oahu's North Shore, now determined to make a name for himself in his childhood haunts. At the time, competitive surfing was pretty much the only avenue available to a talented surfer, but Laird was too big to compete against the increasingly smaller pro surfers riding small surf, and he really didn't like competition, anyway. He had seen his father struggle with judges and he wanted to avoid

Riding Giants into the Big Time

Stacy Peralta on Making the Great Modern Surf Film

R*iding Giants* is Stacy Peralta's second big-screen documentary, a mature sibling to his skateboarding flick *Dogtown and Z-Boyz*. Peralta's first attempt won awards at the 2001 Sundance Film Festival, had a successful theatrical release, and enjoyed a healthy DVD run. *Dogtown* was made for pennies but earned a nice dollar, which gave Peralta the leverage to procure seven-figure financing for his documentary on the origins and pioneers of big-wave surfing.

Riding Giants is the best-crafted big-screen surf movie since *The Endless Summer*. Written by Peralta and Sam George, directed by Peralta, and edited by ace Englishman Paul Crowder, it divides big-wave surfing into three eras and focuses on a pioneer from each of those eras: Act One stars Greg Noll as surfing makes the pilgrimage from California back to Hawai'i and that first day at Makaha.

Act Two stars Jeff Clark, who surfed Maverick's all alone for more than fifteen years, bringing big-wave surfing back to California and the new Golgotha off Pillar Point Harbor. Where Act One is bright and bubbly, Act Two is dark and somber, because Maverick's is dark and somber—a frightening wave that proved deadly to Mark Foo.

Laird Hamilton is the star of Act Three, introducing the era of tow-in surfing into giant waves: Men using machines to boldly step into the Unridden Realm. The surfing footage of Jaws and Teahupoo, shown large on a big screen surrounded by thunderous sound effects, is knuckle-busting even to the most jaded observer.

Riding Giants is a triumph. Peralta has emerged as the leading auteur of what some would call Action Sports and others call X Sports. His work is thoroughly modern but grounded in the four-wall surf movies of the 1970s and the surf and skateboard video revolution of the 1980s—which he helped to establish.

Peralta is all about embracing new technology and new tricks. While *Riding Giants* is grounded in the flow of 1970s surf movies and the fury of 1980s skate videos, this documentary is also state of the art in cinematography, special effects, and sound. The documentary makes equal use of the best still photography and video and film cinematography. *Riding Giants* has surfing filmed from every imaginable angle; Peralta even used a Rotoscope 3D effect to give size and depth to static, familiar still photos. Working with an AVID Media Composer at Big Time Studios in Santa Monica, Paul Crowder alchemized thousands of hours of interviews and action with hundreds of still photos into an intense ninety-five minutes.

Riding Giants got off to a Cinderella start at the 2004 Sundance Film Festival, as it bubbled to the top of more than five thousand entries to be chosen as the premiere movie for the whole deal, the first time a documentary—let alone a surfing flick—has been awarded such an honor. *Riding Giants* rocked the house, received thunderous ovations louder than a Waimea closeout, and sent deal memos and big-dollar offers zinging into the stratosphere.

Here's what Stacy Peralta had to say about riding giants into the big time.

Act One is all about the transition from California to Hawai'i—Makaha, and then Greg Noll leading the Happy Few to Waimea Bay.

Greg Noll stole the show. You know the part of the film where Greg Noll talks about how stupid those '60s films were? The Sundance audiences erupted.

That gets the biggest laugh?

The two biggest laughs in the film. The place erupts. Every time.

You say Greg's comments got the biggest laugh. What else gets the biggest reaction? Noll said there were times when you could hear a pin drop and other times when you couldn't have heard a nuclear bomb.

This is one of the strangest things and one of the most amazing things I have ever seen. When Laird makes that wave at Teahupoo? The crowd erupted in applause as if you were watching Rocky knock out Apollo. That happened the first time, and Sam George, Paul Crowder, and I thought, 'Oh my God, that was amazing, but that was a fluke.' But it happened at every screening after that.

Did it go silent for Foo?

Absolutely. That was the pin drop. Absolutely dead calm.

Act Two is somber. Your movie goes high and low, loud and quiet.

Well the ocean is emotional. Surfers are emotional. Act Three starts with Laird and Billy Hamilton and their story about how they adopted each other as father and son. You can just hear people's hearts beating. You can hear women going "Ahhhhhh!"

So here is a dumb, high-school-level question: Do you consider yourself a skateboarder or a surfer first and foremost?

Well, I was a skateboarder first, but I would say I love them equally. I rode a box-cart-scooter when I was about 3 or 4, then moved up to a skateboard at approximately age 6. I can still remember the feeling of gliding down the sidewalk. I was arrested by the feeling. I needed to do it daily. The first place I surfed was Toes, a left that broke in Ballona Creek just south of Marina Del Rey—a really weird yet unique wave. From there I began surfing Santa Monica—Bay Street to be exact. I got kicked out of POP with Nathan Pratt when we were 14 years old. Our lives were threatened by the leading Mafioso-surfer. I later surfed the T's which broke on the north side of POP as opposed to the Cove which broke on the south side. I'm goofy-foot so I preferred the T's.

What spurred you to do a surfing film?

The success of *DT* provided some form of caché to get me in doors that previously I was unable to get into. As well, I was deeply interested in doing a surf doc as I felt I'd never seen one done that had any balls or provided any context as to why surfing is so magical. Unfortunately and generally, surfers can be a fairly inarticulate bunch and have difficulty in describing why surfing is so special. They all know it; they just don't necessarily know how to communicate it. I wanted to try to do that.

Well you accomplished it. The interviews are as articulate as the action is active. You did a good job of prying eloquence and sincerity out of a bunch of surfers.

When Dave Kalama talks about getting rescued and he says, "Man, when you get rescued and you look at your partner and you just go, 'Man, I love you. Thanks for getting me out of this mess.'" That's a huge laugh.

Where did Riding Giants *come from? Who are your influences? Kurosawa? John Ford? Ken Burns? Hal Jepson?*

We make films that we like. Period. We don't follow and we don't focus group our ideas. We explore and we take chances and we stay open to all the wonderful mistakes that veer us off course to better ideas.

Riding Giants *is in HD now and will be in 35mm eventually. How many formats did you use to make the movie?*

We had 35 mm, 16 mm, Super 16, Super 8, Regular 8, DV, three-quarter-inch video, and every imaginable kind of photograph—as well as the 3D photographs and all that stuff.

What's next?

I don't know. I have no plans right now.

Go surfing?

Yes.

those same hassles: "How do you judge art?" Hamilton scoffed to *Outside* magazine. "I would snap if I was letting someone other than the audience determine my fate."

As a waterman, Laird was something of a polymath, a world-class sailboarder and one of the first

Life is just like surf. It comes up, it goes down, but there's always something happening. Perhaps the greatest lesson of surfing is the gift of spontaneous reaction—flowing with it on a wave is much easier than flowing with it back on the beach.

— *Gerry Lopez in Drew Kampion's* The Way of the Surfer, *2003*

to experiment with kiteboarding—using a parapente as a sail to get dragged around the oceans of Oahu, Kaua'i, and Maui. At twenty-two, he entered a speed-sailing competition in Port Saint-Louis, France, beating the French champion and setting a European speed record of thirty-six knots.

In 1987, Laird had a memorable role as a buff, egomaniacal dickhead named Lance Burkhart in the movie *North Shore*. Laird/Lance was the bad guy, and he was believable. Some people said Laird was acting, some people said Laird was being Laird. He was an ever-growing young man with a love of the ocean and something to prove. He and his friends had spent the 1980s surfing, sailboarding, jumping off cliffs, snowboarding, and riding bigger and bigger waves. Their happy hunting grounds were becoming overloaded with surfers, and they began to look for new pastures and different ways to mow them.

In 1990, Laird was bumming around Europe with Buzzy Kerbox, a talented surfer from Oahu who also worked as a Ralph Lauren Polo model. Laird and Buzzy were like Butch Cassidy and the Sundance Kid—movie-star handsome and on the prowl for adventure. They found it when they attempted to paddle the English Channel. And like outlaws, they didn't bother telling anyone what they were up to or get official clearances; they just dreamed it up and did it. And nearly got killed. "When a huge freighter or tanker or oceanliner is coming at you, it's hard to get out of the way," Kerbox remembers. "There were a couple of close calls, but we made it to the other side with only a little bit of hypothermia."

After that misadventure, Laird and Buzzy got the wild hair to paddle from Corsica to Elba: "This was Laird's idea," Buzzy says. "But I was game. We looked at a map and saw the number '27' between Corsica and Elba. We figured 27 kilometers, no problem. So we took the ferry from Marseilles to Corsica and checked it out and even found a high cliff to jump off. We looked at the map again and saw that same 27 and thought, 'No problem.' We started paddling from Corsica followed by a French film crew in a helicopter. They were going to shoot our adventure, then meet us on Elba with our clothes, money, and a bottle of champagne for my birthday. We paddled for hours but Elba wasn't getting any closer . . . Turned out it was 27 *nautical miles*, not kilometers."

Back safely home in Hawai'i, Laird, Buzzy, and fellow wildman Darrick Doerner were looking for the next big thing. Laird remembers in *Riding Giants*, "We were freeboarding behind a boat in the summer and then there was a little swell and we were using swells for ramps and then we started like taking speed and catching waves and that was when a little light went off one summer day and we were like: 'Oh wow, we can catch waves. We might be able to ride bigger waves.'"

They might, just might, be able to ride *much* bigger waves.

In December 1992, Laird, Buzzy, and Darrick motored out in a sixteen-foot inflatable Zodiac to a surf spot called Backyards, just beyond Sunset Beach on Oahu's North Shore. Backyards is a grand piece of ocean real estate with lots of giant, shifting bluebirds that are beauties to observe, but not easy to catch when the surf gets huge. Laird and gang went after them on their traditional big-wave boards from a towrope behind their Zodiac. They swung into those waves from way, way outside, got into them early, and streaked all the way through the Boneyard that usually keeps surfers from making the connection to Sunset Beach. The pack at Sunset were shocked as the trio came flying past them at flank speed, then kicked out into the channel to be picked up by the boat and taken out to the back of Backyards to do the whole quarter-mile ride all over again.

Where past big-wave surfers were content to catch maybe a wave an hour, Laird, Buzzy, and Darrick were catching as many waves as they could handle—ten giants an hour. They gorged where, for

so many years, big-wave surfers had gotten scraps. The boat was wrong and their boards were too long and they didn't yet have straps on their feet, but the times were about to change dramatically for big-wave riding.

After that one afternoon on Oahu's Backyards, surfing would never be the same again.

Laird and company were not riding waves significantly bigger than what Greg Noll and other guys had ridden in the past. It was *how* they were surfing those waves. Riding big waves was limited not by the size of wave, but the need for speed to *catch* the wave. Laird put on his Dr. Science cap in *Riding Giants* to explain: "As waves increase in size, they also increase in speed. So the bigger the wave, the faster it's moving, the faster you need to be going to catch it." Now, trading in their Zodiac for a Jet Ski, they had the speed to catch even larger waves, and this radical new way of being whipped into a wave came to be known as "tow surfing." Darrick Doerner explains the allure: "You get the slingshot from the towrope and you let go of the rope and there you are, on this beautiful wave with no one anywhere near you!"

Through the rest of 1992 and into 1993, Laird, Buzzy, and Darrick were quickly getting the hang of it. They were now towing behind WaveRunners, giving them access to more intimate parts of the wave, but they were still using traditional big-wave boards. At some point, they got hit by another lightbulb.

Snowboarding provided the impetus. On sleek, tiny snowboards with their feet strapped in for control, they were riding snowy mountains—why not do the same on mountainous waves?

Surfboard-builders Dick Brewer, Gerry Lopez, and Laird's dad Billy cut the trio's big guns by three feet. Then Laird, Darrick, Buzzy, and the rest of their crew bolted on footstraps. Now, they had the control for the supreme speed and tremendous turbulence of riding waves that towered over thirty feet. As Laird explains in *Riding Giants*, "The small board was really the big breakthrough. I think that's really where we shifted gears. All of a sudden now we really had the speed."

Back at Backyards, the entire North Shore crowd and all the lenses and pens of the surf-industrial complex could see what

Above, **Dale Velzy 1990 "Malibu Express" Longboard:** A retro longboard, Dale Velzy's "Malibu Express" was the best of old and new. (© Malcolm Wilson) SPECIFICATIONS: 9' 2" LONG; 22½" WIDE; 2½ THICK; 20 POUNDS

Left, **C. J. Hobgood:** There was a time when East Coast surfers were the Rodney Dangerfields of surfing. Now, guys like C. J. Hobgood get plenty of respect for their surfing in danger spots around the world. (Photo © Jeff Divine)

Laird, Buzzy, and Darrick were doing. With too large an audience watching, they moved their show to the relative privacy of Maui. But the game was too exciting; others saw what was happening and wanted in, and they were soon joined by a group of guys who called themselves the Strapped Crew: Rush Randle, Pete Cabrinha, Mike Waltze, Brett Lickle, and Dave Kalama, the son of Hawai'ian legend Ilima Kalama. Laird and gang had their PWCs wired, they had surfboards that were somewhere between water skis and snowboards, and they were riding them using footstraps derived from snowboarding and sailboarding. They were doing flips, twists, and full rotations in small surf and they had gone well beyond the limits of paddle surfing in the big stuff. Now they were looking for something even bigger.

> My dad used to tell me that surfers are bums and that I would never make any money. So, from the first time I ever tried to surfing, I knew I wanted to go all the way with it.
>
> — *Sunny Garcia, 2005*

Be careful what you wish for.

One day, Gerry Lopez pulled Laird aside and whispered in his ear, "I got something you might wanna see." Lopez's secret was a promised land for big-wave surfing, a wave that any other generation of surfers would have watched in disbelief and written off as unrideable even in their wettest dreams.

The wave was named Peahi, but better known by the aptly descriptive moniker of Jaws. Sited off Maui's northern coast, Jaws broke like rolling thunder far out at sea. "The biggest difference between this wave and Waimea is that this wave is about five Waimeas," Laird says in *Riding Giants*. Adds surfer Brian Keaulana, "You take Makaha, Sunset, Pipeline, Kaena Point, Maverick's, put them all together and mix then in a pot and that's what you get—and more!" For Darrick Doerner, it was a dream come true: "We knew that we had discovered the real unridden realm."

Riding out far into the ocean on a PWC to catch the wave, Laird dropped his towrope and dropped into Jaws. He skimmed down the front at speeds estimated above thirty-five miles an hour, the curl chasing after him like the jaws of a monstrous beast wanting to eat him alive.

When films and still photos of this newfangled surfing circled the world to an unbelieving crowd of surfers, tow surfing had come of age.

In 1994, the world watched what the whole Strapped Crew were up to on the big screen in the movie *The Endless Summer II*. Rumors and whispers and sneak peaks came true when Laird and Darrick and Buzzy and Pete Cabrinha exploded out of the ocean, doing things no one had ever seen on a wave.

On one of the first waves, Laird and Cabrinha got crossed up on the same peak. Laird was behind, Cabrinha couldn't see him, and Laird had two choices: Turn and run and maybe take Cabrinha out, or take the pain.

Laird took the pain, straightened out, and got the *el kabong* from one of the meanest waves in the world: "I couldn't believe how hard it hit me, and I couldn't believe I lived," Laird said later, when the bells were no longer ringing and the tweetie birds had stopped circling: "It was like getting hit by four dump trucks at once."

In 1995, Laird again used a PWC to put himself in mortal danger while working on the Kevin Costner megafeature *Waterworld*. Laird, Buzzy, Brian Keaulana, and practically every other talented waterman in Hawai'i worked as stuntmen on this show, because they needed guys who knew how to drive PWCs on the water to do stunts as the villainous Smokers—the disciples of Dennis Hopper who operated from the hulk of the *Exxon Valdez*.

In 1996, the Strapped Crew released a movie called *Wake-Up Call* and gave just that to the surfing world. This movie showed how far tow-surfing had progressed in just four years. In small waves, the Strapped guys were using that thirty-five-mile-per-hour boost to do flips and full rotations. Featuring some amazing helicopter photography from Dave Nash, it gave the world a God's-eye view of just how big these waves were—and how fast Laird and all of his adrenaline-junkie friends were traveling.

When Laird Hamilton isn't out slaying dragons, he becomes something of a dragon himself. Endorphins are a stronger drug than heroin, and that can turn an extreme athlete like Laird into something similar to a manic-depressive. His big body and big philosophical drive need a lot of fuel, and when he doesn't get that from the ocean, he begins to feed on himself and everyone around him. When he is

A Safe Harbor for Surfing History

Inside the Surfing Heritage Foundation Collections

In the second century BC, it was the ambition of Ptolemy I to build a library in Alexandria, Egypt, to store all of mankind's literature under one roof—math, medicine, astronomy, navigation, history, philosophy, maps of heaven, schemes of the universe, everything the known world had produced. The collection rose to an estimated four hundred thousand scrolls—all subsequently lost when the library burned as the Romans torched the harbor.

Twenty-three centuries later, the Surfing Heritage Foundation is attempting to do something similar with all the gathered knowledge of surfing history and culture: books, maps, videos, posters, photographs, surfboards, magazines, indexes, interviews, stickers, patches. Everything associated with surf culture from before Captain Cook to Laird Hamilton and beyond will soon have a home under one spacious roof in San Clemente, California. Here are a bunch of guys with their hearts and minds in the right places, and the funding to do it justice.

The Surfing Heritage Foundation is the brainchild of Dick Metz, a longtime surf industry stalwart who was the brains behind Hobie Sports. Metz has an extensive personal collection of surfboards and other memorabilia. Over the years, he has joined with Spencer Croul, Steve Pezman, Bob Mardian, Bill Blackburn, and other like-minded folk to create a tax-exempt foundation for the collection and preservation of surfing heritage.

Walking into the Surfing Heritage Foundation loaded with more than a hundred historic surfboards is like being the first archaeologist gazing into King Tut's tomb. The board collection is truly amazing, beginning with Hawai'ian *olo* and *alaia* and going through all the ages to Pacific System Homes, Kivlins, Quiggs, Simmons, Nolls, Velzys, Currens, Brewers, Lightning Bolts, and all the way to Laird Hamilton's tow board. The collection grows monthly, and will probably blossom when the world sees what these guys are up to.

The list of Surfing Heritage Foundation projects stretches off into the future. The first big project is to digitize the photo files of LeRoy Grannis, updating LeRoy's current system of negative storage. "We also plan to digitize every surf magazine ever made, and have it indexed," Metz said. "Matt Warshaw has already donated his index and we are going to perfect that."

The Surfing Heritage Foundation archive in San Clemente will grow with the help of the surfing community and the surf-industrial complex. They are providing a safe, permanent home for surf culture and are looking for contributions of time, money, and artifacts from the surfing world.

challenging himself and getting his kicks, all those liqueurs of fear soothe him into the nicest guy in the world. But when those thrills are not forthcoming and the chemicals are left to stew, the result is a witch's brew. By summer 2000, Laird and Gabby Reece's marriage was heading for the dry reef.

Laird, meanwhile, was standing alone by the ocean, looking south over the horizon. He had heard word of a new kind of dragon that had reared its head on a reef in Tahiti, in the old Society Islands where Captain Cook had first seen someone sliding a wave so many centuries before. Now, Laird set sail, crossing the equator on a quest that would either thrill him or kill him.

Teahupoo is a freak. Other big waves like Jaws, Maverick's, and Waimea break in deep water. Teahupoo crashes onto a shallow, razor-edged coral reef, making a wave that is gracefully cylindrical yet so thick and so powerful it's like a tsunami breaking again and again. While not as high as Jaws, it's much more ferocious. And if the wave doesn't get you, there's always that treacherous reef waiting.

On a gloriously sunny Tahitian day in 2001, Darrick Doerner towed Laird into Teahupoo—and

then had a moment of doubt where he regretted his action. "It was to the point where I almost said: 'Don't let go of the rope!' Doerner remembers in *Riding Giants*. "And when I looked back, he was gone."

Laird rode Teahupoo as if the end of the world was chasing him down. The wave is the apocalypse, a maelstrom biting at his heels, seemingly gaining on him all the way. The hydrodynamic power was so intense, so hungry, that Laird was forced to drag his back hand along the *opposite* side of his board to keep himself from getting sucked down the wave's immense gullet. As he explains in *Riding Giants*, "I had a little voice going, 'Jump off right now. You're not gonna make this wave. You should jump off.' And another side of me was going: 'Well, I can't make it unless I just stay on.'"

It wasn't a ride he could practice a couple times to get the hang of it—but then again, his whole life had been practice for this one ride.

Laird's Teahupoo wave was the single most significant ride in surfing history. Surfing could now be classified as Before or After Teahupoo. It was mind-blowing, epoch-shattering—a wave of change, forever redefining our perception of surfing's limits. It suddenly seemed that riding any wave, anywhere, of any size, was possible.

That single ride at Teahupoo made Laird arguably the most famous surfer since Duke Kahanamoku. He earned acclaim from inside and outside the surfing world. In *Riding Giants*, Laird was Act Three and that Teahupoo "Millennium Wave" was the Grand Finale. As surf historian Matt Warshaw noted, "What could be heavier than that?"

In the dozen years since the Teahupoo ride, specialized big-wave surfers have been chasing that question, from Teahupoo to Mavericks to Dungeons and at outer reefs and "slabs" around the world. Every year, the Billabong XXL Awards bestows $50,000 for "Ride of the Year," but Laird has never taken an interest in the acclaim or the money. As the big-wave world followed in his manly wake, Laird went on to other things. Beginning around 1997, he discovered that standing up on a big surfboard and propelling himself with a paddle got his legs ready for big surf—standup paddle-boarding was simply a good workout. Since then, the sport of standup paddling has taken off and is sweeping the nation.

Meanwhile, Laird is still married to Gabrielle Reece, a woman taller than he is, and together they have two lovely daughters—who are being watched carefully by the United States Olympic Committee and the Coast Guard.

Left, **Ross Williams:** Hawai'ian surfer Ross Williams feeling right at home over a reef deep in the Tahitian Islands. (Photo © Jeff Divine)

Following pages, **The Wave:** Laird Hamilton deeply involved at Teahupoo, in the middle of the single most significant ride in surfing history. Had Laird fallen in the middle of this wave, he would have become a permanent part of the coral reef. (A Frame XX)

Something Wild

The Wave of Surf Culture • *Through the Centuries*

The supreme pleasure of surfing is a truth that can be felt by anyone willing to take a bit of a risk, cross that line in the sand, and plunge into the deep, dark blue ocean. Catch a wave and you'll be sitting on top of the world, the Beach Boys said. It may have been just a corny song lyric, but it was also true.

Go back to the ancient Polynesians and then through the centuries and the decades and the years and think of all the weird, wild, and wonderful things surfing has inspired: Listen to Dick Dale rocking out on "Miserlou"—that's Dick setting aside his Stratocaster to play that trumpet solo, too—and get the chills at one of the great rock'n'roll performances. Check out Sean Penn as Jeff Spicoli "talking about Cuba and having some food" and laugh at one of the comic icons of the twentieth century. Listen to the Clash's "Charlie Don't Surf" and think of Robert Duvall as Colonel Kilgore leading his all-American surfing soldiers.

Surfing is an image of pure romance, a wave rolling through the centuries, carrying a rhythm and a message and a lifestyle from ancient Polynesia to the twenty-first century. It's a true image, a truth that can be heard when Jack Johnson strums his ukulele onstage in front of ten thousand; a truth that can see been in the delirious, joyful surfing and water antics of Laird Hamilton; a truth that can be experienced vicariously in the beautiful surfing movies of Stacy Peralta, Dana Brown, Thomas Campbell, and Chris Malloy.

Think of Frankie Avalon's manic Potato Bug, John Philbin's underdog Turtle, Brian Wilson getting a C on a surfing sonata in high school. Think of a thousand high school and college marching bands doing the most famous drum beat in the world from "Wipeout." Think of a bunch of kids from Minnesota rocking a midwestern dancehall with "Surfin' Bird." Where did it all come from? Add together a thousand years of surf art, poetry, songs, movies, and fashion, and there is so much energy and creativity and innovation coming from this thing people do at the beach. Where does that energy come from?

Go out and catch a wave, and you'll begin to understand. That weird energy comes from the waves themselves, because there are few stranger energies on earth than a wave.

To catch a south swell at Malibu or a north swell at Mavericks or a nor'easter on Long Island or a west swell at Pipeline is to tap into the final few moments of something wild. These waves were all spawned by storms a world away, across the equator, in the Southern Ocean or the Gulf of Alaska or the Indian Ocean or in the hurricane lanes of the Atlantic. The intensity of the storms that produce these waves is scarcely to be credited; they spawn lines of energy that roll through the immense friction of the ocean without losing energy, the chaos of that storm lining up like little soldiers as it moves across the equator, traveling for a week and thousands of miles to show up on beaches and cause havoc on land. When the surf is up, responsible men and women go berserk, betray their spouses, abandon their work and studies, forsake everything to run to the ocean and grab some of that energy.

There must be something to it, because so many people have caught the surf fever, tapping not only into that weird and wild ocean rhythm, but also all the rhythms it has inspired in human culture—music, movies, fashion, art.

Facing page, **Dave Kalama:** The son of Hawai'ian master Ilima Kalama, Dave Kalama was one of the pioneers of tow-surfing at Jaws in the late 1990s. He remained dominant through the first decade of the twenty-first century. (Photo © Ron Dahlquist)

That cultural wave that has rolled through the centuries, from the Polynesian's sport of kings to today has been great inspiration over the years:

Kumai! Kumai! Ka nalu nui mai kahiki mai,
Alo poi pu! Ku mai ka pohuehue,
Hu! Kaikoo Loa....

"The above diversion is only intended as an amusement, not a test of skill, & in a gentle swell that sets on must I conceive be very pleasant, at least they seem to feel a great pleasure in the motion which this Exercise gives...."

"Where was solid water beneath it, is now air, and for the first time it feels the grip of gravity, and down it falls, at the same time being torn asunder from the lagging bottom of the wave and flung forward...."

Wave-Rider, 1930s
(Voyageur Press Archives)

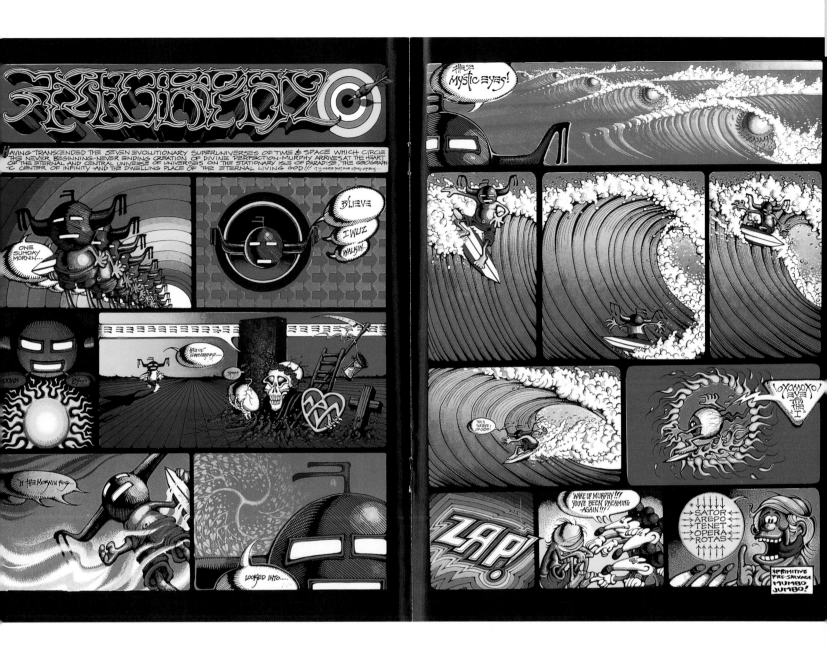

"The great Kahoona showed me the first time how to get on my knees, to push the shoulders up and slide the body back—to spring to your feet quickly, putting them a foot apart and under you in one motion. That's quite tricky. . . ."

A papapapapapapapapapapapa oo ma mow mama papa oo mow mow. . . .

"Charlie don't surf!"

"All I need are some tasty waves and a cool buzz, and I'm fine. . . ."

So many songs and words and dances and tributes produced over the centuries, but it all goes back to the first recorded sighting—and then be-

yond into prehistory—Captain James Cook walking down a beach in Otaheite, on the other side of the world, thousands of miles and thousands of perils away from England, with a million things on his mind—the safety of his crew, the success of his mission, a knighthood if he pulls it off. There is Captain Cook exploring the world with the weight of it on his shoulders, stopping to watch a lone Polynesian man getting his kicks from the same ocean, without a care in the world:

"I could not help concluding that this man felt the most supreme pleasure while he was driven on so smoothly by the sea . . . ."

Exactly.

Surfing Nirvana: Rick Griffin's colorful centerfold in 1972's *Tales From the Tube* defined 1970s surfing stoke. (Used by permission of Ida Griffin/Steve Pezman Collection)

Acknowledgments and Sources

I'd like to thank the Academy for . . . oops, wrong speech.

The first person to blame, er, *thank* is Steve Hawk, who handed this project off so he could free up personal time to play *Tony Hawk's Pro Skater* with his kids.

Hawk handed me off to Michael Dregni at Voyageur Press, who could not have known what he was getting into. *Surfing USA!* was supposed to be a fifty-thousand-word book with a deadline of October 2004. Instead, it was a two-hundred-thousand-word manuscript that took many more months to write and edit back down to fifty thousand words—finishing, appropriately, on April Fool's Day 2005.

Michael Dregni had all the qualities desirable in an editor: patience, communication, patience, style, and patience. He did a good job editing this book, considering he is from Minnesota—and because he was from Minnesota I could not hear his screams. Editing this book was like fighting a Malibu fire in 100-mph offshore winds. As soon as he had it batted down to a reasonable size, I would submit a forty-thousand-word chapter on surf music, and he had to suit up again.

My thanks as well to Margret Aldrich, copy editor extraordinaire, for keeping me honest.

Chapter 1: Catching the First Waves

Some of this chapter was taken from a history I wrote for the *Surfing for Life* website (www.surfingforlife.com/history.html); thanks are due to Matt Warshaw and David Brown.

Thanks to James D. Houston and Ben Finney for their surf scholarship in *Surfing: A History of the Ancient Hawaiian Sport*. (In the 1970s, I ran for student body president of Del Mar Junior High in Santa Cruz against Houston's daughter, Cori, and lost, which ended my political career; I want to thank Cori for that.)

The sidebar on Greg Noll is reprinted from my article in *Hawaii Magazine*. Thanks to Greg Noll, his wife Laura, and son Jed for letting me prowl in the woodshed—and for the fresh-caught and -cooked salmon. Thanks to Drew Kampion and Jorge Salas for their woodshed photos.

"The First Surfers in California" was first printed in the Santa Cruz *Sentinel*. Thanks to Rich Novak of NHS/Santa Cruz Skateboards for permission to use his illustration.

Thanks to Bishop Museum archivists DeSoto Brown, Judith Kearney, Ron Schaeffer, Leah Pualaha'ole Caldeira, Janet (B. J.) Short, and Patrice (Patty) Belcher for letting me raid their archives.

Information for the *Lurline* sidebar came from the Matson Lines website (www.matson.com/corporate/about_us/history.html), Maritime Matters (www.maritimematters.com/matson.html), and Lynn Blocker Krantz's *To Honolulu in Five Days: Cruising Aboard Matson's S.S.* Lurline.

Chapter 2: From Here to Honolulu

While working for *Surfer* magazine in the 1990s, I surfed Mala Wharf with Woody Brown. He was ninety-one at the time, and remains one of the most interesting chaps I have ever met.

For images, thanks go to David Brown (no relation) and Woody's daughter, Mary Sue Gannon.

The aloha shirt sidebar borrowed from a number of sources, including Dale Hope and the websites for Kahala, www.coffeetimes.com, www.mauishirts.com, and other shirt manufacturers. Thanks to Brian Chidester for his input.

Chapter 3: The Golden Years

Chapter three was written about Malibu, in Malibu, either at the Cross Creek Starbucks or the bar of the Beach Café at Paradise Cove. The story was cobbled together from articles I wrote for the *Surfer's Path*, *Surfer's Germany*, *Surfer*, the *Surfer's Journal*, and *Malibu Monthly* magazine.

The Tubesteak interview first appeared in the *Surfer's Journal*, so thanks to Tube S. Steak, Pez, Scott the Hulet, and also to Tube's wonderful wife, the concrete heiress and former Miss Phyllis French.

Thanks here and elsewhere to LeRoy Grannis for being on top of it for so many years.

Thanks to Sol and Jay at the Paradise Cove bar for not always charging me for raiding the salad bar to load up my baked potato.

Chapter 4: The Surfer Stomp

The first draft of chapter four could have been a book on its own. Information came from the website dedicated to the music of the Frankie and Annette movies, www.beachpartymoviemusic.com. I also got input from Phil Dirt at www.reverbcentral.com and Beach Boys aficionado Andrew Doe at www.btinternet.com/~bellagio/. Jan & Dean's website (www.jananddean-janberry.com/) and www.theventures.com were essential.

The final draft was thoroughly combed over by Brian Chidester, a true aficionado of surf music who can tell you who the third bongo player was on any song you choose.

Thanks to Patti McGee and Gordon McClelland for sharing memories.

Special thanks to Jim Fuller and Tony Andreason for talking about "Wipe Out!" and "Surfin' Bird."

Dick Dale and Dean Torrence were kind and willing proofreaders.

Chapter 5: Blue Screen

The main text was taken from an article I wrote called "The Price of Gas" that appeared in the *Surfer's Journal.*

A lot of the information about the Beach Party movies came from the www.beachpartymoviemusic.com website. Thanks to Mikey Mars.

Terry Dufoe was nice enough to let us use his interview with William Asher.

John Philbin was ever so kind to take time out from his jet-setting to sit at the Malibu Starbucks and talk about *North Shore* and *Point Break.*

Chapter 6: Going Vertical

Much here comes from the horse's mouth: Kelly Slater's autobiography *Pipe Dreams.*

For information on the surf industry, thanks go to Danny Kwock, Bob McKnight, Gordon Merchant, Gary Dunne, Claw Warbrick, Paul Naude, Pat O'Neill, Dick Metz, Shaun Tomson, Steve Pezman, and Bob Hurley.

Information on Rick Griffin came from a *Surfer's Journal* article that appears on Ira Opper's www.surfhistory.com. Quotes from Ida Griffin, Jerry Garcia, and R. Crumb were used, with permission, from www.drowningcreek.com/ 06_manifesto/09_griffin/griffin_6.html. Bits and pieces were also gathered from an online piece by Tim Stephenson at www.myraltis.co.uk/rickgriffin/bio.htm.

Gordon McClelland is the author of a book on Rick Griffin, and was kind enough to edited this chapter. Thanks to Steve Pezman for his *Tales from the Tube.*

Thanks to Cindy Love for faxing me the tribute to John Severson I wrote for the *Waterman's Ball.*

And special thanks to Ida Griffin for proofreading and granting us permission to reprint Rick's work.

Chapter 7: The Sport of Queens

Background information came from the www.legendary-surfers.com website as well as Matt Warshaw's *The Encyclopedia of Surfing.*

History on Marge Calhoun and Mary Ann Hawkins came from hangtags I wrote for Malibu Shirts. Thanks as well to Gary Lynch for info on Hawkins.

My sidebar on Hollywood's treatment of women surfers also appeared in *Foam* magazine.

Thanks to Barry Haun and the Surfing Heritage Foundation for the Hawkins photos, and also Dr. Norman Ball for letting us use his dad's photos.

Chapter 8: Monster

Thanks to Laird Hamilton and Jane Kachmer for letting us run the story and photos of Laird. Background information came from Dan Duane's article in the December 2004 *Outside* while quotes were taken with permission from *Riding Giants*, Stacy Peralta's excellent documentary. Thanks to Stacy for sitting for our interview.

Thanks to Jack Johnson, Chris Malloy, Thomas Campbell, and all the talented artists who are keeping the culture alive.

Thanks to Barry Haun, Spencer Croul, Dick Metz, and Steve Pezman of the Surfing Heritage Foundation for keeping the past alive and preserved.

And once again, I can't thank enough the Surfing Heritage Foundation, Matt Warshaw, Brian Chidester, Michael Dregni, the Noll family, Steve Hawk, and the staff of the *Surfer's Journal.*

My appreciation to Malcolm Gault-Williams at www.legendarysurfers.com and Keith Eshelmann for sharing their research and collections.

Thanks as well to Jeff Divine, Ron Dahlquist, Jeff Hall at A-Frame Photo, Ben Seigfried, and LeRoy Grannis.

And thanks to the likes of Gregg Brilliant, Bill Kalmenson, Karen Gallagher, Jay Butki, and the charming and glamorous Kristie Griffith.

Speaking of Kristie, special thanks to Robin and Jim Griffith for letting me invade their home, watch their TV, do my laundry, and eat all their Wheat Thins, ice cream, Nick's Burritos, and whatever else was around.

And, of course, my thanks to old King Neptune for providing the waves.

Index

About the Author

Ben Marcus grew up surfing in Santa Cruz in the 1970s, during a time when everyone wore puka shells and O'Neill Supersuits or Animal Skins, had long blond hair, and rocked out to Honk, Blind Faith, and Jimi Hendrix. An era like that will hook anyone on surfing for life, and Ben was a stoked gremmie, surfing the east side of Santa Cruz at Pleasure Point and also the Santa Cruz Yacht Harbor and River-mouth in the winter.

Author Ben Marcus, left, hanging with the world-famous Robert "Wingnut" Weaver.

After graduating from high school, Ben traveled the world in search of the perfect wave. In the 1980s, he wrote a short story about a surfing adventure on the Spanish Basque coast and submitted it to *The Surfer* magazine. *The Surfer* hired him as associate editor, where he remained for ten years, writing about many of the changes in surfing—the discovery of Maverick's, the debut of tow surfing, the arrival of the New School, and stars such as Lisa Andersen, Kelly Slater, and Laird Hamilton.

Now here in the twenty-first century, Ben still surfs and travels as much as possible, writing for *The Surfer's Journal* and other publications.

Surfing USA! was inspired by an interview Ben did with Jim Fuller—guitarist for the Surfaris and coauthor of "Wipe Out!"—while riding in a limo from Santa Monica's Viceroy Hotel to the Hollywood Bowl to see a James Brown concert. Fuller's story of a bunch of kids from Glendale writing a song that would be played eight million times on the radio over the next forty years got Ben thinking about all the other pioneers of surf culture and their stories. Many of them are in this book.